101 Wines
to Try Before You Die

101 Wines
to Try Before You Die
Margaret Rand

CASSELL
ILLUSTRATED

An Hachette UK Company
www.hachette.co.uk

First published in Great Britain in 2018 by Cassell,
a division of
Octopus Publishing Group Ltd
Carmelite House
50 Victoria Embankment
London EC4Y 0DZ
www.octopusbooks.co.uk
www.octopusbooksusa.com

Distributed in the US by
Hachette Book Group
1290 Avenue of the Americas, 4th and 5th Floors
New York, NY 10104

Distributed in Canada by Canadian Manda Group
664 Annette St, Toronto, Ontario, Canada M6S 2C8

ISBN 978-1-78840-052-7

A CIP catalogue record for this book is available from the
British Library.

Printed and bound in China

10 9 8 7 6 5 4 3 2 1

Group Publishing Director Denise Bates
Senior Editor Pauline Bache
Copyeditor Hilary Lumsden
Design and layout Jeremy Tilston
Junior Designer, Octopus Jack Storey
Picture Research Manager Giulia Hetherington
Picture Researcher Claire Gouldstone
Production Controller Dasha Miller

The UK Health Department recommends that you do not
regularly exceed 2–3 units of alcohol in a day, a unit being
defined as 10ml of pure alcohol, the equivalent of a single
measure (25ml/¾fl oz) of spirits. Those who regularly
drink more than this run an increasingly significant risk of
illness and death from a number of conditions. In addition,
women who are pregnant or trying to conceive should avoid
drinking alcohol.

The U.S. Department of Health and Human Services
recommends that men do not regularly exceed 2 drinks a
day and women 1 drink a day, a drink being defined as 0.5oz
of pure alcohol, the equivalent of 1.5oz of 80-proof distilled
spirits. Those who regularly drink more than this run an
increasingly significant risk of illness and death from a
number of conditions. In addition, women who are pregnant
or trying to conceive should avoid drinking alcohol.

Contents

Introduction

These are not the 101 most iconic wines in the world, nor the 101 highest-scoring wines in the world, though many of them are iconic, and many are high-scoring. (I should also point out that they are not in order of preference, or quality, or any other order. The numbers are there purely for convenience.) Instead they are the wines that, when I have had the chance to taste them, have given me the greatest pleasure.

If there is a thread running through these choices it is one of balance, elegance, poise and precision. I don't like overripeness, I don't like overextraction and I don't like overoaking. I love freshness, I love acidity and I love a sense of authenticity. This last point is difficult to explain, but is to do with a sense of risk, a sense of individuality – a sense of place, yes, but also a feeling of energy. It is the opposite of the safe, the industrial, the reliably crowd-pleasing.

Risk is important in winemaking, and is an element in the greatest and most exciting wines, but it is hard to define in tasting except as the feeling of walking a tightrope. Wines need to taste confident, but wines that taste routine are dull, and wines that taste as though they're trying too hard are tiresome, like a show-off at a party.

In winemaking, spontaneous fermentation (a factor in a fair number of my 101 wines) is a risk: it means allowing your must to ferment with an unknown population of different wild and ambient yeasts, a population that will vary every year as different climatic and vineyard conditions favour different yeast strains, and it runs a risk of spoilage if there are unfriendly ones in there, or of a fermentation stopping too early. Those who prefer it believe it expresses their terroir better than using an off-the-peg laboratory yeast; to me it seems to increase complexity and give a different texture, a different feel. It also produces wines that taste of salt and stones, earth and wild herbs, rather than conventional fruit-forward flavours of peach or plum or cherry. Wines that taste of wine, you might say.

The greatest risk factor of all, though, is where you plant your vineyard. The maxim that great wines are made at the climatic margin still holds true. Consumers with any serious interest in wine relish the vintage variation that results: some years are ripe, some are crisp, some are opulent and some are linear. But being on the margin means that some years will be poor: unripe, thin, rained-on or hailed-on.

You see the problem: for the grower, risk is a luxury that might be unaffordable. In the chilly 1970s German growers in the Mosel reckoned on having three good years, four dreadful and three mediocre ones in any ten-year period; since the late 1980s, however, poor years there have been a rarity. Climate change has favoured not just Germany but most of Europe – though better viticulture has also been a huge factor. Regions that were dangerously marginal for vines 50 years ago are now comfortable, and wine journalists like to stir things a little by asking if Champagne, or Chianti Classico, or any famous region you can think of, will become too warm.

The answer, so far, is that there are other, more marginal sites – northeast- or east-facing, higher, cooler – that could be planted. That's already happening in some places. But nobody wants to go back to a time when only a third of vintages were good. Vintage variation is more interesting than the monotony of one predictably hot year after another, but the truth is that we've become accustomed to less of it, and we prefer it this way. In addition, since better viticulture and better winemaking enable winemakers to handle risk with ever-greater precision, weather conditions that might have been ruinous 30 years ago are now often merely problematic. (Hail is the exception: that can still be catastrophic.)

As wine around the world gets better and better, it's reasonable to wonder how perfect a wine should be? Defining perfection is subjective, and changes with time: some flavours that were explained as "terroir" 30 years ago are now dismissed as faults. But technical "perfection" in the winery, with all the analyses just how you want them, is possible. So the pendulum is swinging again, towards "natural" wines, which may embrace the very faults that technical winemakers despise. I'll go along with the natural-wine movement part of the way – there are some wonderful natural wines – but I don't want faults dressed up as virtues, I don't want wine to taste of cider or beer, and I don't want bottle variation. That's not part of the journey of the wine, or the wine expressing itself, it's just bad winemaking. (Or sometimes variable corks. The problem of TCA has been almost eradicated from cork, but it's still a natural product and no two corks are identical.)

Great wines – wines that have something worthwhile to say beyond the safe clichés spouted by industrially made wines – are being made all over the world. Some are unexpected: most people laugh when I say that I've included a Lambrusco here. And why would you look for Riesling in Oregon? The answer is the same in both cases: taste it.

I have not included an example of every highly reputed region, or wine. The reason, often, is that there wasn't room. Also, wine is changing constantly. Five years ago my selection might have been different; in five years time it might be different again.

I owe a very big thank-you to all the producers whose wines I've tasted over the years, and an apology to those whose wines I've loved but haven't included here. There are many I would like to have added in. I nearly asked the publishers if we could stretch to 111. But alas, I knew the answer.

A note about prices: the price bands refer to current vintages. Older vintages may be more expensive, or cheaper. If you find an old vintage, ask if it has been stored properly (bearing in mind that not everybody will be honest about this, or even know the answer). If it is a very rare and expensive wine, bear in mind also that forgeries and fakes can be a problem.

Many of the wines here are very expensive. I wish they weren't, but top wines are expensive just as top footballers are expensive. But there is, in wine, no precise correlation between price and quality. Which is lucky, because it means that there's still a role for wine writers.

KEY:
....

* Up to £30 / US$40 per bottle retail
** £30–60 / US$40–80
*** £60–100 / US$80–140
**** £100–200 / US$140–270
***** £200-plus / US$270-plus
This is a guide only, based on UK prices. Customs duties and sales taxes vary from country to country.

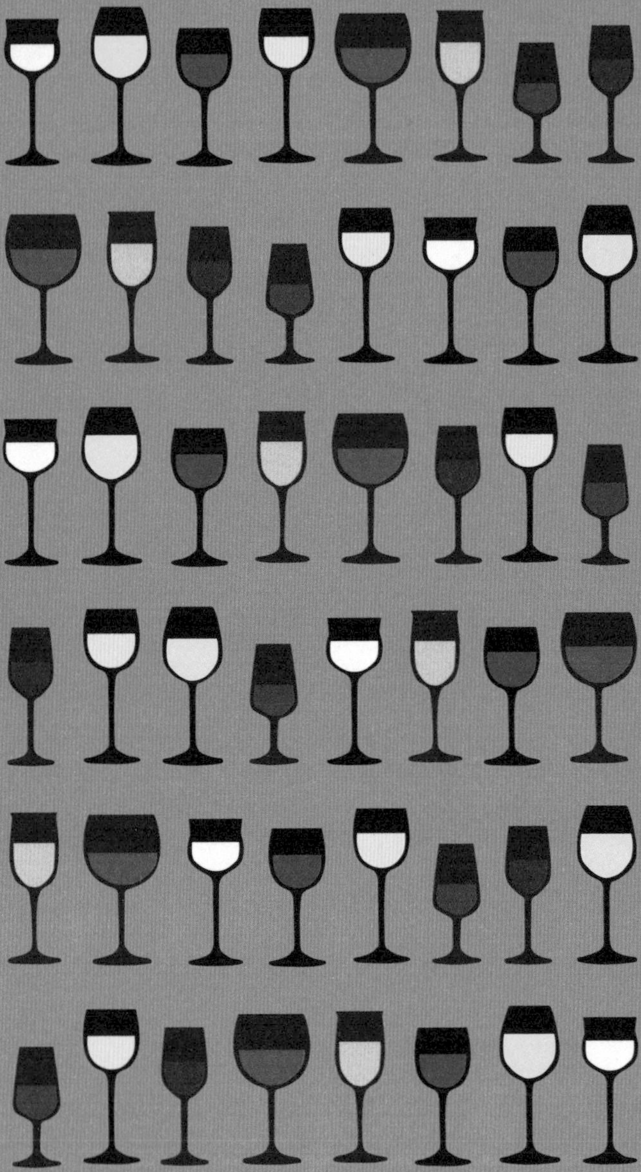

101 Wines

1

Domaine de Chevalier Blanc

REGION

Pessac-Léognan, Bordeaux

COUNTRY

France

GRAPES

Sauvignon Blanc, Sémillon

PRICE

***

DRINK WITH

Seafood, cheese; older wines take bigger flavours than younger, tighter ones

An estate that seems incapable of getting it wrong. Domaine de Chevalier red is a lovely, underrated and even underpriced wine; but the white is one of the great wines of the world. Tight and citrus in youth, it broadens and deepens with the years to flavours of beeswax and toast, dried apricots and honey, lemons and pears. Drink it too young and you don't get the full spectrum: this is a wine that needs time to show its paces.

There's nothing flashy about Domaine de Chevalier. The estate is tucked away on the edge of the Landes forest, those endless pine trees that stretch all the way to the Atlantic coast. This is good for shelter, but bad for frost, and the wind-machines in the vineyard show that this is a real problem. Some of the buildings are old, some new, but they all harmonize. This estate is not about bling. Director Olivier Bernard, whose family own the château, is obsessed with viticulture. "Ninety per cent of the choices are in the vineyard," he says. "In the cellar you are just following the fruit."

Bernard has been running the property since his family bought it in 1983; he asked the previous owner Claude Ricard to stay on for a few years because he wanted continuity. Details have changed, of course, and viticulture and winemaking have become more precise. Says Bernard, "the biggest challenge is, with all the changes we've seen, to stay with the same style on the same road. If I do a vertical tasting of the last 50 years, they are all on the same road. Techniques are the easiest mistake. They're easy to use, especially in this region. And whites are even more sensitive to techniques."

BEST AGE TO DRINK

15 years-plus

TROPHY VINTAGES

1978, 1984, 1985, 1986,
1990, 1998, 2001, 2004,
2005, 2007, 2008,
2009, 2010

DECANT

No need

CHILL

Serve it cool

**WHAT TO SAY IF YOU
MEET THE OWNER**

When should I drink
the 2016?

AND WHAT NOT TO SAY

I drank it yesterday

PAUPER SUBSTITUTE

Esprit de Chevalier
Blanc is the second wine

2

Château Haut-Bailly

REGION

Pessac-Léognan, Bordeaux

COUNTRY

France

GRAPES

Cabernet Sauvignon, Merlot, Cabernet Franc

PRICE

*** →****

There are plenty of big, overstated, shouty, tarty wines out there. They're seldom very interesting, and when you've tasted one you've tasted them all. The interesting wines are the ones that don't shout because they don't need to. They are the ones you come back to again and again in an attempt to understand what makes them so fascinating.

Haut-Bailly is unfailingly stylish. The vineyard soils are complex, and Merlot is planted where there is more clay, but the subsoil is fossil-rich limestone. A research programme initiated by owner Robert Willmers, who bought the property from the Sanders family in 1998, revealed that the roots don't actually go down that deep here, so drought years tend not to be the best. There is also a three-hectare plot of very old ungrafted vines, survivors of phylloxera, which includes some Malbec and Carmenère, grapes that fell from favour in Bordeaux after phylloxera. Director Véronique Sanders is gradually replacing Cabernet Franc in the vineyard with Cabernet Sauvignon, as the terroir is perfect for it.

The style of the wine is, as you might infer, elegant, fresh, concentrated and precise. It has tannic grip but it is never a blockbuster. It's in the classic mould of red Bordeaux: all those flavours that are supposed to be typical of red Bordeaux – cigar boxes, lead pencils – are present, together with black cherries, black plums, smoke and earth, a touch of liquorice, and with age, some truffle and undergrowth notes. One goes to Pessac-Léognan for a certain moreishness, an appetizing, refreshing quality. Haut-Bailly has it in excelsis.

DRINK WITH

Roast lamb

BEST AGE TO DRINK

Ten years-plus

TROPHY VINTAGES

1945, 1947, 1955, 1959,
1961, 1964, 1978, 1983,
1985, 1990, 1998, 2000,
2005, 2009, 2010

DECANT

Yes

CHILL

No

**WHAT TO SAY IF YOU
MEET THE OWNER**

Is Haut-Bailly a
feminine wine?

AND WHAT NOT TO SAY

I really like oak flavours

PAUPER SUBSTITUTE

The second wine is La
Parde de Haut-Bailly

3

Château Margaux

REGION

Margaux, Bordeaux

COUNTRY

France

GRAPES

Cabernet Sauvignon, Cabernet Franc, Merlot, Petit Verdot

PRICE

**** →*****

Margaux, Margaux – so good they named it twice. This château, the greatest in the Margaux appellation and one of the four Médoc First Growths, is the most elegantly graceful of them, with the texture of silk and a note of violets on the nose. The vineyards are on the deep gravel beds that mark the Médoc's best sites: Quaternary gravel from the Pyrenees and the Massif Central, swept here by floods as the Pleistocene ice sheets melted and froze and melted again, and now, a couple of million years later, settled into a gently undulating and utterly undramatic landscape beside the flat expanse of the Gironde River.

Gravel matters: it drains well, and well-drained soil is warm soil, which helps the late-ripening Cabernet Sauvignon. Where there is more clay, Merlot flourishes. Petit Verdot, in small quantities, is a hallmark of the château, adding extra floral perfume. But all the focus on aroma and elegance shouldn't distract one from the fact that Margaux is also a wine of concentration and density. It's just that it wears it so lightly. You are aware of poise, of tension, of walking a tightrope with vast depths beneath – and you're hardly aware of the muscular strength needed. It is both delicate and sumptuous, lush and fresh in youth and complex and harmonious with age. People call it feminine because of its finesse; crystalline might be a better word. It is owned and run by Corinne Mentzelopoulos. She and director Paul Pontallier made a brilliant team, steering the wine past the overextracted fashions of the last couple of decades while never losing critical acclaim. Pontallier died in 2016; his successor is Philippe Bascaules.

DRINK WITH

The very best shoulder of lamb you can find

BEST AGE TO DRINK

15 years-plus

TROPHY VINTAGES

1945, 1947, 1949, 1953, 1959, 1961, 1983, 1985, 1990, 2000, 2009, 2010, 2015

DECANT

Yes: maybe an hour ahead; less if it's very old

CHILL

Only if you're in the tropics; but too cool is better than too warm

WHAT TO SAY IF YOU MEET THE OWNER

How's Zorba? (Zorba is a beagle)

AND WHAT NOT TO SAY

Margaux must be a lovely place to relax (she doesn't, ever)

PAUPER SUBSTITUTE

The second wine is Pavillon Rouge

4

Vieux Château Certan

REGION

Pomerol, Bordeaux

COUNTRY

France

GRAPES

Merlot, Cabernet Franc, Cabernet Sauvignon

PRICE

*** →****

DRINK WITH

Roast rib of beef or haunch of venison. Or grouse

The 14 hectares of vines here (properties are small in Pomerol) are divided into 23 parcels for maximum precision, maximum reflection of the character of each vintage. Not every winemaker, even every top winemaker, wants as much honesty in his wines as Alexandre Thienpont. He says, "for 20 years I was preaching in the desert. In the 1990s the index of tannins was the parameter. Now authenticity is coming back. Balance is the next thing." Which is not to say that vineyards should be allowed to do as they please. "An *enfant naturel* is an *enfant sauvage*. It's a question of balance." He is a man who combines diffidence with rigour and great intelligence, and as ever, the wine reflects the winemaker. You can't get him to praise himself; all credit goes either to nature, or to his son Guillaume, who now works with him, and who he says is "much more intelligent than me".

Merlot is the main grape here, not surprisingly, and planted on clay, but unusually for Pomerol it forms only 60 per cent of the vineyard. There is Cabernet Franc and Cabernet Sauvignon where there is gravel, and this gives elegance to the blend; elegance, finesse, even delicacy, allied to concentration and density, are the hallmarks of VCC. The wine, tasted in extreme youth from barrel, is dazzling in its beauty, its depth and its refinement. With time it can acquire notes of orange peel, chocolate, toasty black fruits, spice and minerality, always underpinned by a firm structure and a silky, restrained opulence. Some critics described the 2009 as the greatest wine they'd ever tasted. The 2010 is, if anything, even better.

BEST AGE TO DRINK

12 years-plus, depending on the vintage

TROPHY VINTAGES

1945, 1947, 1948, 1950, 1982, 1990, 1995, 1996, 1998, 2000, 2005, 2009, 2010, 2011

DECANT

Yes

CHILL

No, unless your house is very hot

WHAT TO SAY IF YOU MEET THE OWNER

Wines should have soul, emotion, shouldn't they?

AND WHAT NOT TO SAY

Tell me about yourself

PAUPER SUBSTITUTE

The second wine is Le Gravette de Certan

5 Château d'Yquem

REGION

Sauternes, Bordeaux

COUNTRY

France

GRAPES

Sémillon, Sauvignon Blanc

PRICE

*****

DRINK WITH

Roquefort or foie gras

Yquem is so iconic that people who don't even know what colour it is have heard of it. It's been famous for centuries, and yet the price is lower than that of equivalent red Bordeaux. Fashion has moved away from sweet whites. Current owner LVMH pushes the price, but it's still a (relative) bargain.

The detailed harvesting techniques at Yquem and the tiny yields produce sweet wines of incredible complexity and concentration: shrivelled, super-sweet, nobly rotten berries are the pickers' target, though enough semi-shrivelled and even green berries must also be picked to keep the balance right: picking is berry-by-berry. Each vine yields a single glass of wine.

What makes it all possible is the terroir: much of the vineyard faces north, towards the river Garonne, from which come the morning mists that encourage the *Botrytis cinerea* fungus. The vineyard is the highest point in Sauternes, and catches the breezes that keep the grapes healthy. The soil is clay, gravel and sand over limestone, and so varied is the vineyard that its 113 hectares are divided into 150 different parcels. Intricacy and complexity in the final wine is the target.

Yquem always balances concentration and opulence with freshness. In youth it tastes of pineapple, honey and lemon zest; with age the colour darkens through caramel to mahogany and the flavours become more honeyed, toasty, spicy, and the tropical fruit gives way to crème brûlée. Is it the best of all Sauternes? The bar is set high these days, but Yquem is hard to beat.

BEST AGE TO DRINK

Start when it's young,
and continue for one
hundred years or more

TROPHY VINTAGES

1784, 1811, 1847... more
recently, 1921, 1929,
1945, 1949, 1955, 1959,
1967, 1975, 1983, 1989,
1990, 2001, 2009, 2011

DECANT

You don't have to, but
it looks wonderful in
a decanter

CHILL

Slightly

WHAT TO SAY IF YOU
MEET THE DIRECTOR

How many pickers do
you need at Yquem?

AND WHAT NOT TO SAY

Is Yquem now
a luxury brand?

PAUPER SUBSTITUTE

There's no second
wine; try Château de
Fargues, owned by
Comte Alexandre de
Lur-Saluces, previous
owner of Yquem

6

Chablis Grand Cru Les Clos, Domaine René et Vincent Dauvissat

REGION

Chablis, Burgundy

COUNTRY

France

GRAPE

Chardonnay

PRICE

****

Here, a tossed coin has decided the particular vineyard, and indeed the grower. In Chablis it could have been Raveneau; but it came down heads, and so it's Dauvissat. These two are the leading lights, the *sine qua nons* of the appellation.

So: Dauvissat. Les Clos or Les Preuses? Heads again. Les Clos is perhaps a more complete wine, whereas Preuses is richer, more instantly seductive, and needs time to show its detailed complexity; but it's so enveloping it's easy not to care that actually, it's too young and you should wait. You have to wait for Les Clos: it's tighter, with reticent power. There is huge weight there, and it reveals itself only slowly. Most Chablis-lovers would say it's the greatest of the Grands Crus, and it's also the biggest. The Dauvissat holding is 1.7 hectares of the total 26.96 hectares.

René and Vincent are father and son, and the domaine was first established by René's father Robert in the 1920s. Everything is meticulous and quite a lot might look rather old-fashioned: "classic" might be a better word. Viticulture is biodynamic (it wasn't always, but Vincent has introduced it), yields are kept right down, and the juice is fermented in a mixture of steel vats and oak barrels – but this is old oak, which leaves no mark on the wines except an extra layer of complexity and depth. These are wines of immense concentration, tightness and purity; if you want real, classic Chablis steeliness, that will develop into honey-over-steel, toast-over-steel, minerality-over-steel, it's here.

DRINK WITH

Grilled Dover sole or turbot

Chablis Grand Cru
"Les Clos"
APPELLATION CHABLIS GRAND CRU CONTRÔLÉE

Mise à la Propriété

SARL Vincent DAUVISSAT, VITICULTEUR À CHABLIS (YONNE) FRANCE 13% ALC./VOL.

BEST AGE TO DRINK

Not before ten years,
and then for another ten

TROPHY VINTAGES

2002, 2007, 2010,
2014, 2015

DECANT

No

CHILL

A little

**WHAT TO SAY IF YOU
MEET THE WINEMAKER**

Why isn't all Chablis
this exciting?

AND WHAT NOT TO SAY

Why don't you just
make more?

PAUPER SUBSTITUTE

The Dauvissats'
basic Chablis

7

Le Chambertin, Domaine Armand Rousseau

REGION

Côte de Nuits, Burgundy

COUNTRY

France

GRAPE

Pinot Noir

PRICE

*****

DRINK WITH

Guinea fowl or duck

Picking the burgundies for this book was the most difficult of all: so many good producers, so many glorious wines. Picking one meant leaving out half a dozen others.

This estate is now run by Eric, Armand's grandson, with Eric's daughter Cyrielle, but the wines haven't changed much in style. Viticulture is more precise and more organic; cellar work is still non-interventionist. Most of the grapes are destemmed and the wine is aged in 100 per cent new oak, mostly from cooper François Frères.

Chambertin is the most famous vineyard in the village of Gevrey, which is why the village appends the name to its own. There are nine Grand Cru vineyards in all, and all are confusingly called Chambertin: as well as Le Chambertin there is Chambertin-Clos de Bèze, Mazis-Chambertin, Latricières-Chambertin and so on. Armand Rousseau has 2.15 hectares of Le Chambertin, as well as holdings in many of the others. The Chambertin vines are in three plots, all on soil with a high limestone content.

And the wine? Very difficult to describe. Extraordinary complexity and intensity, yet with such finesse: there's spice, savouriness, a texture like silk velvet; it's imposing and seductive, intellectual and sensual, thrilling and compelling. The weight is barely perceptible: all is balance, tension and length. The apotheosis of Pinot Noir? More likely the apotheosis of Chambertin: like all great burgundies, it's about the terroir, not the grape.

8

Chevalier-Montrachet, Domaine Leflaive

REGION

Côte de Beaune, Burgundy

COUNTRY

France

GRAPE

Chardonnay

PRICE

*****

Domaine Leflaive, under the stewardship of Anne-Claude Leflaive, was one of the greatest names in Burgundy. It has been fully biodynamic since 1997, and its wines are a byword for incredible poise and refinement, richness and precision. They're among the greatest white wines of Burgundy; and those from the Montrachet vineyards are as great as Chardonnay gets. The wines are, as ever, like their maker, and Anne-Claude Leflaive was brave and strong. Her biodynamism was passionate and lived: her house was specially designed to make minimum impact on the environment, and she set up a wine school in Puligny-Montrachet to pass on her beliefs. She died in 2015, and her cousin Brice de La Morandière has taken over the management of the estate.

The Chevalier-Montrachet holding is slightly bigger (1.92 hectares) than the estate's other Montrachet vineyards. They are all superb. Burgundy expert Jasper Morris suggests that the Chevalier-Montrachet is more chiselled, its Bâtard-Montrachet most restrained in youth, Bienvenues more sensual. Any and all of them will dazzle and seduce.

From the 2014 vintage all the wines are bottled under Diam: a "technical cork", which it is hoped will help to ward off premature oxidation (premox), and which is still not properly understood. If you're thinking of buying any bottle of old white burgundy you should be aware of the risks.

DRINK WITH

Truffled chicken, perhaps

BEST AGE TO DRINK

From eight years to
about twenty-five

TROPHY VINTAGES

2002, 2005, 2008,
2010, 2012, 2014, 2015

DECANT

No

CHILL

A little

WHAT TO SAY IF YOU
MEET THE WINEMAKER

Did you grow up with
Anne-Claude?

AND WHAT NOT TO SAY

Would Anne-Claude
have have switched from
natural cork closures to
Diam technical corks?
(Presumably she would,
since she initiated trials)

PAUPER SUBSTITUTE

Bourgogne Blanc from
the same estate

Corton-Charlemagne, Domaine Bonneau du Martray

9

REGION

Côte de Beaune, Burgundy

COUNTRY

France

GRAPE

Chardonnay

PRICE

**** →*****

Corton is a single hill with more appellations than you could shake a stick at. Nine of them can call their white wines Corton-Charlemagne, and they face in all directions from south to west. This estate's massive 9.5 hectares of Corton-Charlemagne are at the heart of the appellation, in the En Charlemagne and Le Charlemagne vineyards, west-facing and with lots of sunshine; viticulture is biodynamic and all 15 parcels are vinified separately with natural yeasts, and aged separately. Only about a third of the oak is new. The estate has recently been sold to American businessman Stanley Kroenke, owner of Napa's Screaming Eagle. Before this it had been owned by the same family for over 200 years.

The wine can be enigmatic in youth, and combines concentration with a feeling of weightlessness and utter effortlessness. Yes, there are white fruits, yes, there is stony minerality and acidity and tension, yes, there is salt and earth and lime flowers and spice – but none of these tell you much about the perfect harmony that gathers in the glass. The previous owner, Jean-Charles Le Bault de La Morinière, used a painting analogy. Montrachet, he said, reminded him of Veronese: sumptuous, full, but balanced. Corton-Charlemagne he thought was more Vermeer: apparently modest, but full of light. A colleague of mine once summed up this wine by quoting John Donne: "no darkness nor dazzling but equal light, no noise nor silence but one equal music." I don't think I can do better.

DRINK WITH

Sweetbreads or poached wild Scottish salmon

BEST AGE TO DRINK

From ten years

TROPHY VINTAGES

2002, 2005, 2008,
2010, 2012, 2014, 2015

DECANT

No

CHILL

A little

**WHAT TO SAY OR NOT
SAY IF YOU MEET THE
WINEMAKER**

At the time of writing
it wasn't clear who the
winemaker would be
in the future

PAUPER SUBSTITUTE

The estate only makes
two wines, this and
(red) Corton

10

La Romanée, Domaine du Comte Liger-Belair

REGION

Côte de Nuits, Burgundy

COUNTRY

France

GRAPE

Pinot Noir

PRICE

*****

This estate makes wines of ethereal delicacy and penetrating intensity, intricacy and majesty, power and lightness. To have all this in a single bottle is remarkable; but that's what great burgundy is. It's also exceedingly expensive.

Vosne-Romanée makes reds of refinement and perfume, and it boasts a substantial clutch of Grands Crus. Of these, remarkably, La Romanée is a monopole: Domaine du Comte Liger-Belair owns all 0.85 hectares of it, making this a very rare wine indeed. It is actually the smallest appellation in France. It sits immediately above La Romanée-Conti Grand Cru, on a slope of 11 or 12 degrees, and has slightly more clay in the soil; there's tannin in the wine, and a sinewy strength, wrapped up, in youth, in sweet, fleshy fruit, haunting perfume, with exquisite purity and transparency. It will last and improve for years.

This is a relatively new domaine, in one sense: the family first bought vineyards in 1815, and indeed owned La Romanée, until everything was put up for sale in 1933 because of succession problems. Just a few vineyards were saved for the family, including this one. In 2000 Vicomte Louis-Michel Liger-Belair started taking vineyards back in Vosne-Romanée and Nuits-St-Georges as lease agreements expired. He believes in minimum intervention, maximum care and light extraction in the winery: ploughing is by horse to avoid compacting the soil, the grapes are entirely destemmed and fermentation is with natural yeasts. The vines are about 50 years old.

DRINK WITH

Best roast chicken, something simple to show off the wine

BEST AGE TO DRINK

After about ten years, then for at least another twenty

TROPHY VINTAGES

2002, 2005, 2006, 2010, 2012, 2015

DECANT

Yes

CHILL

No

WHAT TO SAY IF YOU MEET THE WINEMAKER

How's the horse?

AND WHAT NOT TO SAY

Is it cheaper to use a horse?

PAUPER SUBSTITUTE

The estate's village Vosne-Romanée

11

L'Avizoise Extra Brut Blanc de Blancs Grand Cru, Champagne Agrapart & Fils

REGION

Champagne

COUNTRY

France

GRAPE

Chardonnay

PRICE

***

It would be invidious not to include a grower Champagne, but which one? There are enough outstanding growers in the region to make the choice very difficult. Why Agrapart? Because in the end the wines are invariably compelling. The difference between grower Champagnes and Champagnes from the big houses can be overstated, but it does exist. Each play to their strengths. The houses source grapes from all over the region to make a consistent style year after year. The growers, with only their own parcels of vines at their disposal, focus on terroir and make a virtue of inconsistency: vintage and terroir variation are to be celebrated here, whereas for the houses, they must mostly be blended away.

Pascal and Fabrice Agrapart's 12 hectares are mostly in the Côte des Blancs villages of Cramant, Oiry, Oger and Avize; they are divided into 50 different plots. No chemical pesticides or weedkillers are used, fermentation is with natural yeasts, and this wine is aged in big, old, oak barrels for a gentle roundness, a bit of extra weight, and left on its lees in bottle for five years before disgorgment. Not that weight is what you think of when you taste it. It has a crystalline tension, yet feels effortless; utter purity, yet great richness. It is a vibrant, elegant wine that gains power from its 55-year-old vines and a mixture of clay in the chalk soil. Minéral is a lighter expression of Avize, from chalkier soil in the same village. Dosage is low, at four grams per litre (g/l), but the wine has no hint of austerity.

DRINK WITH

Rich fish dishes

BEST AGE TO DRINK

From eight years or so,
according to the vintage

TROPHY VINTAGES

None

DECANT

No

CHILL

Yes

**WHAT TO SAY IF YOU
MEET THE WINEMAKER**

How long did it take
you to understand
your vineyards?

AND WHAT NOT TO SAY

How can Champagne
be a terroir wine?

PAUPER SUBSTITUTE

Les 7 Crus NV, from,
as you might guess,
seven villages

12 Cristal, Roederer

REGION

Champagne

COUNTRY

France

GRAPES

Pinot Noir, Chardonnay

PRICE

****

DRINK WITH

To show off the wine, scallops with saffron beurre blanc

Expensive Champagnes abound, but Cristal is unmissable. The Roederer style is a taut balance between reductive and oxidative, flirting with both: reductive but open, expressive but tight. That house style carries through into this prestige cuvée, which combines brioche and tarte-tatin flavours with freshness and liveliness. With age the freshness lasts and lasts, and the palate develops notes of crème brûlée, white truffles and white chocolate. And that tension is always there. If you want a prestige cuvée that dances, this is it. Chef de cave Jean-Baptiste Lecaillon aims, in blending, to get flavour and texture coming in waves on the palate, with a certain sparkiness that comes with just the right amount of malic acid.

Is Cristal (or, for that matter, any prestige cuvée) properly appreciated by most of its drinkers? Probably not. You'd think it might be dispiriting (or might induce cynicism) to have your finest wine drunk, in the main, far too young, and/or without the attention it deserves. But the quality of Cristal cannot be faulted. It is made in most years these days – 2000, 2002, 2004, 2005, 2006, 2007 – and quantities are substantial, though a lot less than Dom Pérignon (see page 36). It is possible because of meticulous (and increasingly biodynamic) viticulture – Roederer owns a lot of vineyards – and precise winemaking. The bottles are aged for six years in the cellar and given a further eight months' ageing after disgorgement. Further ageing is up to you. But do keep the bottles in the dark: that clear glass offers no protection against light damage, to which Champagne is particularly prone.

BEST AGE TO DRINK

Not before 15 years;
1955, 1959, 1962, 1964
still going strong

TROPHY VINTAGES

Recently, 1988, 1995,
2002, 2004, 2006, 2007

DECANT

No

CHILL

A bit; don't serve too cold

**WHAT TO SAY IF YOU
MEET THE WINEMAKER**

How do you define
perfect ripeness
in grapes?

AND WHAT NOT TO SAY

What do you think
of Dom Pérignon?

PAUPER SUBSTITUTE

Roederer NV: rich,
taut, compelling

MILLIONAIRE SUBSTITUTE

Late-release Cristal,
currently 1995

13

Plénitude Rosé, Dom Pérignon

REGION

Champagne

COUNTRY

France

GRAPES

Pinot Noir, Chardonnay

PRICE

*****

To have a prestige cuvée is no longer enough: Champagne houses now must have something even more spectacular to tempt the punters. Plénitude is Dom Pérignon's late-release series: the normal release is P1; P2 is the same vintage, released later and late-disgorged; P3, ditto and even later. Late-disgorged wines are fresher than those you keep in your own cellar. The idea is that maturity goes in waves rather than in a straight line, and an old wine will be perfectly poised and expressive, but different, at different points in its life.

Dom Pérignon is tight and compact in youth; it needs years to show the depth and breadth of which it is capable. The extra weight of age, and the extra breadth and depth of good rosé, makes this a good food match; and DP rosé ages to glorious creamy flavours of mandarin and lemon, raspberry, spice, mushrooms, coffee and earth. The vintage character comes through strongly: it's the antithesis of a NV blend.

The rosé is a different blend to the white – different from the word go, with fewer components, and with about 20% of red Pinot added. DP has been working hard on the quality of its Pinot Noir in recent years: the role of Pinot in a Champagne blend is to give structure and body to white and, in addition, aroma and colour to rosé. So you want aromatic ripeness, proper colour and good concentration, but not too much tannin; and that particular balance has to be achieved in the vineyard, with clever viticulture.

DRINK WITH

Smoky, spicy, earthy, complex dishes, but easy on the chilli

BEST AGE TO DRINK

On release, or keep;
current releases are
20-plus years old

TROPHY VINTAGES

1993 is pretty good

DECANT

Could do, but you'll
lose the bubbles

CHILL

A bit. Don't serve
too cold

WHAT TO SAY IF YOU
MEET THE WINEMAKER

Tell me about the
aromatic complexity

AND WHAT NOT TO SAY

How much DP do you
make?

PAUPER SUBSTITUTE

The standard DP is a
pauper wine compared
to these prices

14

Vieilles Vignes Françaises, Bollinger

REGION

Champagne

COUNTRY

France

GRAPE

Pinot Noir

PRICE

*****

If you live in Chile, or Washington State, the idea that vines should be planted on their own roots won't be the least surprise. In Europe, however, it's a rarity; and an even greater rarity is vines grown *en foule*, and propagated by layering, which went out when phylloxera killed Europe's vines and made grafting onto rootstocks necessary. It involves partly burying a cane, and once it has grown roots, cutting it from the mother vine. The vines are astonishingly densely planted: up to 30,000 per hectare, compared to around 8,000 in the rest of Champagne.

Bollinger does it in just three small plots of Pinot Noir because that's what it has: for whatever reason, these 36 ares have not been infected with phylloxera. Whether it's being ungrafted that makes the difference, or the high density of planting, or the very low yields, who can say? But this is the most extraordinarily burgundian of Champagnes. Put your nose in the glass and you could be in the Côte d'Or: aromas of red fruits, spice, undergrowth, truffles, brioche, butter, smoke, toast and nuts; the palate has Bollinger weight and concentration, precision, compactness and tremendous length. It is a Champagne like no other. You could portray it as a forerunner of the fashion for Blanc de Noirs, and a forerunner of terroir-driven Champagnes, but actually it's too rare to be anything other than a collector's item. Only 2–3,000 bottles are made, and not every year.

DRINK WITH

Pigeon – always good with Pinot

BEST AGE TO DRINK

Any age, really; on
release, then onwards

TROPHY VINTAGES

All of them; 1973, maybe

DECANT

No

CHILL

A bit; don't serve too cold

**WHAT TO SAY IF YOU
MEET THE WINEMAKER**

Does it remind you
of Musigny?

AND WHAT NOT TO SAY

Shall we open
another bottle?

PAUPER SUBSTITUTE

Bollinger NV;
a heavyweight
Champagne that dances

15

Gewurztraminer Furstentum Cuvée Laurence, Domaine Weinbach

REGION

Alsace

COUNTRY

France

GRAPE

Gewurztraminer

PRICE

** →***

Gewurztraminer is a bit of a Marmite grape, but at its best it's a great deal more than the face-cream-and-lychees flavours of what the simple examples might suggest. This is Gewurz at its finest. It's slightly off-dry, and from the Furstentum vineyard, a south-facing Grand Cru with shallow, clay-chalk-sandstone soil: the clay gives power and retains the water that Gewurz needs, the sandstone elegance and what the French call *nervosité*. It gives freshness to a grape naturally low in acidity; getting powerful Gewurz is easy. What you want is power that is tucked into filigree delicacy; structure that runs in a fine, taut line through the wine. What you want, too, is a terroir so imposing that it shines through the grape, so that all the aroma and spice and lushness of the grape is a window onto a particular hillside, a particular year.

Weinbach's wines are like no others in Alsace. They're extreme wines – not in the sense of weight or power or showiness, but in their wininess, their minerality. They're sturdy yet elegant, structured but with great finesse. Because for many years the domaine was run entirely by women it would be easy to say that they are feminine; but feminine in the sense of being intellectual, resilient, detailed.

This wine, in youth, combines richness with a citrus note of mandarin, rose spice and crystallized fruit, and it ages to flavours of jasmine, truffle and mirabelle plum. With time it becomes less sweet: the sweetness seems to be absorbed into the wininess.

DRINK WITH

Foie gras
or Munster cheese

BEST AGE TO DRINK

Start young and go
on for 15 years

TROPHY VINTAGES

2010, 2012, 2013, 2015

DECANT

No

CHILL

Yes

**WHAT TO SAY IF YOU
MEET THE WINEMAKER**

How do you define
vineyard character?

AND WHAT NOT TO SAY

Will this go with curry?

PAUPER SUBSTITUTE

The estate's standard
Gewurztraminer
Vendanges Tardives

16

Pinot Gris Clos Saint Urbain, Rangen de Thann, Zind Humbrecht

REGION

Alsace

COUNTRY

France

GRAPE

Pinot Gris

PRICE

***

Clos Saint Urbain is a tiny enclave within a small vineyard, and in the middle of it is an even tinier chapel dedicated to the patron saint of those who work in wine, where Mass is said once a year, on the last Saturday of June. The whole Rangen de Thann vineyard is just over 22 hectares; the Clos just 5.5 hectares. The Clos is owned by Zind Humbrecht, and Olivier ZH reports that Pinot Gris grown above and below the chapel have different characters: the higher part is cooler and later ripening, with rockier soil, and gives more acidic, leaner wines; the lower part gives richer, more powerful wines. The difference in soil pH between the top of the slope and the bottom, even in this small vineyard, is 2.5–5.5 at the top, 7 at the bottom. If you want to see the differences that terroir can make to the flavour of wine, put your boots on and scramble to the top of Rangen.

It's a hot site, in the far south of Alsace, with dark, rocky, volcanic soil, and it's so steep that if you stand in some parts and stretch your arm out, your hand will touch earth. It shines through the character of the grape, so that Zind Humbrecht's Pinot Gris is tense and mineral, salty and sparky, with spice and opulence woven into a brisk structure. Olivier is a great grower and winemaker: his wines have been getting drier in recent years, and while his Pinot Gris from Clos Saint Urbain can have quite high residual sugar it often feels only off-dry. And it ages superbly. The 1988, tasted in 2015, was fresh, stony and truffley.

DRINK WITH

Risotto or pasta with truffles – push the boat out

Riesling Schoelhammer, Hugel

17

REGION

Alsace

COUNTRY

France

GRAPE

Riesling

PRICE

***

This wine should be an Alsace Grand Cru. Should be, but isn't. It comes from the Schoenenbourg vineyard, a Grand Cru that rises in a steep slope just outside the medieval walls of the town of Riquewihr; the vines are in fact a nugget of 30 south-facing rows in mid-slope, as good as you can get. But it's not a Grand Cru because Hugel, having been instrumental in driving the Grand Cru classification in Alsace, then boycotted it because Johnny Hugel believed that the Grand Cru vineyard boundaries had been drawn too generously, allowing in unsuitable sites.

He was right, but on the other hand the classification has done more good than harm to Alsace and its wines. So the current generation at Hugel has edged round, and in future years this wine might be declared as a Grand Cru. Until the 2007 vintage it went into Hugel's Jubilee range: now, allowed to shine on its own, it reveals extraordinary tension and minerality. It's not about the flavour of Riesling; it's about the flavour of this particular south-facing 63 ares of clay-marl soil, sloping at 25 degrees, expressed by a company that has always favoured the austere, the slow-to-develop, over the ebullient and come-hitherish.

The first vintage was 2007, released in 2015. It's a wine of crystalline purity and transparent depth: it's like looking into a perfectly clear river to the stones beneath. Flavours of tangerine peel, earth, white flowers, apple, spice, salt and herbs, intensely bright and penetrating.

It's pronounced "Shell hammer", by the way.

DRINK WITH

Dover sole, turbot;
something special

BEST AGE TO DRINK

On release, or keep for
a decade or two

TROPHY VINTAGES

2007, 2008

DECANT

It wouldn't hurt

CHILL

A little

**WHAT TO SAY IF YOU
MEET THE WINEMAKER**

Why is Alsace terroir
so varied?

AND WHAT NOT TO SAY

Is it German?

PAUPER SUBSTITUTE

Riesling Jubilee,
from other plots in
the Schoenenbourg
vineyard

45

Châteauneuf-du-Pape Blanc, Roussanne Vieilles Vignes, Château de Beaucastel

18

REGION
....
Southern Rhône

COUNTRY
....
France

GRAPE
....
Roussanne

PRICE
....
** →***

This is one of the most famous whites of the Rhône, from an estate that traces its history back to the 16th century, now being run by the fourth and fifth generation of the Perrin family. The Perrins teamed up with Brad Pitt and Angelina Jolie to make their Provence rosé.

Roussanne is a difficult, finicky grape to grow, and most Châteauneuf producers hedge their bets with Clairette, Bourboulenc and Grenache Blanc; this, though, is 100% Roussanne, from a parcel of vines planted in 1909. The flavours are astonishingly complex: orange blossom, verveine, lime blossom, fresh herbs, citrus, honey, pepper, and a gingerbread richness at the core. It's exotic and elegant, concentrated, opulent: bone dry, yet with enormous richness; relatively low in acidity, yet fresh.

The soil is the classic Châteauneuf *galets*, the rounded alluvial stones that make it look a bit like a reclaimed beach. Since the Rhône once ran through here, a reclaimed beach is pretty much what it is. The vines are bush-trained in the style called *gobelet* ("goblet", which tells you the shape of the vine), this suits the climate: hot in the summer, and subject to the Mistral, which whips through here. The estate was an early convert to biodynamics and isn't a fan of oak flavours, so the herb and floral flavours shine through. If you want to age it be aware that it tends to shut down after a few years, and it can be hard to predict when it will re-emerge. In youth it is so splendid that it's debatable whether it gains much.

DRINK WITH

Best ham, pasta with spring vegetables, coquilles St Jacques, turbot with beurre blanc

The producers recommend drinking it within three years or after fifteen

TROPHY VINTAGES

2009, 2010, 2011, 2013, 2014, 2015

DECANT

No

CHILL

Yes

WHAT TO SAY IF YOU MEET THE WINEMAKER

Are you unusual in growing all 13 Châteauneuf varieties?

AND WHAT NOT TO SAY

What are Brad and Angelina really like?

PAUPER SUBSTITUTE

The Perrins' Coudoulet de Beaucastel Blanc is famously good value for the quality

19

Châteauneuf-du-Pape, Château Rayas

REGION

Southern Rhône

COUNTRY

France

GRAPE

Grenache

PRICE

*****

It's difficult to know if Rayas would be quite so fascinating if its maker wasn't so famously elusive and eccentric. It is now run by the elusive Emmanuel Reynaud, nephew of the elusive Jacques Reynaud; Jacques was the son of the elusive Louis Reynaud, who used to jump into a ditch and hide to avoid visitors. Emmanuel is a hair's-breadth less elusive, but only that.

The winery is also famously eccentric: ramshackle, and with less focus on antiseptic cleanliness than is usual these days. There is dust, and there are cobwebs, and not much light, and to find the place at all you need a touch of second sight because (obviously) it's not signposted from the main road.

The wine, however, is even more unexpected. It comes from a vineyard of the same name, ten hectares in size, with sandy soil, and it's firmly in the traditionalist Châteauneuf camp: don't expect dark colours and new oak here. Instead the wine is pale, perfumed, subtle, redolent of lavender and honeysuckle, sandalwood and spice. It has proper muscle at its heart when young, and is intense, compelling, with sweet fruit, tannin clothed in flesh, and great purity and succulence. It is essence of Grenache; and wine made from 100% Grenache is rare in Châteauneuf. Few producers grow the full 13 varieties, but nearly all favour blends. Rayas is in a class of its own.

DRINK WITH

Roast pork

20

Condrieu Vertige, Yves Cuilleron

REGION

Northern Rhône

COUNTRY

France

GRAPE

Viognier

PRICE

** →***

A wine whose name means "vertigo" is already telling you something about its vineyard. The steepness of the slopes in Condrieu, and the difficulty and expense of working them, meant that in the mid-20th century the appellation went into decline, and by 1965 only eight hectares of vines were left in this great, classic spot. Viognier, the only grape planted in Condrieu, was fast vanishing from the map.

Time for a revival. In Condrieu, it's very hard to beat Yves Cuilleron. He's charming, unassuming and focused. He has ten hectares of Condrieu (yes, more than was planted in the whole appellation in 1965). Vertige comes from a single parcel of vines, planted at a density of 8–10,000 per hectare, which is a lot. The soil is granite, which gives freshness to wine, and the vines are in the great south-facing amphitheatre of the Coteau du Vernon. The wine is fermented with natural yeasts in barrique, and aged for another 18 months on the lees in barrique.

What emerges is a wine of tense exoticism, of restrained opulence. Viognier is good at opulence, but it can be too tarty, too oily and obvious. Cuilleron's Condrieu is never obvious. Yes, there are the spiced, dried-apricot flavours that everyone loves in Viognier, and a richly textured palate that might otherwise signal a sweet wine, but this is mineral, dry, all stones and salt, honey, peaches, white blossom, citrus pith; it's compact and expansive at the same time, a miracle of contrasting textures. Much good Viognier has the exuberance of a baroque palace; this is more like the perfect pace of a Nash terrace in Bath.

DRINK WITH

Tender spring peas and beans with pasta

51

21

L'Ermite Blanc, Ermitage, M. Chapoutier

REGION

Northern Rhône

COUNTRY

France

GRAPE

Marsanne

PRICE

*****

I defy you to find a Marsanne better than this. Chapoutier makes three Sélections Parcellaires (single-vineyard wines) from Hermitage; Le Méal Blanc is the most powerful, De L'Orée Blanc the most yellow-fruited, but this has, for me, the perfect balance of aromas, silkiness and tautness. It is from the top of the Hermitage hill, around the chapel, where the granite soil turns to granilite, which is alkaline, with a pH of 7.5–8, and Michel Chapoutier loves it. It gives a wine of seamless tension, great concentration and elegant lightness, with flavours of honeysuckle and yellow peach, almonds and beeswax, complex, concentrated and extremely long. It also has remarkable freshness in spite of Marsanne's low acidity. It's because of the grape's high tannins, says Chapoutier: "the bitterness of Marsanne is like the tannin of a red wine, and gives the potential for ageing."

The vines are around 140 years old; all of the vineyards are farmed biodynamically, and fermentation is with natural yeasts. Chapoutier has cut back on the amount of new oak he uses: the barrels are 600-litres, for less oak influence, and he does some *battonage* but very gently, so as not to lose the carbonic gas. He claims that the L'Ermite bottling was born because when he suggested to Philippe Jaboulet that they might swap some vines – some of Jaboulet's vines in Méal for some of Chapoutier's in L'Ermite – Jaboulet refused because the L'Ermite vines were too young. This wine was Chapoutier's riposte.

DRINK WITH

Chicken with truffles

Up to at least 30 years,
probably more

TROPHY VINTAGES

1999, 2000, 2003,
2004, 2006, 2009,
2010, 2011, 2012 (Michel
Chapoutier's favourite),
2013, 2014, 2015

DECANT

It would look
pretty decanted

CHILL

A little

WHAT TO SAY IF YOU
MEET THE WINEMAKER

Would you like a glass
of Bollinger? (He always
has one before or after
London press tastings,
claiming it's the only
way his UK agents ever
pay him)

AND WHAT NOT TO SAY

Can I have one too?

PAUPER SUBSTITUTE

Chante Alouette
Hermitage is also
100% Marsanne

22

Hermitage, Domaine J.-L. Chave

REGION

Northern Rhône

COUNTRY

France

GRAPE

Syrah

PRICE

★★★★ →★★★★★

The meticulous, artisanal Hermitage of J.-L. Chave is not the showiest wine of the appellation: the perfection is in the detail, the harmony. It is always a blend – Chave's only other Hermitage is Cuvée Cathelin, based on a parcel in Les Bessards, bottled in the very best vintages, years that can stand up to the 100 per cent new oak ageing. Is it better than the standard Hermitage? With only 200 cases released, it's difficult to form a judgement. But the standard Hermitage is exceedingly hard to beat. It is sturdy, full of tannin and toasted spice, flesh and backbone and muscle, minerality, cassis intensity, herbs and stones, iodine and pepper, black olives and charred steak, sweet raspberry fruit and violets. It has an endearing velvet gentleness to its power, and enlivening freshness.

That harmony comes from Syrah in eight different *lieux-dits* in Hermitage, with the blend done a year after the vintage. Around 10–20 per cent of the oak is new; most of the grapes are destemmed and there is no filtration. The winemaking has evolved over the years, of course, but remains pretty traditional. Everything in the winery is minimal intervention, so that what shines through is the vineyards.

The eight *lieux-dits* give a variety of styles: Bessards and Greffieux give tannic wines with backbone; Le Méal gives density; Beaumes and L'Ermite give aroma; lower sites like Péléat are more opulent. Harmony, believes Chave, comes from blending.

DRINK WITH

Venison, wild boar, ox cheek

It takes six to ten years
to come round, and then
lasts for fifteen to twenty

TROPHY VINTAGES

1990, 1991, 1995, 1998,
1999, 2000, 2001, 2005,
2006, 2007, 2009, 2010,
2012, 2015, 2016

DECANT

Yes

CHILL

No

**WHAT TO SAY IF YOU
MEET THE WINEMAKER**

Have you really handed
everything down from
father to son since 1481?

AND WHAT NOT TO SAY

How did you manage to
have enough sons?

PAUPER SUBSTITUTE

Côtes du Rhône Mon
Coeur; it's from the
Southern Rhône,
so mostly not Syrah,
but you get the Chave
perfectionism

23

Chinon Vieilles Vignes, Philippe Alliet

REGION

Chinon, Loire

COUNTRY

France

GRAPE

Cabernet Franc

PRICE

*

DRINK WITH

Veal, pigeon

If you want enlivening, appetizing reds that sing; plenty of aroma, lots of fruit and a few flowers, a sense of minerality and terroir, some grip and a touch of spice and cedar and a streak of pepper, the Loire is where to look. Cabernet Franc, when it goes south to Bordeaux, gets riper and sleeker but is still fresh, and is usually blended: see Vieux Château Certan, page 18. Here in the Loire, and particularly in Chinon, it retains a crunch.

The Alliet *chai* is dug into the tuffeau rock that rises steeply above the Vienne River (I know I said Loire earlier: the Vienne joins the Loire). From the outside it's a cross between a fairytale and a theatre set: a creamy-yellow rock face with an impeccable wooden door and windows. It looks as though the rock is growing back over the smooth masonry of the façade; that if you stayed inside too long you might never get out again. But these troglodyte cellars and houses are extremely comfortable: dry, with a stable temperature. They're ideal for making and ageing wine.

Alliet's Vielles Vignes is given a long fermentation here and aged in old barriques for about 18 months, having been grown on the deep gravel terraces that border the Vienne. The vines are 50 years old; yields are low, ripeness is perfect, and the grapes are destemmed to remove any hint of the greenness that can bedevil Loire reds. The result is full of cherries and tobacco, bay and raspberries, powerful and fresh, seductive, polished and with a sense of ease; Alliet wines never seem to have to try.

BEST AGE TO DRINK

Up to a decade

TROPHY VINTAGES

2005, 2009, 2010, 2015

DECANT

Yes

CHILL

No

**WHAT TO SAY IF YOU
MEET THE WINEMAKER**

Which Bordeaux wines
inspire you most?

AND WHAT NOT TO SAY

Do you think you're
making typical Chinon?

PAUPER SUBSTITUTE

The basic Chinon
is a lovely vibrant,
appetizing wine

24 Pouilly-Fumé Silex, Didier Dagueneau

REGION

Pouilly-Fumé, Loire

COUNTRY

France

GRAPE

Sauvignon Blanc

PRICE

→*

DRINK WITH

Something that will show off the wine; a goat's cheese soufflé, perhaps

Didier Dagueneau was known as the wild man of Pouilly – lots of hair, lots of ideas, not one to suffer fools gladly – and when he was killed in a microlight accident at the age of 52 the wine world went into shock. His son Louis-Benjamin – who had been about to set up his own domaine – is now in charge, and while he has (so far) less hair he is committed to running the estate in the same way. This means very low yields; working the soil with horses instead of tractors; everything of the most meticulous.

Pouilly-Fumé is across the river from Sancerre, and usually Sancerre is better. Dagueneau never minded telling his fellow-vignerons so, either: he was, and his domaine is, the exception, a shining light of quality to show what Sauvignon Blanc can be.

What it can and should be in the Loire is terroir-driven, ripe and tense, tasting of citrus and salt, and capable of ageing. It's the opposite of most New Zealand Sauvignon Blanc. It's wine for grown-ups.

"Silex" refers to a type of soil, the flint soil that is found in parts of Pouilly-Fumé (and parts of Sancerre too). It produces long-ageing and relatively slow-maturing wine with a certain sparkle, which could just be my overheated imagination, but I always find it. Dagueneau's Silex is rich and full, tense and mineral; utterly confident and resonant. It is not about the flavours of the grape; not at all. There's cream and exotic fruits, all wound round a tight core. It needs time to unwind. It's also in great demand, so if you want to buy some, good luck.

BEST AGE TO DRINK

Not before five years

TROPHY VINTAGES

2005, 2008, 2009, 2010, 2012, 2014, 2015

DECANT

No

CHILL

Yes

WHAT TO SAY IF YOU MEET THE WINEMAKER

How are the horses?

AND WHAT NOT TO SAY

I love New Zealand Sauvignon

PAUPER SUBSTITUTE

There's the Blanc Fumé de Pouilly, if you're a rich pauper; Asteroide, from ungrafted wines, if you're a rich millionaire

Savennières Clos du Papillon, Domaine du Closel

25

REGION

Savennières, Loire

COUNTRY

France

GRAPE

Chenin Blanc

PRICE

**

DRINK WITH

Fish or white meat, truffles, mushrooms, cheese

If a vineyard happens to be butterfly-shaped, what would you call it? Quite. Clos du Papillon perches mid-slope in a little valley, facing southwest towards the Loire. The soil is shallow, and full of schist and quartz; the site is prone to botrytis, and the final blend is a mix of botrytized and unbotrytized grapes, the former for richness, the latter for freshness. So it's quite an exotic butterfly, aged in old oak for about 16 months on the lees: there's weight to balance the acidity.

Closel is a beautiful property: a turreted château tucked behind high walls on the edge of the town, with a landscape garden of trees and water, and cattle wandering in the grounds; if you didn't already know you might guess that organic is the rule here. Low intervention in the cellars and biodiversity in the vineyards is the mantra.

But what is Savennières? Simply, the best dry Chenin Blanc there is. You could say that dry Vouvray rivals it; but Savennières at its best has a mineral intensity matched with a taut lightness-yet-fullness that is hard to beat. Climate change is being kind to it, too; ripe years are in the majority now. It can be a difficult wine to grasp, for the novice. High acidity, intense minerality and the sort of tension that takes a few years to round out, mean that it can be quite tight in youth, bright and dark at the same time. Give it time and it turns to honey, albeit honey of a rather intellectual sort; honey on a shard of rock, with baked quince and beeswax. It's thrilling and compelling.

BEST AGE TO DRINK

From about five years
to about fifteen

TROPHY VINTAGES

2001, 2002, 2004,
2005, 2006, 2007, 2008,
2009, 2010, 2011, 2013

DECANT

No

CHILL

Yes

WHAT TO SAY IF YOU
MEET THE WINEMAKER

You come from a line
of women winemakers

AND WHAT NOT TO SAY

Is this a wine for women?

PAUPER SUBSTITUTE

La Jalousie is earlier
picked, fresh and light

26

Vouvray Moelleux, Huet

REGION

Vouvray, Loire

COUNTRY

France

GRAPE

Chenin Blanc

PRICE

****

This is the gerontophilia spot. Huet *moelleux* and demi-sec last as near forever as makes no difference, so I'm going to say: hunt down an old vintage. The estate was bought in 2003 by businessman Antony Hwang, who also owns the Királyudvar estate in Tokaj, Hungary. The new management sold a lot of old bottles from the cellar when it took over, and Berry Bros & Rudd (BBR) in London bought the lot. Make BBR your starting point. Don't worry about age: Huet sweet Chenins will live a hundred years.

I haven't specified a cuvée because all the demi-sec and *moelleux* wines from here will please: take what you can find. When young the wines are tight, all lemon curd, apple and honey on the nose, plus melon, apricots, nuts and herbs; they're very concentrated, rich and tense. The palate is full of cream, lime and herbs, great complexity. As they unwind with age they keep their tension and the complexity builds; the intensity becomes if anything more immediate, more insistent, and the honey and cream notes develop. There are flavours of baked apple, vanilla, nectarine, apricot and toffee, all spiked with intense linear acidity. Extraordinary wines from probably the greatest terroirs in Vouvray, made by a hugely experienced team.

DRINK WITH

Best on its own after dinner. If you must, then very best cheese, but it will only distract from the wine

27 Bandol Rosé, Domaine Tempier

REGION

Provence

COUNTRY

France

GRAPES

**Mourvèdre,
Grenache, Cinsault**

PRICE

* → **

The main problem with selecting the wines for this book was just that – selecting. The estates jumped out; but having decided that Domaine So-and-So had to be in, which wine to choose?

Domaine Tempier demands inclusion for the transcendent *joie-de-vivre* of its wines; their mineral, precise, dancing depth. Tempier led the revival of Bandol and established it as a wine of individuality and complexity; everything Tempier makes is splendid. And so here, for your consideration, is the rosé.

A bit of a south of France cliché, no? Not this one. This will age for up to 20 years, which (assuming you're fairly young now) gives you plenty of time. Rosé is not normally expected to age, and most Tempier rosé is drunk young, to the mild regret of the owners. In youth it's stony and pure, with flavours of *garrigue*, rosehips, redcurrants, and it ages to cream, wet earth and roses, complex and structured. It's got the backbone and complexity to deal with the pungent food of Provence at any age, so you won't lose out if you drink it young. But if you happened to forget about a couple of bottles in the cellar…

Winemaker Daniel Ravier has made a few changes that have paid dividends: the vineyards are now farmed biodynamically and fermentation is spontaneous, with no laboratory yeasts. The rosé is made by direct pressing, as is usual in Provence, and is based on the characterful Mourvèdre grape: Bandol is the only appellation in the world to demand 50% Mourvèdre. The rosé also sells out fast, so if you happen not to be able to find any, take a Tempier red instead. You'll be happy either way.

DRINK
WITH

**Pungent fish or
vegetable dishes,
tapenade,
ratatouille**

BEST AGE TO DRINK

Young or with up to
20 years' age

TROPHY VINTAGES

None

DECANT

No

CHILL

Only slightly

**WHAT TO SAY IF YOU
MEET THE WINEMAKER**

Tell me about
Mourvèdre, the key
grape of Bandol

AND WHAT NOT TO SAY

I prefer a different shade
of pink

PAUPER SUBSTITUTE

It's not overpriced

28

Quintessence du Petit Manseng, Domaine Cauhapé

REGION

Jurançon,
Southwest France

COUNTRY

France

GRAPE

Petit Manseng

PRICE

****

There are not very many sweet wines in this book and this, I confess, is because I don't have a sweet tooth. My annual consumption of sweet wines does nothing to keep the industry solvent.

So when I do drink one I want it to be amazing. This, from the remote southwest of France in the foothills of the Pyrenees, is from the Petit Manseng grape. Manseng, according to a local ampelographer, was a name given locally to the best varieties; there's also Gros Manseng, which is related, and Manseng Noir, which isn't. (The worst local grapes were apparently known as "Bordelais", which might have been a local joke.) Domaine Cauhapé is the leading producer in Jurançon and has done more than anybody to put the wines and the region in the spotlight. The dry wines, usually from Gros Manseng, are remarkable – lime-scented and apricot-fruited. The sweet ones are all that, plus plus plus. This is the top cuvée of several, picked in the second half of December when the grapes are shrivelled and super-ripe, and the wine is almost savoury in the way that Seville orange marmalade can be almost savoury: intensely concentrated, with high acidity to balance the sweetness. These wines are from grapes that are *passerillé*, shrivelled on the vine, rather than from grapes affected by noble rot, though in some years there might be some noble rot. The flavour from *passerillé* grapes is different – purer, perhaps; more direct. This is a rare, distinctive wine.

DRINK WITH

Foie gras, powerful
blue cheese

Arbois Vin Jaune La Vasée, Domaine André & Mireille Tissot

29

REGION

Jura

COUNTRY

France

GRAPE

Savagnin

PRICE

** →****

There are just two hectares of the La Vasée vineyard at Domaine Tissot, so there's not a lot of this wine about. Vin Jaune is a Jura speciality, and it's rare because it involves putting young wine from the high-acid Savagnin grape into barrel, leaving it for six years while it grows a thin veil of flor, in the manner of Fino Sherry, and then bottling it; the barrels aren't topped up, so what is left in a 228-litre barrel divides neatly into 228 x 62cl bottles called *clavelins*.

The key differences between this and Fino are there is no solera system and the Savagnin grape has enormous acidity compared to the low acidity of Palomino. So while the flor affects the flavour, the results aren't the same. You get a similar wet-earth-after-rain note, similar nuts, hay and apples, but allied to steely acidity.

Stéphane Tissot's wine is remarkable stuff: aromatic, linear, austere, pungent and in flavour part-way to malt whisky (Tissot, a great innovator, has even experimented with ageing Vin Jaune in an ex-whisky cask from Isle of Jura), with iodine, salt, pickled lemon and cheese notes, savoury and stony. It's also quite restrained: it doesn't shout and you need to spend time with it to get to know it, perhaps over a meal. It's a natural with the local Comté cheese, and if you were feeling flush you could use it in the classic dish of chicken with Vin Jaune and morels, with more Vin Jaune in your glass.

DRINK WITH

Poulet au Vin Jaune,
in an ideal world

Vin Jaune 2009 "La Vasée"

BÉNÉDICTE & STÉPHANE TISSOT

ARBOIS

BEST AGE TO DRINK

From about ten years old to thirty or more

TROPHY VINTAGES

None

DECANT

It needs to breathe, so either decant or open in advance

CHILL

The producer recommends serving it at 14°C (57°F)

WHAT TO SAY IF YOU MEET THE WINEMAKER

How much extra work is it to be biodynamic?

AND WHAT NOT TO SAY

Why are you always experimenting?

PAUPER SUBSTITUTE

If I was going to be wicked I'd say Fino Sherry

30 Barbaresco, Angelo Gaja

REGION

Barbaresco, Piedmont

COUNTRY

Italy

GRAPE

Nebbiolo

PRICE

*** →****

Angelo Gaja is one of the giants of Italian wine, with an ego to match: he was the driving force in the revival of Piedmont in general and Barbaresco in particular. He's often thought of as being an arch modernist but in fact he's only semi-modern: he uses new-oak barriques for example, but also old Slavonian oak *botti*. This is indisputably a trophy wine, beloved of collectors and label-drinkers.

Which doesn't mean that the rest of us aren't allowed a go. Gaja makes wines of grace and beauty, of vast depth and concentration that make it all look easy. It's a point to remember: great wines shouldn't be hard work to taste or drink – unless they're going through a youthful closed period, which is different. Great wine should be invigorating, not tiring.

Gaja's wines are never tiring. They're balanced and rich, always fresh, always aromatic. The Nebbiolo grape in Barbaresco is less massive than it is in Barolo, and the tannins less pronounced, but the florality of the grape, those seductive rose and peony perfumes, the notes of herbs, are still there. This is easily the equal of any Barolo in terms of quality, but it's more approachable and matures a bit younger; it's superbly elegant. It's a blend of up to 14 vineyards; there are also three single-vineyard Barbarescos (Sorì Tildìn, Sorì San Lorenzo and Costa Russi); Angelo Gaja took them out of the Barbaresco DOC in order to be able to add a touch of Barbera to them, but from 2013 his daughter, the remarkably named (and very able) Gaia Gaja has taken them back to Barbaresco.

DRINK WITH

A good chunk of well-aged beef

BEST AGE TO DRINK

Give it at least six years; but it will last for decades

TROPHY VINTAGES

1989, 1990, 1996, 2000, 2001, 2004, 2010, 2011, 2012, 2013, 2015

DECANT

Yes

CHILL

No

WHAT TO SAY IF YOU MEET THE WINEMAKER

What's it like working with such a powerful, dynamic father?

AND WHAT NOT TO SAY

Why are you called Gaia?

PAUPER SUBSTITUTE

This is the pauper wine; sorry – the single-vineyard wines are far more expensive

31

Barolo Monfortino, Giacomo Conterno

REGION

Barolo, Piedmont

COUNTRY

Italy

GRAPE

Nebbiolo

PRICE

*****

It's invidious, at this level, to say that one wine is better than another: a particular bottle may be better, or a particular vintage. But a wine? And this is probably as good as wine gets: Giacomo Conterno's Monfortino bottling is only released in the best years. It's aged for seven or eight years in cask, and it emerges with flavours of dried porcini, walnuts, coffee, chocolate, dried figs, tar, liquorice and haunting notes of peony. It has endless depth and power balanced by freshness, elegance and precision. It feels like the silky purr of a very expensive engine, and it's one of the great wines of the world.

The grapes are a selection from the 14-hectare Cascina Francia vineyard, facing mostly west to southwest, in Serralunga d'Alba, which the family bought in 1974. Monfortinos before that date were made from bought-in grapes. It was easier to buy good grapes in those days, Roberto Conterno, Giacomo's son, points out. Now it's clear that buying that vineyard was one of the best things they ever did. It often outpaces poor vintages by producing far better quality than the year would suggest; it also gives wine of a sensual, exotic character that is thrilling in youth, muscular and dense, and ages to a silky savouriness, seamless and harmonious. It should also be noted that Giacomo Conterno is an arch-traditionalist – no new oak, no temperature control in fermentation – and Roberto is following the same principles. Giacomo's brother Aldo – the family split over their vision of wine, as has happened in rather a lot of Italian families – is also a traditionalist, though becoming more modern now, and also very good. But Giacomo takes the crown.

DRINK WITH

The best lamb, beef or game

Start at about ten years, and then just keep on going

All of them, but especially 1970, 1971, 1978, 1982, 1985, 1999, 2001, 2004, 2006

Yes

No

Is fashion moving away from flashy wines?

Is it difficult to work with your family?

Barbera d'Alba Cerretta; different grape, same winemaker

32 Barolo La Serra, Roberto Voerzio

REGION

Barolo, Piedmont

COUNTRY

Italy

GRAPE

Nebbiolo

PRICE

***

If you want to talk about modernism and tradition in Barolo (and it is less relevant than it was, as most producers adopt a bit of both), then you would put Roberto Voerzio in the modernist camp. The wines have bright, black fruit, great minerality – there's a real feeling of stoniness – and there are new-oak barriques in the cellar, which reveal themselves in the wine as a certain toastiness. But it's not overdone and doesn't exceed 30 per cent; the rest of the oak is old barriques and *botti*, and extraction of tannins is very gentle. These are not muscle-monsters; instead they are fine-grained wines of great precision. They are a different aspect of Barolo to Giacomo Conterno (see page 73). Barolo can be more than one thing.

The winery was founded in 1986 in La Morra, a village that gives some of the most elegant Barolos; La Serra is a great terroir, southeast-facing and thus slightly cooler than some, and giving more floral wines. (The name means "the greenhouse", which admittedly doesn't sound that cool.) Davide Voerzio, Roberto's son, is now in charge, and treats his vineyards with meticulous care. Yields are low, and then he prunes each cluster to get rid of any berries that don't match up. This might sound a tad *garagiste*, but what he's after is purity of expression. There is no filtration. Yeasts are wild, and the wines have a lightness and finesse that belies their power. You won't stub your palate on a brick of tannins here, nor will you find a gap on the palate between structure and aroma. These wines are seamless.

DRINK WITH

White truffles would be good

BEST AGE TO DRINK

Start at five or six years
old, and continue for
twenty or more

TROPHY VINTAGES

1990, 1996, 2000, 2001,
2004, 2010, 2011, 2012,
2013, 2015

DECANT

Yes

CHILL

No

WHAT TO SAY IF YOU
MEET THE WINEMAKER

Half a kilo (1lb 2oz)
of grapes per vine
isn't much

AND WHAT NOT TO SAY

Why don't you increase
your production?

PAUPER SUBSTITUTE

Langhe Nebbiolo di
San Francesco from
the same producer

33

Case Basse, Gianfranco Soldera

REGION

Tuscany

COUNTRY

Italy

GRAPE

Sangiovese

PRICE

**** –*****

To call Gianfranco Soldera an outsider would be an understatement. The wine from the estate he started from scratch in 1972 has been at various times Brunello di Montalcino, Brunello di Montalcino Riserva, Rosso di Montalcino and Vino da Tavola; and when he resigned from the local *consorzio* in 2013 it retaliated by sacking him. (From 2006 all the wine is Toscana IGT.) In 2012 much of the already tiny production of his nine hectares, maturing in old oak *botti* in his cellars, was lost when an intruder opened the taps to let the 2007–2012 vintages run away; a disgruntled ex-employee was later convicted.

The wine, sold under the single name of Case Basse (from 2006), is extraordinary. It demands total concentration; it rewards with endless complexity. It can be enigmatic; you might write one tasting note at the beginning of a glass, another at the end. Descriptors like "fruity" or "spicy" aren't adequate; you'll find yourself writing flights of fancy that will make you wonder, the next day, what you were on. Simple: you were on Case Basse. To talk of harmony, poetry, music and, more mundanely, elegance and precision, will give an idea.

Winemaking is with indigenous yeasts (he's fascinated by yeasts) and involves minimal intervention; there is no temperature control at fermentation, for example. The wines age in casks for between 48 and 75 months. Viticulture is all about biodiversity and the avoidance of artificial pesticides, fungicides and herbicides. There's not much made, and even less available with the loss of most of six vintages. But if you do find a bottle, get it. And then listen to it.

DRINK WITH

Best beef rib

From release onwards, with no end in sight

TROPHY VINTAGES

The first vintage was 1975; Soldera thinks the 1976, 1989 and 1992 were slightly under par, but he's known for making great wine even in difficult years

DECANT

Yes, just before serving; then let the wine open in the glass

CHILL

Soldera recommends serving at 17–18°C (63–64°F)

WHAT TO SAY IF YOU MEET THE WINEMAKER

I know I'm not allowed to spit

AND WHAT NOT TO SAY

Where's the spittoon?

PAUPER SUBSTITUTE

There's a red lily, *Lilium soldera*, named after the wine, that might be some sort of consolation prize; otherwise nothing

34 Sassicaia, Tenuta San Guido

REGION

Bolgheri, Tuscany

COUNTRY

Italy

GRAPES

Cabernet Sauvignon, Cabernet Franc

PRICE

***

The story of Sassicaia's birth involves an aristocrat, a wine region that wasn't yet a wine region and a love of Bordeaux – the same love of Bordeaux that inspired so many wines around the world, and several in this book. Sassicaia stayed under the radar for several decades: the first vintage was 1941, after Marchese Mario Incisa della Rocchetta planted vines on his land in Bolgheri, near the Tuscan coast. (The cuttings came from the vineyards of an old friend, near Pisa.) It wasn't a wine region because it was too warm for Sangiovese, Tuscany's great red grape; but the Marchese planted Cabernet. Why not? He was in love with Bordeaux.

Only with the 1968 vintage was it launched commercially. The world went mad for it. It changed vinous fashions in Tuscany – suddenly everybody wanted Cabernet, and everybody started planting Cabernet. The name SuperTuscans was coined for those wines that, like Sassicaia, scorned the DOC system because they used the wrong grapes, and were made in the wrong way and in the wrong places.

They won, of course, and now Bolgheri has some of the most expensive vineyard land in Italy, and its own DOC. There are more famous wines here than you could shake a stick at. But Sassicaia is, to my palate, still the best, the most elegant, the most refined. It's savoury, herbal, tasting of roses and spice, violets and graphite. It doesn't have the bright density of some of its rivals, but it has a beguiling delicacy, an almost Pinot-like succulence and precision. You can flirt with other great Bolgheri reds, but you'll always come back to Sassicaia.

DRINK WITH

Rich meat dishes, slow-cooked

BEST AGE TO DRINK

From four or five years,
for ten or twenty

TROPHY VINTAGES

1985, 1988, 1990, 1995,
1998, 2001, 2004, 2007

DECANT

Yes

CHILL

No

**WHAT TO SAY IF YOU
MEET THE WINEMAKER**

What does the
name mean?

AND WHAT NOT TO SAY

What are you trying
to copy?

PAUPER SUBSTITUTE

Le Difese, from the same
estate, has the same
floral, herbal character

35

I Capitelli, Anselmi

REGION

Veneto

COUNTRY

Italy

GRAPE

Garganega

PRICE

* (50cl)

This is Recioto di Soave that isn't Soave: Roberto Anselmi left the Soave DOC in 2000 (with a decidedly outspoken open letter) in protest at the relaxation of regulations in the region. He preferred to plant more vines per hectare (7,000 instead of the usual 1,200), take a lower yield per vine (three clusters instead of the usual fifteen) and make wine his way unhindered by a DOC, which, he said rather firmly, had got it wrong.

So this is Recioto di Soave as it ought to be, but minus the official name. What Anselmi produces is a sweet wine that is like drinking spiced pears in syrup with Jersey cream: it is utterly seductive and delicious. It's not intensely sweet, but it is concentrated and fresh, with notes of lemon, tangerine, apricot and wildflowers. It's complex, and very, very long on the palate. It's made in the same way as Recioto: ripe bunches are put to dry on racks, in a single layer. They shrivel and concentrate, and in November begin to show signs of noble rot. (The skill is in managing the temperature and humidity so that the rot is noble, not the related grey rot, which ruins the grapes.) The biochemistry of the process is complicated, but it's far more than mere raisining, and it produces a myriad of new flavours.

In February the grapes are pressed and the juice fermented naturally in oak barriques, and then aged in barrique for about 16 months. Everything is done with minimal intervention and maximum sensitivity.

DRINK WITH

Crème brûlée, cheesecake, sticky toffee pudding

BEST AGE TO DRINK

About five years, and
then for easily ten more

TROPHY VINTAGES

None

DECANT

No

CHILL

Yes

**WHAT TO SAY IF YOU
MEET THE WINEMAKER**

Are there any
vineyards in Soave
better than yours?

AND WHAT NOT TO SAY

Don't you miss the DOC?

PAUPER SUBSTITUTE

This is really good value

36 Soave La Rocca, Pieropan

REGION

Soave, Veneto

COUNTRY

Italy

GRAPE

Garganega

PRICE

*

The best view of Soave is from the vineyards; and this view, if you get well up into the hills, also tells you all you need to know about the difference between great Soave and run-of-the-mill Soave. Down on the flat plain there are long rows of vines producing lavish quantities of grapes. Up on the hills, where you're standing among outcrops of black volcanic rock and pale, weathered limestone, it looks quite simple: black and white, even. Yields are lower up on the hills. Flavours are intense. Good single-vineyard Soave, and Pieropan's La Rocca is the benchmark, is a serious wine for the long term.

La Rocca is calcareous, terraced and faces southwest. The grapes are entirely Garganega – one of Italy's great white grapes, giving wine of substance and depth, structured and creamy. And while Italians have never been fond of extravagantly aromatic whites, Garganega is nevertheless aromatic in a pears and apricots, lemons and almonds sort of way. It is not showy, but it has presence and even a touch of opulence, balanced with savoury acidity. There are no barriques involved in this wine: it's all steel and old oak, for subtlety and elegance.

The first time I became aware of just how well La Rocca ages was in a restaurant in Venice, when there was a 20-year-old bottle on the list. It seemed like a bit of a punt – it was the only old vintage they had – but it was amazing: rich, nutty, silky, vigorous, winey. I've forgotten the vintage and I've forgotten the restaurant, but I remember the taste.

DRINK WITH

Fish, poultry, cheese;
it's versatile

BEST AGE TO DRINK

It will last a couple
of decades or more,
and deserves at least
a few years

TROPHY VINTAGES

Not really

DECANT

No

CHILL

Yes

**WHAT TO SAY IF YOU
MEET THE WINEMAKER**

Is La Rocca the best
vineyard in Soave?

AND WHAT NOT TO SAY

Would you ever sell it?

PAUPER SUBSTITUTE

The estate Soave

37

Valpolicella Classico Superiore, Quintarelli

REGION

Valpolicella, Veneto

COUNTRY

Italy

GRAPES

Corvina, Rondinella, Molinara

PRICE

**

Quintarelli is a bit of a legend in Valpolicella. Bepi Quintarelli, who died in 2012, was thoroughly traditional: the tasting room looked as though it hadn't been tidied for a hundred years, never mind updated. The light was so dim you could hardly see, and spitting was banned. Quintarelli is regarded as the leading "traditionalist" grower in the region (one fellow-grower calls Quintarelli the Ferrari of the traditionalists, with several Maseratis just underneath), as opposed to the "modernists" who favour more fruit-forward wines. Bepi's daughter and grandchildren are now in charge, with the same winemaking team and the same insistence on tradition. What has changed is the attitude towards quality control – now a lot tighter – and, um, hygiene. It's really clean now. There's a car park. But still no spitting.

The wines are remarkable: long ageing in wood produces silky, filigree wines of elegance and finesse and no shortage of concentration, with balsamic notes, herbs, aromatic cherries, spice and pepper.

Will the style gradually change? At the moment all the available wines date from Bepi's reign – it's because of that long ageing. There are some new oak barrels in the cellars, which are apparently so well integrated into the ageing programme that the style of the wine will not be affected. We shall see.

DRINK WITH

Pork, well-flavoured

BEST AGE TO DRINK

On release

TROPHY VINTAGES

None, really

DECANT

No

CHILL

No

WHAT TO SAY IF YOU MEET THE WINEMAKER

How much can you change and still stay the same?

AND WHAT NOT TO SAY

Where's the spittoon?

PAUPER SUBSTITUTE

None

38

Valpolicella Superiore Maternigo, Tedeschi

REGION

Valpolicella, Veneto

COUNTRY

Italy

GRAPES

Corvina, Corvinone, Rondinella

PRICE

* →**

Valpolicella has been steadily improving its quality, steadily learning more about its grapes, which are unique to the region, and steadily identifying its best sites. Amarone has the glamour, Ripasso has the sales; but standard Valpolicella has the immense drinkability.

However, you don't get many "standard" Valpolicellas as distinctive as this. Tedeschi has carried out a detailed study of the soil in its 31-hectare Maternigo estate, and the 7 different zones revealed by the study are being cultivated in different ways: some parts have ground cover, some have been planted with growth to increase the soil's carbon content, some are monitored for humidity, some for drought. More detailed viticulture leads (in the right hands) to more detailed wines. This wine comes from a plot called Impervio because of its steepness, and is remarkable for its character, elegance and delicate forcefulness. It's "traditional" in style, which basically means aged in big old Slavonian oak casks rather than the smaller French oak favoured by modernists, and it has lots of acidity, a linear shape in the mouth, great concentration and flavours of black fruit and herbs, brisk and energetic.

The estate is so named because it used to have a home, an ex-monastery, for unmarried mothers. One hopes they were given something decent to drink while they were there, but of course it might have been the local wine that landed them there in the first place.

DRINK WITH

Roast meat, pasta, mature hard cheese

BEST AGE TO DRINK
....
At three to four years
old to ten or more

TROPHY VINTAGES
....
None

DECANT
....
No

CHILL
....
No

WHAT TO SAY IF YOU
MEET THE WINEMAKER

What makes a single-
vineyard wine special?

AND WHAT NOT TO SAY

Isn't Valpol for students?

PAUPER SUBSTITUTE
....
Tedeschi's Lucchine
Valpolicella Classico
has the same tightness
and freshness

39

Ribolla Gialla, Josko Gravner

REGION

Collio, Friuli-Venezia Giulia

COUNTRY

Italy

GRAPE

Ribolla Gialla

PRICE

** →***

Ribolla Gialla is a high-acid white grape that has been known in northeast Italy since at least the 13th century. Josko Gravner hasn't been making it for quite that long, but in 2003 he took a big step and started making everything in clay amphorae. Everything. Out went the barriques; in came amphorae imported from Georgia, sealed with beeswax.

The inspiration was originally a disillusioning trip to California, which depressed him by the lack of authenticity in the wines; he decided to look in the direction where wine began, in the Caucasus. He couldn't get to Georgia until 2000; but after that there was nothing to stop him.

The amphorae are buried underground; there is no temperature control, no added yeast and the white grapes are crushed, put into the amphorae and left to ferment. The new wine macerates with the skins for up to seven months before being racked off; wine has been made like this for 5,000 years. It is the oldest method there is. Amphorae have since become super-fashionable, and white wines fermented with their skins are dubbed "orange"; but they all tip their caps to Gravner.

What does this Ribolla Gialla taste like? Tannic, of course; nutty, fresh, mineral, citrus; but hugely complex, serious and winey. This is not just white wine with tannin and a dark colour: it feels like a more complete transformation of grape into wine, as though fruity, pale wines are just a case of arrested adolescence. There is more depth, focus and power, and an unmistakable authenticity, an honesty that demands attention. There's nothing gimmicky; everything simply feels right.

DRINK WITH

Meat, fish or vegetables. It's hard to think of something this wouldn't go with

BEST AGE TO DRINK

On release and for some years; the wines age to a lovely beeswax character

TROPHY VINTAGES

The very idea would be anathema to Gravner

DECANT

No

CHILL

Only slightly

WHAT TO SAY IF YOU MEET THE WINEMAKER

"Thank you", probably

AND WHAT NOT TO SAY

Is this just a passing trend?

PAUPER SUBSTITUTE

None, alas; there's no cheap way of doing this

40 Vintage Tunina, Jermann

REGION

Friuli-Venezia Giulia

COUNTRY

Italy

GRAPES

Chardonnay, Sauvignon Blanc, Malvasia Istriana, Ribolla Gialla, Picolit

PRICE

**

This will make you wonder why you ever thought single-varietal wines were a good thing. Northeast Italy is where the country's white wines turn into something much winier and grown-up than usual; both qualities are emphasised here, perhaps because it's a field blend, with everything grown together, picked together and fermented together. When that happens the modern idea of optimum ripeness for everything goes out of the window. But somehow co-fermented wines end up as more than the sum of their parts. The flavour has a less direct relationship with any single variety, and there's a complexity and a richness of texture, a voluptuousness and a multi-faceted character, that goes way beyond conventional flavours. It's tightly knit, focused and savoury; you can find notes of white blossom in there, almonds and confit apricots, and it ages to beeswax and spice; it feels a long way from the original varieties.

The vineyard, incidentally, used to belong to a woman called Tunina, a local diminutive of Antonia, and as far as Silvio Jermann is concerned it pays homage to Casanova's poorest lover, a governess in Vienna, who was also known as Tunina. Of the grapes in the wine, Chardonnay and Sauvignon are familiar and international; Malvasia Istriana is a native of Croatia and makes lovely honeyed, zesty wines; Ribolla Gialla is high in acidity and goes back at least to the 13th century; and Picolit was a bit of a cult grape in 17th-century Venice.

DRINK WITH

White meat, or complicated, rich fish dishes; truffles, too

BEST AGE TO DRINK

It will go on improving
for up to ten years
or more

TROPHY VINTAGES

None

DECANT

No

CHILL

Only slightly

WHAT TO SAY IF YOU
MEET THE WINEMAKER

Remember to pronounce
his name as "Yerman"

AND WHAT NOT TO SAY

"Are you German?"
(No, he's not)

PAUPER SUBSTITUTE

You could try the
straightforward Pinot
Grigio or Sauvignon

41

Lambrusco Fontana dei Boschi, Vittorio Graziano

REGION

Emilia-Romagna

COUNTRY

Italy

GRAPE

Lambrusco Grasparosso

PRICE

*

This is what Lambrusco should be like, and once upon a time was. These days nearly all Lambrusco is industrial. Vittorio Graziano prefers to go in the other direction: instead of massive yields from irrigated, battery-chicken vineyards he has much lower yields (one bottle per vine) from unirrigated vines on the hills. Instead of high-volume, low-cost fermentation techniques he uses what he terms the Metodo Ancestrale, which involves wild yeasts, fermenting the juice on the skins for three or four days to get colour, bottling in the spring with a bit of sugar and yeast and leaving it in bottle to continue its fermentation to dryness. Eighteen months' or two years' ageing on the lees gives more complexity. Some is then disgorged off the lees, which means the wine pours clear. Some is not, and is sold *sur lie*, and therefore is potentially cloudy. It tastes totally different like this: less fruit, more weight. You can have two wines in one bottle.

This is real artisan wine: wild, unpredictable, tasting of savoury blackberries and herbs, with high acidity, a touch of green, and a bit of tannic grip. Unlike industrial Lambrusco, it ages beautifully. Of course it does: it's authentic wine, made as Lambrusco used to be made before the lure of mass production and cost-cutting. For a while Graziano was the only one making artisan Lambrusco; now a few others have joined in. It'll be a cult one of these days.

DRINK WITH

Local salami
and cheese

92

BEST AGE TO DRINK

Young, or age it for up to seven years to become sleeker and less grippy

TROPHY VINTAGES

None

DECANT

No

CHILL

Yes

WHAT TO SAY IF YOU MEET THE OWNER

Tell me about the Lambrusco Grasparosso grape

AND WHAT NOT TO SAY

I like wine to be predictable

PAUPER SUBSTITUTE

Honestly, you don't need one

42

Verdicchio Classico Riserva, Villa Bucci

REGION

Marches

COUNTRY

Italy

GRAPE

Verdicchio

PRICE

* →**

There's nothing showy about Verdicchio; it's resolutely unflashy. If you were tasting casually you might not notice anything remarkable about it: structured white, you might think; dense, nutty, rich. Nice with the food. And then you might look again, and think, hello! This is rather good. In fact it's very good. Where's the bottle?

This is the point of Verdicchio: it's subtle. It's discreet. It requires attention. For Italians it's one of those whites – which they rather like – with the structure of a red: plenty of backbone and weight.

Not all Verdicchio is as serious as Villa Bucci, however. These are wines of complexity, made for ageing; yields are low, vines are old, with an average age of between 40 and 50 years, and the grapes come from 6 vineyards, all with different exposures and at different altitudes. This variety of blending material gives extra complexity. Soils are a mix of limestone (for good, elegant acidity) and clay (for weight), and it's aged in big old Slavonian oak barrels for a year or more.

And those subtle flavours? There's beeswax and apricots, spice, honey, rosemary, lavender and flint, herbs and nuts. Acidity is high, and a there's a firm, tight backbone and plenty of richness and depth. It's hugely characterful, and ages from its initial leanness and tightness to more honeyed notes while keeping its freshness. Don't be deterred by the comment of the staff at the local *enoteca* one day when I asked for a sample: "Ah, the ladies like this one".

DRINK WITH

Strong flavours – the local fish stew is good with it, as is *stocafissa* (dried, salted cod)

BEST AGE TO DRINK

It will last for ten years, but it's good young, too

TROPHY VINTAGES

This cuvée is only made in good years

DECANT

No

CHILL

Yes

WHAT TO SAY IF YOU MEET THE WINEMAKER

It's Armani rather than Versace

AND WHAT NOT TO SAY

I'm more high street, myself

PAUPER SUBSTITUTE

The lighter, more straightforward, fruity Bucci

43

Rampante Etna Rosso, Pietradolce

REGION

Sicily

COUNTRY

Italy

GRAPE

Nerello Mascalese

PRICE

*

There's a pleasure in being surprised by a wine. Sicily, we all know, is hot. So it should make massive wines, right? Broad-shouldered, swaggering reds that are great for the first half-glass and tiring thereafter. Well, no. For one thing, Sicily has mountains, including Mount Etna, which, being a volcano, has slopes of stony volcanic soil. I'm not going to attempt to explain why, but volcanic soil seems to impart a certain sparky vitality to wines. Etna also has the indigenous Nerello Mascalese vine – lovely name, lovely grape. It's quite light in colour, it has supple tannins, and pure, floral, herbal, cherry aromas and flavours. For this one, imagine the juiciest cherries steeped briefly in creosote. It has the most appetizing tarry-cherries flavour, with touches of wild herbs, all vibrant and energetic and extremely moreish. There would be no question of only drinking half a glass.

Pietradolce is a young company, family-owned, with 11 hectares of steep, terraced slopes on the northern side of Mount Etna. The stone walls supporting the terraces are overgrown with moss and vegetation, and the bush vines (which are 80–100 years old) have a slightly random look to them. But they produce great grapes. Age is one factor and altitude is another: these vines are at 850m (2,790ft). This terroir comes through in the wine, in its freshness and liveliness. French oak is used for ageing and it's so well tucked in you wouldn't know it was there, which is how it should always be, in a perfect world. If you love Pinot Noir but are horrified by the prices, then look here for an alternative.

DRINK WITH

Almost anything

BEST AGE TO DRINK
....
At about four years,
and certainly for
another ten

TROPHY VINTAGES
....
None so far

DECANT
....
No

CHILL
....
No

WHAT TO SAY IF YOU
MEET THE WINEMAKER
....
What's it like living
under a volcano?

AND WHAT NOT TO SAY
....
What would you do
if it buried your vines?

MILLIONAIRE
SUBSTITUTE
....
There's a grander,
bigger, more
concentrated wine
if you want to push
the boat out: Vigna
Barbagalli; only
2,000 bottles made,
sold on allocation

44

Brauneberger Riesling Kabinett, Fritz Haag

REGION

Mittelmosel, Mosel

COUNTRY

Germany

GRAPE

Riesling

PRICE

* →**

If you want a classic Mosel Riesling, all crystalline purity and tense delicacy, it's very difficult to beat Fritz Haag. Based in the village of Brauneberg, in the heart of the Mittelmosel, the vines stretch in a steep, unbroken wall along the northern bank of the Mosel. There is perfect exposure to the sun: this is one of several vineyards along the Mosel with sundials, and you can't have a sundial without sun.

The style of Fritz Haag often involves a bit of residual sugar, which emphasizes the fruitiness: whether you seek this wine as a Kabinett Trocken, a sweeter Spätlese or a properly sweet Auslese is really a matter of taste. There is also Beerenauslese (BA) or Trockenbeerenauslese (TBA) when the year permits, and all have their sweetness balanced by ripe but piercing acidity. Expect laser-like definition, smoky notes, ripe, floral fruit that will become honeyed with age, and power tucked into a filigree exterior.

The longer you keep the sweet versions the less sweet they will seem: the impression is of honey and gingerbread rather than sweetness. The age to drink them is likewise a matter of taste: a Spätlese at 15–20 years will be a good match for certain dishes – a subtle fish curry redolent of coconut, perhaps – whereas a Kabinett will be good younger, perhaps with chicken-liver pâté. BA and TBA will work with apple or quince desserts, or just with a perfect peach.

DRINK WITH

For the drier wines, pâté, trout, scallops

FRITZ HAAG

Brauneberger
Riesling Kabinett

BEST AGE TO DRINK

After two or three years
for Kabinett, up to ten
for a BA; and then for
many, many years

TROPHY VINTAGES

There's been no bad
vintage for years

DECANT

No

CHILL

Yes

**WHAT TO SAY IF YOU
MEET THE WINEMAKER**

How do you work such
steep vineyards?

AND WHAT NOT TO SAY

If you fall over, do you
land in the river?

PAUPER SUBSTITUTE

The village
Brauneberger Riesling

Idig Grosses Gewächs Riesling Trocken, A. Christmann

45

REGION

Mittelhardt, Pfalz

COUNTRY

Germany

GRAPE

Riesling

PRICE

**

Somebody once asked me how to understand Riesling – a complicated question as it's so varied. I'd say that Riesling is about tension. There are a number of Rieslings in this book, and they are all very different, but they have in common a tensile line on which flavours are poised like a tightrope-walker. A Riesling without that tension is not doing its job.

Tension is what you notice when you taste a Christmann wine. It's more than just acidity, it's more than just vigour: it's a thread of piano wire running through the wine from beginning to end. The detail of the wine is the other thing you notice: everything is perfectly defined. There's no blurring, and yet it is seamless. You can't do this without very good sites, very good viticulture and very good winemaking.

Christmann is situated in the Mittelhardt region of the Pfalz, the region where Riesling still dominates the vineyards, and where it makes wines of weight and muscle. The Idig vineyard comprises four hectares of chalk, clay, basalt and red sandstone over limestone, facing south-southeast, and (for the Pfalz) relatively steep; all is farmed biodynamically. The limestone gives a lovely line of acidity that runs alongside saltiness and a refined backbone; it's a ripe, rich yet dry wine with scents of summer meadows, apricots and yellow plums, minerality and a dancing liveliness. It is serious and singing, concentrated and light, all at the same time.

DRINK WITH

Scallops, sea trout

BEST AGE TO DRINK

After about five years,
for at least twenty

TROPHY VINTAGES

2005, 2008, 2010,
2012, 2015

DECANT

No

CHILL

Yes

WHAT TO SAY IF YOU
MEET THE WINEMAKER

Is Grosses Gewächs
the equivalent of
Burgundian Grand Cru?

AND WHAT NOT TO SAY

Much cheaper, though

PAUPER SUBSTITUTE

The Ruppertsberg
Riesling is wonderful;
or there's the entry-level
Pfalz Riesling

46

Serriger Schloss Saarsteiner Riesling Kabinett, Schloss Saarstein

REGION

Saar, Mosel

COUNTRY

Germany

GRAPE

Riesling

PRICE

*

Schloss Saarstein is a heavy-walled, slate-and-sandstone house perched on a promontory that juts into the landscape like a nose. The wind whips round it and the river Saar curves around and away. It's an uncompromising, austere site. Yet the Rieslings from here are filigree – tense, taut, fine and resilient as piano wire, but filigree.

The Saar region is one of Germany's coldest, and it has benefited greatly from climate change. That, and the canalization of the Saar in the 1980s has tempered the climate and the grapes are riper as a result: because the river is not very wide, and the slopes are high and steep, canalizing the river was like installing a heating system. The grapes have more tartaric acid at picking than in the chilly mid-20th-century decades, and less sharp malic acid. Riesling here has, for the first time in decades, moved into its comfort zone – a golden age for Saar Riesling.

So much so that it's even becoming possible to make balanced dry Rieslings here. Owner Christian Ebert, however, still prefers the style that Germans term "fruity": crystalline, a bit of residual sugar offset by acidity. "For me," he says, "a really great wine from here can only be sweet, mineral, with acidity and low alcohol." In fact his Kabinett is so tight and lean that it feels barely off-dry, its concentration and taut complexity just leavened by some interwoven sweetness. It has the texture of silk over a core of the slate on which it is grown.

DRINK WITH

On its own, or with trout, scallops or crab

BEST AGE TO DRINK

After a couple of years,
and then for another ten

TROPHY VINTAGES

2005, 2011, 2015

DECANT

No

CHILL

Yes

WHAT TO SAY IF YOU
MEET THE OWNER

How do you get such
concentration at
8% alcohol?

AND WHAT NOT TO SAY

Just don't call it
"Riseling"

PAUPER SUBSTITUTE

You don't need to be rich
for this

47

Walporzheimer Kräuterberg Spätburgunder, Meyer-Näkel

REGION

Ahr

COUNTRY

Germany

GRAPE

**Spätburgunder
(Pinot Noir)**

PRICE

***

**DRINK
WITH**

Pork, game,
beef; perhaps in
the Hofgarten
restaurant, run
by Werner's
brother

The story of the rise and rise and Meyer-Näkel is a classic. The scion of a wine-growing family sees no future in a world of low prices and low quality, which was the Ahr in the 1970s. So he leaves, only to be brought back to the winery when his father becomes ill. And he never leaves again. Instead he modernizes, improves quality, buys vineyards, improves quality some more...

The Ahr used to make pale, wishy-washy Pinot of no great appeal. Werner went to Burgundy and bought barrels; he reduced yields and set about making Pinot that tasted like Pinot. German Spätburgunder now has a brand-new reputation for quality and interest, and Meyer-Näkel is one of its leaders. And Werner's daughters, Meike and Dörte, are not going anywhere.

Climate change favours the Ahr. These are wines of elegance and finesse, ripe and racy: Werner wants aroma and concentration, but not obvious power, and certainly not obvious oak. The wines are aged in barrels, but the oak is perfectly integrated; it doesn't show except in the form of a little extra structure.

My favourite is the Kräuterberg vineyard in the village of Walporzheim, a Grosses Gewächs site where terraces are patched onto a steep, rocky hillside and soak up the sun. The wines are intensely aromatic, tight, spicy and mineral, full of black fruits, incense, thyme and wild herbs, very balanced, very pure. The Romans cultivated this hillside; everything is simply reinvention.

BEST AGE TO DRINK

Meike recommends
ageing them for eight
to ten years, then for
probably another ten

TROPHY VINTAGES

Not really

DECANT

Yes

CHILL

No

WHAT TO SAY IF YOU
MEET THE WINEMAKER

Are you glad you
gave up teaching?

AND WHAT NOT TO SAY

Teachers have
good pensions

PAUPER SUBSTITUTE

The entry-level
Pinot Noir

48

Westhofener Morstein Riesling Grosses Gewächs, Weingut Wittmann

REGION
....
Wonnegau, Rheinhessen

COUNTRY
....
Germany

GRAPE
....
Riesling

PRICE
....
**

The Rheinhessen was not, traditionally, the place you went for serious Riesling. A couple of generations ago it was a byword for enormous yields of cheap, sweetened-up plonk, with just a handful of good producers struggling to put across an alternative view. That opinions are very different now has a lot to do with Wittmann.

A couple of generations, however, is nothing in German vineyard terms. Morstein has been recognized as a great site for centuries: the first documented reference was in 1282. It is clay-limestone over more limestone, on a gentle south-southeast-facing slope to the northwest of the village, where the Wittmanns have been involved in viticulture since 1663; they have about four hectares. And the Wonnegau region is where the excitement in the Rheinhessen is concentrated now.

Wittmann has been biodynamic since 2004, having begun with organic methods in the early 1980s, which makes it a pioneer. Fermentation is with natural yeasts in big old oak casks, and the wines have extraordinary delicacy and definition, allied to a raciness and tension that seems to have something of the Mosel about it, though the weight and body of this wine takes you towards somewhere warmer. There's spice on this wine, and it seems almost too rich to be dry, although dry it is. It's mineral and sappy, with wonderful depth and tension, full of summer fruits and chalky rock, often closed when young but maturing to graceful complexity.

DRINK WITH

Wild Scottish salmon, preferably one you caught yourself yesterday

BEST AGE TO DRINK

After about five years,
for twenty or more

TROPHY VINTAGES

2002, 2007, 2008,
2009, 2012, 2014,
2015, 2016

DECANT

No

CHILL

Yes

WHAT TO SAY IF YOU
MEET THE WINEMAKER

How much more work is
biodynamic viticulture?

AND WHAT NOT TO SAY

It's easier in a warm
climate, surely?

PAUPER SUBSTITUTE

Westhofener Riesling
Trocken will give a taste
of the Wittmann style

49 Achleiten

REGION

Wachau

COUNTRY

Austria

GRAPES

**Riesling or
Grüner Veltliner**

PRICE

***

There are reasons why I haven't specified a producer for this wine. Achleiten is a vineyard – a very great vineyard – and it's one of the few in the world where the character of the site overrules the grape variety. The growers tell you that if you try to guess, blind, whether an Achleiten is Riesling or Grüner Veltliner you will get it wrong. (Yes, I tried. And yes, I got it wrong.) The other reason is the impossibility of deciding who is best among the small number of growers who bottle Achleiten. Can I say that Prager is better than Josef Jamek, or Jamek better than Toni Bodenstein, or either of them better than Rudi Pichler or Domane Wachau (right)? And frankly, there's not that much Achleiten about. Find any of the above and you can congratulate yourself.

Achleiten is a high, steep, terraced hillside that looms over the Danube. The terraces negotiate with the rock, weaving back and forth, stopping where the rock juts out. The rock in question is gneiss, magmatic higher up, sedimentary lower down; and the lower terraces, near the road, are not part of Achleiten but are Ried ("vineyard") Klaus. Exposure varies from southwest to south to southeast, and Achleiten's 19 hectares are worked by about 30 growers. Some sell grapes, some sell their wine via their own Heurigen.

It's not a homogeneous site, but, says Toni Bodenstein, "the flinty-mineral structure of the wine is inimitable". There's a dark, smoky, peppery aspect, some citrus, peach characters and notes of tea. Rudi Pichler describes it as "the dust of weathered rocks after warm rain". It ages to honey and tea and caramel, still bone-dry, and almost delicate over its sinewy structure.

DRINK WITH

Whitebait or
fritto misto

BEST AGE TO DRINK

It's a wine for the long term; think in decades

TROPHY VINTAGES

1969, 1982, 1986, 1990, 1993, 1997, 1999, 2001, 2005, 2007, 2009, 2013, 2016

DECANT

No

CHILL

Yes

WHAT TO SAY IF YOU MEET A WINEMAKER

How long did it take you to get to know Achleiten?

AND WHAT NOT TO SAY

It can't be that difficult to work

PAUPER SUBSTITUTE

None; start saving

50 Gemischter Satz, Wieninger

REGION

Wien (Vienna)

COUNTRY

Austria

GRAPES

Any of Weissburgunder, Grauburgunder, Chardonnay, Neuburger, Welschriesling, Grüner Veltliner, Sylvaner, Zierfandler, Rotgipfler, Traminer, Riesling

PRICE

*

Gemischter Satz is the speciality of Vienna's own vineyards, grown in various villages within the city boundaries. The vineyards consist of several different grape varieties all mixed up. It used to be simply the house wine of every grower's Heurige, where locals would go to eat simple home-produced food with a half-litre (18floz) of wine. Several varieties were grown as a form of frost and disease insurance, and the particular mix became each grower's hallmark.

Grapes that are picked and fermented together – some ripe, some overripe, some a bit green – produce a result that is totally different from the standard practice of growing, picking and fermenting varieties separately and then blending: the wine is more complex, less grape-driven, more "winey". Whether it expresses the terroir better, as the growers claim, is a moot point, but there's no doubt that co-fermentation has interesting effects on flavour.

Fritz Wieninger's grapes are in the Bisamberg, Nussberg and Rosengart vineyards. All are cultivated biodynamically. The soils are all different, and the wines different every year. The flavours are always exotic – lime blossom, citrus peel, herbs, held together with good acidity and a silky texture.

Weininger was the driving force behind the revival of Gemischter Satz: 20 years ago it was dying. Now it's ultra-fashionable and even has its own organization, Wien Wein, with half a dozen young members committed to Gemischter Satz. Weininger has his own Heurige in Stammersdorf: taste it there, in view of the vineyards, for the full experience.

DRINK WITH

A plate of local cured meats

BEST AGE TO DRINK

Young

TROPHY VINTAGES

None; take what
you find

DECANT

No

CHILL

Yes

**WHAT TO SAY IF YOU
MEET THE OWNER**

How random
is your choice
of grape varieties?

AND WHAT NOT TO SAY

Why don't you
want it to be the
same every year?

PAUPER SUBSTITUTE

It's pretty cheap
already, unless you
include the airfare
to Vienna

51

Riesling Ried Heiligenstein, Schloss Gobelsburg

REGION

Kamptal

COUNTRY

Austria

GRAPE

Riesling

PRICE

* →**

"Ried" means "vineyard" in Austria, and the Heiligenstein vineyard is a 250-million-year-old geological island. Riesling is planted on the exposed, rocky terraces; lower down, where the slope flattens out and the soil becomes rich, is the Lamm vineyard with Grüner Veltliner. A single hectare of vines in Ried Heiligenstein would cost around €250,000, compared to €50–80,000 round about. Heiligenstein, Holy Mountain, is one of Austria's great vineyards.

Schloss Gobelsburg is one of Austria's great producers. It is run by Michael Moosburger, intellectually rigorous, affable, witty and absolutely determined to produce the Platonic ideal from every site. Wine is about origins, he says; grape varieties are merely the conduit for the site. He's obsessed with texture, far more so than with aroma; these are wines of structure and subtlety. "You're not paying for Riesling when you buy Heiligenstein," he says; "you're paying for the best expression of Heiligenstein, in the same way that Grüner Veltliner gives the best expression of Lamm. It's all about vineyards.

So what is the character of Heiligenstein, refracted through Riesling and Moosburger's intellect? Lean to the point of austerity, pure, transparent, tense; notes of spice, smoke; ripe yellow fruits; intensely mineral. Taut, transparent wines, made with wild yeasts and minimum intervention. After about seven years you have celestial honey and lemon; or wait longer for more honey and no loss of tension or structure.

DRINK WITH

Fish with plenty of flavour, or goose or pork

BEST AGE TO DRINK

It's good young but will age for decades. The 1973 was superb, all wildflower honey and rich dryness, in 2014

TROPHY VINTAGES

None

DECANT

No

CHILL

Yes

WHAT TO SAY IF YOU MEET THE WINEMAKER

Wine reflects its winemaker as well as its site

AND WHAT NOT TO SAY

Do you ever take shortcuts in winemaking?

PAUPER SUBSTITUTE

Straightforward Schloss Gobelsburg, fine and complex

52

Spitzerberg Blaufränkisch, Muhr-van der Niepoort

REGION

Carnuntum

COUNTRY

Austria

GRAPE

Blaufränkisch

PRICE

**

Blaufränkisch is Austria's best red grape, and it makes grown-up, elegant wines. Dorli Muhr's are particularly elegant. Her winery partnership with Dirk Niepoort (whose Tiara is on page 136) continues, though they're no longer married, and produces wines of delicacy and structure, beautifully poised, very precise, floral, subtle and powerful, with lovely silky tannins. They come from several small plots on the Spitzerberg, and the soil is sandy limestone, not water-retentive. So hot, dry summers (like 2009, 2011, 2012, 2013 and 2015) give juicy, more opulent wines, and cool, humid years give savoury, peppery wines. Muhr's preference is for the latter: "They show the finesse and delicacy of the Spitzerberg from the first moment on," she says. You have to wait a bit longer for the others.

Everything is picked by hand, and every overripe berry is selected out: she hates jammy notes in her wine. Some of the grapes are destemmed, but 15–30 per cent are fermented as whole bunches, which gives well-defined tannins and a spicy note. The cellar is small, even rustic. There's no pumping-over, for example: instead it's done with buckets. All fermentation is with natural yeasts – that's the case with a lot of the wines in this book. Laboratory yeasts are safe and give predictable results; spontaneous fermentations are riskier but seem to give a finer texture, and a less controlled feel. Most winemakers feel that they are a truer way of expressing a particular terroir.

DRINK WITH

Pork, duck

BEST AGE TO DRINK

Give it a couple of years, and then for another ten

TROPHY VINTAGES

None

DECANT

Yes, or open in advance

CHILL

No

WHAT TO SAY IF YOU MEET THE WINEMAKER

These are your family vineyards?

AND WHAT NOT TO SAY

You'll be giving up the day job, then? (She's a leading PR in Vienna)

PAUPER SUBSTITUTE

The Carnuntum bottling is made from younger vines

53

Cava Celler Batlle Gran Reserva, Gramona

REGION

Penedès, Catalonia

COUNTRY

Spain

GRAPES

Xarel.lo, Macabeu

PRICE

***

A Cava with quality and depth to rival the Champagnes in this book. Gramona and Recaredo (next entry) represent the top of the Cava tree. And it's a tall tree.

Gramona's top wine is a powerful, sleek, complex, winey, smoky, creamy glassful with a note of coffee on the finish; it's very rich. It also has about 7–8g/l dosage, so it's not bone dry. "Batlle" is the family name; it was Pau Batlle who started selling sparkling wine to French merchants in the late 19th century, when phylloxera was destroying the vineyards of France. His daughter married a Gramona, and their son realized after WWII that when French merchants continued to seek stocks in Penedès, what they wanted was aged wines. So that's what he started producing.

They've cut the ageing a bit since then, but as always, Xarel.lo needs age and doesn't show well young. Here it has 25% of Macabeu to flesh it out a little. The vineyards are biodynamic, and soil specialists Lydia and Claude Bourguignon are consultants. The estate grows its own plants for the biodynamic preparations, and the many animals provide good compost. In the cellar they press whole clusters, which gives extra richness and structure. These are big wines. The *liqueur de dosage* (if a French term is allowed here) comes from a hundred-year-old solera of *mistela*, grape juice with a shot of brandy. The solera is run by one man, and only he knows the secret – and he's not telling.

DRINK WITH

Smoky, rich flavours

BEST AGE TO DRINK

On release, but
it will age further

TROPHY VINTAGES

None

DECANT

No

CHILL

Yes

**WHAT TO SAY IF YOU
MEET THE WINEMAKER**

Tell me about the
capacity of roots
to take up flavours
from the soil

AND WHAT NOT TO SAY

Does terroir
really matter?

PAUPER SUBSTITUTE

Ill Lustros Gran Reserva

54 Cava Turó d'en Mota, Recaredo

REGION

Penedès, Catalonia

COUNTRY

Spain

GRAPE

Xarel.lo

PRICE

****

This is the tops, from first-class vineyards planted in 1940 and farmed biodynamically, from Xarel.lo grapes, and aged nine years in bottle before sale. So: one thing at a time.

Xarel.lo is one of the three Penedès grapes commonly used in Cava, and it's the best: structured, powerful, uncompromising, not particularly pretty, but imposing. It's all backbone and no frills when it's young, which is why in wines to be sold young it's softened and fleshed out with Parellada and Macabeu. But not here. Here those nine years in the cellar have a profound effect, so that it emerges as a wine of toast and brioche on the nose, mineral and winey on the palate, with notes of lemon zest and coriander. It's got a phenolic edge, too, which adds to the sensation of freshness, because Xarel.lo is not high in acidity. There's no dosage: it's bone dry. Don't expect it to taste like Champagne: it doesn't. It's not supposed to. It's superbly elegant, with tight power and fine bubbles; but the bubbles are not really the point. This is a fine wine that happens to be sparkling.

The vineyards? A mosaic of plots interrupted by forests and ravines in the Alt Penedès, around the Bitlles River. The soil is mostly chalky, and horses are used to work the land. Many of the plants needed for the biodynamic preparations are grown here, too, and Recaredo is isolating more and more of its own yeasts, so it can match yeasts to plots of vines. The latest innovation is to kick off the second fermentation in bottle with must from the same vineyard, but it's complicated. "I like very much to dream, and it's free!" says director general Ton Mata.

DRINK WITH

On its own, or with guinea fowl, octopus: firm textures, strong flavours

BEST AGE TO DRINK

On release

TROPHY VINTAGES

None

DECANT

No

CHILL

Yes, but not too much

WHAT TO SAY IF YOU
MEET THE OWNER

Xarel.lo seems to keep
young forever

AND WHAT NOT TO SAY

Would you ever put
Chardonnay in it?

PAUPER SUBSTITUTE

Try the Brut Nature
Gran Reserva

55

Gran Reserva 890, La Rioja Alta

REGION

Rioja

COUNTRY

Spain

GRAPES

Tempranillo, Mazuelo, Graciano

PRICE

****

La Rioja Alta makes two Gran Reservas of which it is justifiably proud; this, and the 904. To decide between them I opened a bottle of each with a slow-cooked leg of lamb cooked with plenty of cumin, coriander, garlic and smoked paprika. And dammit, it was still difficult.

The two wines have different flavours, and different shapes in the mouth. Both are aged in American oak, but 904 has less vanilla, more briskness and youth. The 890, tasted without food, offers more of a wall of American oak. But with food that wall melts away and the wine is completely at ease with itself and the food; and the flavour lasts and lasts. So while you won't be disappointed with either wine, I've come down in favour of the 890. It's twice the price. Sorry.

What is that flavour? Think of balsamic notes of herbs and lavender, some violets, some red fruit and dried figs, all held together with silk. It's got plenty of oomph and freshness, plenty of complexity and can handle strong flavours; it's got a lot to say, but it doesn't shout.

It is 95% Tempranillo, with Mazuelo and Graciano added as seasoning. It's named after the year La Rioja Alta was founded, 1890. The bodega is traditionalist, but the wines combine grace with vigour. Some "traditional" Gran Reservas seem as expiringly frail as a consumptive Victorian maiden; not these. Over the years they've gently reduced the age of the oak and the length of time the wines spend in it, thus freshening the style without anyone really noticing. That's how you have to do it in Rioja.

DRINK WITH

Spiced, slow-cooked lamb

BEST AGE TO DRINK

On release, and for
probably ten years

TROPHY VINTAGES

It's only released
in the best years; but
if anyone offers you
the 1904, don't refuse

DECANT

Could do

CHILL

No

WHAT TO SAY IF YOU
MEET THE WINEMAKER

Is it true you make
your own barrels?

AND WHAT NOT TO SAY

Can I buy one
of the old ones?

PAUPER SUBSTITUTE

The 904, which in
terms of quality:price
is very good value

56

Unico, Vega-Sicilia

REGION

Ribera del Duero

COUNTRY

Spain

GRAPES

Tempranillo, Cabernet Sauvignon

PRICE

***** →*****

For years this was the most famous wine in Spain. Perhaps it still is; but it has rivals now. Its current owners, the Álvarez family, bought it in 1982 (without seeing it: David Álvarez apparently just sent in the accountants) and set about a gentle but insistent programme of modernization that was much needed. Before that it was almost as famous for its unreliablity as its quality.

Now the unreliability has been ironed out, while the complicated ageing – big barrels, barriques, old and new, French and American, with the wine going in and out and backwards and forwards according to its evolution – continues, though it is slightly shorter than in the past. The wine's original inspiration was Bordelais, hence the Cabernet Sauvignon. The first winery was built in 1864 and lots of other grapes were planted as well, including Pinot Noir; the first commercial release was 1915, and the ageing, which included wine skins as well as barrels, was long in the Riojan way.

The style still falls outside the normal boundaries. It has never gone down the path of massive extraction and added tannins that often still afflicts Ribera del Duero; it also seems to have better acidity and freshness than much Ribera del Duero, possibly because of its north-facing vineyards of more-or-less calcereous soil, and big diurnal temperature differences. It's a wine of perfect polish and silkiness, endless complexity and apparently endless lifespan. It is certainly dense and concentrated, but with great freshness and a minty, herbal, almost eucalpytus note. There's a delicacy to it, too. In time (30 years plus) it becomes almost burgundian.

DRINK WITH

I had it with ox cheek at the bodega: fabulous

57

Le Naturel
Reposado, Vintae

REGION

Navarra

COUNTRY

Spain

GRAPE

Garnacha

PRICE

*

This is Garnacha as nature intended: organically grown at about 600m (1,970ft) up on limestone clay soils in a cool area – as far north in Navarra as red grapes will ripen, in fact – and aged in old French oak for ten months. This is not overripe, overextracted, overalcoholic, overtannic. Instead it's Garnacha-as-Pinot-Noir: delicate, savoury and transparent. There are layers of flavour, raspberry and blackberry, black cherry, roses, herbs, flowers; there's extraordinary complexity packed into a wine of lightness and purity. It has the filigree texture you find in some whites, or in red burgundy from a good grower. And it has a firm structure, fine as a spider's web and as strong. It builds and develops on the palate, driving forward to a long finish.

It's not the only Garnacha like this in Spain: a raft of young growers are doing similar things, particularly in less famous regions, and particularly in the Sierra de Gredos area, to the west of Madrid. Look out for them, and prepare to be surprised.

Vintae is a family company that produces wine in 15 different regions of Spain, and hunts out old vines and remote locations. Garnacha is a passion, because of the way this grape expresses its site – when it is allowed to. This is from its Bodegas Aroa winery in Navarra. It's made with minimum intervention, indigenous yeasts and no fining or filtration. And most remarkably, no sulphur. That means the winemaker has to take great care at all stages: it's risky. They prefer not to sell it in summer, they say. It has a best-before date on the label, and if you want to store it, keep it somewhere cool and dark.

DRINK WITH

Salmon, partridge

BEST AGE TO DRINK

Immediately or
nearly so

TROPHY VINTAGES

It's only been made
since 2013

DECANT

No

CHILL

No

**WHAT TO SAY IF YOU
MEET THE WINEMAKER**

Will all Garnacha
be like this one day?

AND WHAT NOT TO SAY

I'm going to keep
it in my kitchen

PAUPER SUBSTITUTE

This is very good value

58

La Faraona, Descendientes de J Palacios

REGION

Bierzo

COUNTRY

Spain

GRAPES

Mencía, white grapes, other red grapes

PRICE

*****

I'm not sure if I'm allowed to have two wines from the same family, but they are from different regions, grapes – and in fact different companies. L'Ermita (see page 130) is from Álvaro Palacios' Priorat venture; this company in Bierzo is Álvaro with his nephew Ricardo Pérez. The joint venture was Ricardo's idea, and he is the winemaker; the philosophy seems to be in the genes. As does the addiction to wonderful old vineyards and brilliant grape varieties. The vineyards of Corullón, a town in the west of Bierzo, not only offered old vines and steep slopes, but also a mosaic of soils; it reminded them of Burgundy's Côte d'Or. La Faraona is from a single vineyard, biodynamically worked, with shallow soil and a tectonic fault running down the middle – not bad for a 55-are plot. It's at 850m (2,790ft) altitude, faces southeast, with astonishingly complex soil full of quartz and metals derived from lava. It also fits another Palacios criterion for buying a vineyard: it has a long history influenced by religion – Álvaro reckons the best sites have a monkish background. Bierzo is on the Camino de Santiago.

This one has all the depth of very old vines, worn with poise and elegance. It's concentrated and mineral, earthy, brisk, with an edge of grippy tannins and a texture like silk: think of raspberry silk with an edge and you'll get the idea. There's lavender and blackberry as well, bay and savoury spice; it's both exuberant and perfectly defined.

DRINK WITH

Slow-cooked pork belly

BEST AGE TO DRINK

You could keep it for ten years or more

TROPHY VINTAGES

2007, 2009, 2013, 2014, 2016

DECANT

Yes

CHILL

No

WHAT TO SAY IF YOU MEET THE WINEMAKER

How does a great vineyard speak to you?

AND WHAT NOT TO SAY

What if it says nothing?

PAUPER SUBSTITUTE

Villa de Corullón is cheaper, and comes from 60–100-year-old vines

59

1902 Centenary Carignan, Mas Doix

REGION

Priorat, Catalonia

COUNTRY

Spain

GRAPE

Cariñena

PRICE

*****

DRINK WITH

Lamb

Priorat isn't what it used to be – thankfully. The overoaking has now faded from the scene, and what is left is wines from ancient vines on ancient soils in a unique place.

Priorat is mountains surrounded by higher mountains, in a Mediterranean climate, yet with enough continental climatic influences to give cold winters. The Montsant range keeps the northerly winds off. There's not much rain, and no irrigation. In Poboleda, where Mas Doix is found, it is a bit cooler, a bit damper, a bit later-ripening, but the soil, called *llicorella*, has just two per cent organic material. It is decomposed slate and schist, tawny and silver in colour and hardly soil at all. But it does allow the roots to go deep. (A piece of the stone is glued to every bottle pack, so you can see for yourself.) Bigger, fractured chunks of *llicorella* are used to keep the dry-stone walls of the terraces in good repair – though the soil is so rocky that distinguishing wall from vineyard can be difficult. The vines are bush vines, low to the ground, and for this wine, give just 300g (10oz) of grapes each, which amounts to around 850 bottles. As you might infer from the name, they were planted in 1902.

This is a wine of violet and tobacco flavours, chocolate and undergrowth, damsons and spice, with a touch of tar and herbs and a gloriously silky texture. Acidity is fairly low, but the wine has freshness, even lightness and liveliness: it's 15% alcohol, but you wouldn't guess. The texture is beautiful, the concentration worn lightly.

BEST AGE TO DRINK

From about four years old for another ten

TROPHY VINTAGES

2009 was the first vintage; then 2010, 2012, 2013

DECANT

Yes, at least one hour ahead

CHILL

No

WHAT TO SAY IF YOU MEET THE WINEMAKER

How amazing to have such old Cariñena

AND WHAT NOT TO SAY

Cariñena never used to be thought much good

PAUPER SUBSTITUTE

Les Crestes is for younger drinking

60

L'Ermita de Nostra Senyora de la Consolació, Álvaro Palacios

REGION

Priorat, Catalonia

COUNTRY

Spain

GRAPES

Garnacha, Cariñena, white grapes

PRICE

*****

Álvaro Palacios comes from a Rioja winemaking family – Palacios Remondo is the family business – but he has made his name by reviving (reinventing?) wine in other parts of Spain. It is impossible to overstate his role in creating Spanish wine as it is now; but as the seventh child in a family of nine, he had to make his own way.

He was fascinated by old monastic vineyards; invariably great sites, he believed. He joined forces with Priorat pioneer René Barbier, and he fell in love with the steep terraces, old vines and the sparkly, crumbly *llicorella* schist he found there. L'Ermita (bought in 1993) was precisely the sort of old monastic site he was looking for: it gains its name from the little chapel perched on top of the hill.

History in vineyards is crucial to Palacios: he reconverts vines to bush-training if necessary, because that's how it was always done and that's what suits the climate. He grafts Cabernet Sauvignon over to Garnacha. He works vineyards with mules. He has said that what he really regrets is that "life goes too fast": a winemaker spends his whole life learning from his mistakes.

This wine is less marked by oak now than it was in the past. It is silky on the palate and opens like a butterfly, delicate but with a structure of steel; it tastes of raspberry, blackberry and spice, fresh, taut, graceful and almost filigree.

DRINK WITH

Wild boar

BEST AGE TO DRINK

From youth to about
20 years

TROPHY VINTAGES

2004, 2006, 2008, 2010,
2012, 2013, 2015, 2016

DECANT

Yes

CHILL

No

**WHAT TO SAY IF YOU
MEET THE WINEMAKER**

Is L'Ermita one of the
greatest vineyards
in Spain?

AND WHAT NOT TO SAY

Why is it so expensive?

PAUPER SUBSTITUTE

Gratallops Vi de Vila

61

Extra Viejo Oloroso 1/7 VORS, El Maestro Sierra

REGION

Jerez

COUNTRY

Spain

GRAPE

Palomino

PRICE

**** →*****

El Maestro Sierra might sound like a couple of defunct family cars but in fact it's one of the most remarkable producers in the Sherry country. Nothing is modern here; when Doña Pilar took over from her husband on his death in 1976 she continued doing just as he had done. Now her daughter Mari Carmen is carrying on. No chemicals are used; fining is with egg whites from the local bakery, and when the earth floor of the bodega needs watering twice a day in summer (to keep the humidity at the right level) it's done with well water, not tap water. The bottling line (wines are bottled to order only) is operated by hand, and the corks are banged in with a hammer.

The solera is operated by transferring wine from barrel to barrel, rather than blending to homogeneity in between, as more commercial bodegas do: the individuality of each barrel is the point here. Not surprisingly, the wines have razor-sharp precision and uncompromising character. This Oloroso is surprisingly delicate, perfumed, austere yet rich, and tastes of burned toast, nuts, toffee, coffee, chocolate, burned lemons; it's dense, huge and light all at the same time. The wine is an average of perhaps 70 or 80 years old (it's difficult to be precise with a solera) and when it's bottled it won't be filtered or even cold-settled, but it might be passed through a nylon coffee strainer. That's quite modern, for here.

DRINK WITH

On its own, or with nuts or mature hard cheese

BEST AGE TO DRINK

It's ready when bottled

TROPHY VINTAGES

None; it's NV

DECANT

You could, but you
don't need to

CHILL

A tiny bit, perhaps

**WHAT TO SAY IF YOU
MEET THE WINEMAKER**

You're in the highest
part of Jerez; does the
breeze from the sea
really benefit the wine
in barrel?

AND WHAT NOT TO SAY

How does it compare to
Bristol Cream?

PAUPER SUBSTITUTE

There is also a younger
15 Años Oloroso

62

Tío Pepe En Rama Fino, González Byass

REGION

Jerez

COUNTRY

Spain

GRAPE

Palomino

PRICE

*

Here is a seasonal, fresh-from-the-barrel version of a widely available Sherry brand. If you drink Fino you already know and love Tío Pepe: it's full of true Fino character, those flavours of apples and earth after rain, thin as water in the mouth and fine as a blade. The acidity is low because ageing under flor, the yeast that develops on the surface of Fino in barrel, changes the make-up of the wine. Acidity falls over the four years or so in which the wine progresses through the different stages of the solera; volatile acidity falls; glycerol and dry extract fall. But acetaldehyde, which gives Fino its characteristic aroma, rises. By the time Fino is ready for bottling it has forgotten all the flavour of the grape and turned into something entirely different. That's the point of it, that it doesn't taste of grapes.

For shipping around the world the wine must be stabilized by filtration. That's why you can buy a bottle of Tío Pepe at any time, and it will be good. But if you happen to be in Jerez, sampling wine from the barrel, it tastes different: more intense, more immediate. That's what En Rama is: Fino in its natural state, taken twice a year, in spring and autumn when the flor is most vigorous, given a cool clarification only, and bottled and shipped for drinking within two and a half months. Don't keep it: it will just tire, though it's possible that flor might start to regrow on the surface. To get some you'll need to look online, see who has stocked it before, and put your name down in advance. It sells out quickly.

DRINK WITH

Tapas; or on its own

BEST AGE TO DRINK

Within a few weeks

TROPHY VINTAGES

None

DECANT

No

CHILL

Yes

WHAT TO SAY IF YOU MEET THE WINEMAKER

Sherry is so undervalued

AND WHAT NOT TO SAY

My grandma likes Sherry at Christmas

PAUPER SUBSTITUTE

If you don't know Fino, start with Tío Pepe

63

Tiara Branco, Niepoort

REGION

Douro

COUNTRY

Portugal

GRAPES

About 15, but principally Códega do Larinho, Rabigato, Donzelinho, Cercial

PRICE

∗ →∗∗

Dirk Niepoort doesn't do anything the normal way. He comes from a Port family (yes, a Dutch Port family, in the Douro since the mid-19th century) and as well as making Port, he makes table wines of some eccentricity. This one is relatively conventional: from vines of an average of 60 years old, growing at 600–800m (1,970–2,625ft). Fermentation is with indigenous yeasts, and it goes through the malolactic fermentation. Picking earlier, and taking advantage of those high altitudes, is the answer. The fermentation goes on for what must seem like forever, and is in fact up to a year, at low temperature.

It's a field blend – all Portuguese vineyards at that date were field blends, with lots of different varieties all mixed up. Not many of these vineyards have survived the modernization of the late 20th century, and those that are are treasured by the winemakers who can get access to them. "I'm a great believer that there was experience and logic in what they planted where," says Niepoort. Of course it was partly a protective measure – if one variety was hit by disease the others might survive – but it also means that you pick everything at the same time, "probably 80 per cent ripe, 10 per cent underripe and 10 per cent overripe". That goes against modern thinking, which says that everything should be at optimum ripeness, but Niepoort reckons it gives more complexity. In any case, he says, "I don't give a ∗∗∗∗ about variety; I prefer old vines, and soil character." This is certainly complex; firm, herbal, citrus, with notes of honeysuckle and hay and honey, lowish acidity but a lot of freshness. It's elegant and quite weighty.

DRINK WITH

Grilled fish, roasted vegetables

BEST AGE TO DRINK

It's energetic and vibrant young, but will age for six or seven years

TROPHY VINTAGES

None

DECANT

No

CHILL

Yes

WHAT TO SAY IF YOU MEET THE WINEMAKER

Tell me about your latest project

AND WHAT NOT TO SAY

I haven't got long, though

PAUPER SUBSTITUTE

This is one of Niepoort's cheaper whites

64

Nacional Vintage Port, Quinta do Noval

REGION

Douro

COUNTRY

Portugal

GRAPES

Touriga Nacional, Touriga Franca, Tinta Roriz, Tinta Cão, Sousão

PRICE

*****

DRINK WITH

Nuts, top-quality cheese

This is a one-off: the rarest Vintage Port of all, made in tiny quantities from ungrafted vines of up to 70 years old. They should be an impressive sight, but they look a bit scrawny: these four small plots in front of the house at Noval are the ones you'd pass without a glance on your way to photograph the neighbouring terraces.

Yet the wine from these feeble-looking plants has a vigour, a distinctiveness, an energy that can outshine standard Noval and can make just about every other Vintage Port look subfusc in comparison to its Technicolor precision. It's not showy; it just sings with more power, more grace, more complexity, more focus.

But not every year. "Nacional marches to its own drum," says Christian Seely of AXA Millésimes, the estate's owner. Its great years are not necessarily the same as Noval's great years. Also, the list of trophy vintages (right) has a long lacuna from the late 1960s to the early 1990s. That was the estate's saddest period: family disagreements meant little investment, and the quality of the wines plummeted. AXA, and Seely, took over in 1993 and the revival was swift: Nacional and Noval have both reached new heights, and the difference is smaller than it was.

Why have these vines survived? Nobody knows: Seely tried planting ungrafted vines elsewhere on the estate but they didn't thrive. Could the Nacional vines succumb to phylloxera and die? Presumably. As Seely says, "Buy now while stocks last."

BEST AGE TO DRINK

Either very young, within a year or two of bottling, or at fifteen years-plus

TROPHY VINTAGES

1931, 1963, 1966, 1967, 1994, 1996, 1997, 1998, 2003, 2011

DECANT

Yes

CHILL

No

WHAT TO SAY IF YOU MEET THE WINEMAKER

How did you manage to transform the wines?

AND WHAT NOT TO SAY

So Vintage Noval is second-best?

PAUPER SUBSTITUTE

Standard Quinta do Noval vintage, which is not second-best in any context

65

Procura White, Susana Esteban

REGION
Alentejo

COUNTRY
Portugal

GRAPES
Mixed white

PRICE
*

Susana Esteban is a Spaniard who fell in love with the Douro Valley and ended up making wine in the Alentejo – and the Alentejo, in case you think that wine from the south of Portugal is tourist tat, is a centre of vinous experimentation and free-thinking. After the devastation of phylloxera a political decision was taken that the Alentejo would produce grain, not wine. Up in Portalegre, in the north of the region, there were old vineyards that had survived, but they weren't worth replanting so they were just abandoned. And when the likes of Esteban came hunting for interesting old vines, there they were.

Portalegre is high up, rainy, with cold summer nights and a landscape dotted with huge worn granite boulders. You get good acidity here, and not too much alcohol: Procura white is around 13%. It comes from vines that Esteban reckons are about 60 years old, "and they're all different sizes, from tree-sized to very small". All different varieties, too: this is a classic old mixed vineyard of the sort that Portugal dedicated itself to eradicating when it took to modern viticulture in the 1980s and 1990s. She farms it biodynamically, favours wild yeasts where possible and ages it in old oak barrels.

The wine has a wild feeling, a feeling of unpredictability kept in check by poise and balance; yellow fruits and honey, herbs, stones are all in there, and it's very fresh, structured and long. My notes say that it tastes "determined". I don't think you could isolate a molecule for "determined", but there is a sense of drive and vigour. It is both conventionally delicious and as individual as you can get.

DRINK WITH

Rich fish dishes, of course, but also chicken or guinea fowl

BEST AGE TO DRINK

It's very good young,
but will certainly age
a few years

TROPHY VINTAGES

It's not really
a trophy wine

DECANT

No

CHILL

Yes

**WHAT TO SAY IF YOU
MEET THE WINEMAKER**

Was buying old barrels
from Burgundy more
expensive than buying
new ones locally?

AND WHAT NOT TO SAY

Why bother?

PAUPER SUBSTITUTE

Not really

66

Very Old Madeira

REGION

Madeira

COUNTRY

Portugal

GRAPES

Sercial, Verdelho, Terrantez, Bual or Malmsey, or Tinta Negra

PRICE

****

This is another wine where I'm going to be vague about producers, because quantities of these old Madeiras are tiny, and it just depends what you can get your hands on. Look out for anything from Blandy's, Cossart Gordon (right), Leacock, Henriques & Henriques; if you're on the island the producers' lodges are a good source of old bottles. Some is exported; the producers have realized there's a market and are releasing small quantities. At the time of writing Blandy's had some vintages from the 1970s available. If you find anything older, grab it: I've tasted Madeiras made when Marie-Antoinette was on the throne of France, and they were marvellous; certainly with more staying power than the French monarchy.

The different grapes (listed left) each make their own style, more or less from dry to sweet. Old Sercial is searingly austere and acidic, redolent of preserved lemons, beeswax and leather; Verdelho still dry and acidic but rounder, more walnuts; rare Terrantez usually off-dry and with focus; Bual getting sweeter, more nuts and coffee; Malmsey the sweetest and most opulent. Or the grape might be Tinta Negra, which for years was used for pretty much every style, though I don't think it's ever quite as good. With time all take on a pungent *rancio* character, which is compelling and refreshing.

You can drink a bottle gradually because all the oxidation is done before bottling: they're stable. I can think of no greater vinous treat than an old bottle of Madeira drunk over a wet winter weekend with the one you love.

DRINK WITH

No food is needed; have a glass as an apéritif on a gloomy winter's evening

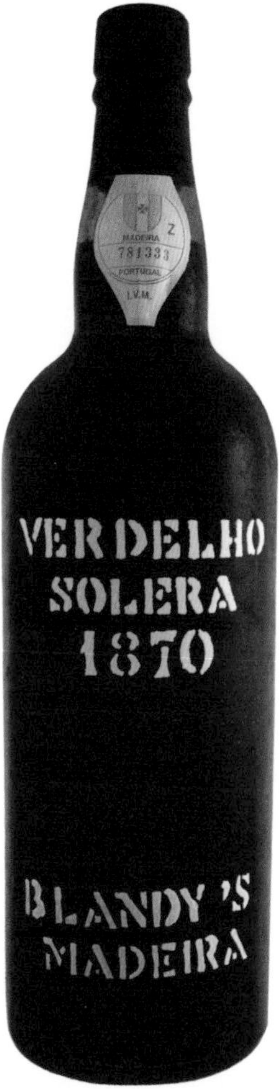
MADEIRA
781333
PORTUGAL
I.V.M.
VERDELHO
SOLERA
1870
BLANDY'S
MADEIRA

BEST AGE TO DRINK

We're looking at 40-plus

TROPHY VINTAGES

Whatever you can get

DECANT

Not unless it's thrown a deposit

CHILL

Probably not

WHAT TO SAY IF YOU MEET THE WINEMAKER

You may be too late to say anything, if the wine is very old

AND WHAT NOT TO SAY

Tell me about the weather that August

PAUPER SUBSTITUTE

A 20-year-old in the style of your choice is probably the nearest substitute

Blanc de Blancs Vintage, Wiston Estate

67

REGION

South Downs

COUNTRY

England

GRAPE

Chardonnay

PRICE

**

English sparkling wine has had a lot of hype recently. Is it worth it? Sometimes, yes.

The key to really good quality – quality that can look good Champagne in the eye without flinching – is chalk. Chalk soil gives a particular feel to the acidity of the wine: a sort of ripe, brilliant linearity that other soils simply don't give. The problem in the south of England is that a lot of the best chalk slopes face north, which is too cold. You want something a bit warmer, a bit sunnier, to ripen grapes in Sussex.

Wiston's 16 acres of Chardonnay, Pinot Noir and Pinot Meunier are on south-facing chalk, cultivated with no herbicides. The wines are fermented in old oak barrels bought from Burgundy, for a bit of extra weight but no oak flavour; so what you get in this 100% Chardonnay Blanc de Blancs, which is from the best, steepest and chalkiest part of the vineyard, is dancing tension, a sort of expansive harmony and the feeling of complexity you get when the flavour comes in subtle waves on the palate rather than all at once. You get that "flavour in waves" in great Champagne as well, and it gives fascination and moreishness .

What this wine needs is bottle age. When it's very young it can be austerely tight, and it needs a few years to unwind a little and fill out and develop its flavours of brioche and butter, citrus and toast.

The estate is new in wine terms – in the family since 1743, it only started making wine in 2008.

DRINK WITH

Seared scallops

BEST AGE TO DRINK

Give it seven years or so
from the vintage date,
and then for another five
or more

TROPHY VINTAGES

2010, and then whenever
the sun shines

DECANT

No

CHILL

Yes

WHAT TO SAY IF YOU
MEET THE WINEMAKER

Is climate change good
news for you so far?

AND WHAT NOT TO SAY

The long-range forecast
is rain, I hear

PAUPER SUBSTITUTE

The NV Blanc de Blancs,
steely and sleek

Kapi Vineyard Tokaji Aszú 6 Puttonyos, Disznókő

68

REGION

Tokaj

COUNTRY

Hungary

GRAPE

Furmint

PRICE

*** →****

Tokaji – pungent, concentrated, botrytized, with piercing acidity – had been famous for centuries, but the long Communist winter had destroyed it. Not just the winemaking but even the vineyards had become debased. The new foreign investors found they had to reinvent everything; and they did so with great sensitivity and attention to detail. Vineyards were replanted with better clones, pruned for lower yields and old winemaking techniques were restored. Here, aszú berries (those shrivelled by botrytis until they are almost violet in colour) are macerated in fermenting must (must that is not fermenting, or finished wine, can also be used) for several days, then all is pressed and left to finish fermentation before being aged in oak barrels.

Disznókő is owned by French insurance company AXA Millésimes. It makes Tokaji of immense freshness and purity, silkiness, subtlety and concentration. Kapi is its top site: it has more limestone in the soil than is usual in this very volcanic region, and gives wines of crystalline purity and whiplash power; not as aromatic as some, but with tremendous elegance. It is always 6 putts (*puttonyos* are the measure of sweetness: 5 putts is sweet, 6 is sweeter), so intensely sweet, with intense linear acidity to balance, and flavours of tea and smoke, preserved lemons, herbs, toast, salted grapefruit, bitter marmalade; it's like drinking fireworks. With age it darkens and takes on more toffeed notes; it was first bottled separately in 1999.

DRINK WITH

Cheese, foie gras, nuts, or on its own

BEST AGE TO DRINK

Not before 10 or 15 years.
If you want a younger
wine, choose a 5 putts

TROPHY VINTAGES

2005, 2011

DECANT

No

CHILL

Yes

**WHAT TO SAY IF YOU
MEET THE WINEMAKER**

Which is the more
classic style of Tokaji,
5 or 6 putts?

AND WHAT NOT TO SAY

Is the Hungarian
government friendly
to foreign companies
these days?

PAUPER SUBSTITUTE

Aszú 5 Puttonyos from
the same producer;
not pauper, perhaps,
but less pricey and
extremely good

69

Clai, Sveti Jakov

REGION

Istria

COUNTRY

Croatia

GRAPE

Malvasia Istriana

PRICE

* →**

If you follow the fertile Mirna River valley inland from the Istrian coast you will see, only an intensively farmed field or two back from the river, a much wilder landscape of forest, of fields carved out wherever the land allows, and the Ucka mountains rising to the north. The cold air coming off the mountain ridge combines with the gentler maritime influence coming in through the Mirna valley to give hot, dry summers but much cooler autumns and cold winters.

This is where Giorgio Clai has his winery and his eight hectares of vines, tucked into a valley 10km (6 miles) from the sea and 30km (19 miles) from the mountains, on limestone that twists and turns to give umpteen different exposures, at altitudes of 150–250m (492–820ft). And it is here that he makes his very particular wines.

You could call this natural wine, you could call it orange wine – it ticks both those boxes. The grapes are crushed and fermented with the skins for two to four months, just like a red wine, in open wooden vats. That's where the tawny colour comes from: not so much orange as the colour of aged Fino Sherry. The texture is so light it's almost ethereal. The nose is – what? Wet clay? Ripening barley? A touch of apples? The acidity is high, ripe and fine. And it doesn't taste of fruit, it tastes of wine. It's a sort of apotheosis of wine, both intellectual and sensual. It's refined, seamless, lively, intense but delicate, structured, but supple as silk. There's a touch of cooked apple, a touch of Victoria plum straight from the tree; and absolute purity, restraint and dancing tension, with some tannin of the most fine-grained sort stitched through it.

DRINK WITH

It seems to work with almost anything

BEST AGE TO DRINK

Up to ten or even
twenty years

TROPHY VINTAGES

None

DECANT

Yes, an hour or more
before drinking

CHILL

A little

**WHAT TO SAY IF YOU
MEET THE WINEMAKER**

How do you get
such finesse?

AND WHAT NOT TO SAY

Shouldn't "orange"
and "natural"
mean "rustic"?

PAUPER SUBSTITUTE

None

70

Haut de Pierre Dézaley, Domaine Blaise Duboux

REGION

Lavaux, Vaud

COUNTRY

Switzerland

GRAPE

Chasselas

PRICE

**

You might think, if you were cynical, that if only one country regards Chasselas as a serious wine grape and all others regard it as primarily a grape for eating, then perhaps the minority should listen to the majority. But in wine the minority voice can often have something worthwhile to say. The Swiss celebrate Chasselas for the minute differences of terroir that it can reflect. When you first encounter it you might think that anything that whispers that quietly hasn't got a chance. But it's a grape that repays the effort of listening.

This is a surprisingly big wine. It combines breadth with freshness, tightness with complexity. The acidity is low but there's a feeling of stoniness, a gentle melon note, a touch of lime blossom and nuts; it's unlike anything else. It's not aromatic and there are no fireworks, but it's a layered, rewarding wine, all earth, sap, stones, with beautiful texture and concentration. To get this subtlety and depth you need good viticulture; Blaise Duboux is biodynamic, focused on expressing every nuance of these mountain slopes.

These vineyards overlook Lake Geneva, and the vineyards were originally planted by 12th-century Cistercian monks; now they're a UNESCO World Heritage Site, and Blaise Duboux is the 17th generation of his family to work them. Was it Chasselas they planted back then? It's impossible to say. The grape almost certainly originated in this area, and it's an old variety, first entering the written records in the 16th century. It's a corner of the wine world that deserves exploration.

DRINK WITH

Fish, mushrooms

BEST AGE TO DRINK

After about a year,
for six or seven years

TROPHY VINTAGES

None

DECANT

No

CHILL

Yes

WHAT TO SAY IF YOU
MEET THE WINEMAKER

You need a head
for heights

AND WHAT NOT TO SAY

What do you do if you
get vertigo?

PAUPER SUBSTITUTE

Not from Switzerland,
no

71

Assyrtiko, Hatzidakis

REGION

Santorini

COUNTRY

Greece

GRAPE

Assyrtiko

PRICE

*

It is extraordinary that somewhere so hot can produce wine with such singing, stinging minerality and acidity, but that's Assyrtiko for you. It is one of the world's great white grapes, yet until we all started to realize how amazing Greece's indigenous varieties are, you could hardly find a bottle of it anywhere.

Santorini is of course a volcano, and volcanic soils seem to give wines with a particular energy, a particular sparkle. The vines here are extraordinary too: there's a local training system called *koulara* that winds the canes in a basket, with the clusters on the inside. Every 50 years or so everything is cut back to the roots, and the vine starts again. This system offers protection to the grapes from the incessant wind; and there's not much rainfall, so dew and mist have to sustain the vines through the hot summer. There's no phylloxera on the island so all the vines are ungrafted, and some are allegedly 500 years old. What is more certain is that many are over 100 years old. Hatzikakis farms its vineyards organically and biodynamically, and the grapes ripen early at the beginning of August. This wine is the standard Assyrtiko; there is also Assyrtiko de Louros, aged in old oak for greater weight and ageability, and single-vineyard Assyrtiko de Mylos. Both are impressive, but I prefer the standard bottling for its purity, clarity and precision.

The wine is substantial, savoury, with keen acidity, and orange peel and floral notes, saltiness and an unmistakeable tannic edge. It's energetic, concentrated and vibrant: a structured, sinewy wine from a unique and difficult place.

DRINK WITH

It's a brilliant match for pungent flavours like anchovies and olives, and will go with both meat and fish

BEST AGE TO DRINK

It needs a couple of years in bottle to open properly, and will be good for five or more

TROPHY VINTAGES

None

DECANT

No

CHILL

Yes

WHAT TO SAY IF YOU MEET THE WINEMAKER

Fashion has come round to Assyrtiko

AND WHAT NOT TO SAY

I prefer Riesling

PAUPER SUBSTITUTE

This is very good value

72 Retsina, Domaine Papagiannakos

REGION

Attica

COUNTRY

Greece

GRAPE

Savatiano

PRICE

*

My husband is a painter, and when I first met him I loved the smell of turpentine that hung about his work clothes and his studio. I would, it follows, adore Retsina. Except that I don't. It's too coarse, too obvious, too oily. Apart from this one. Delicate, filigree even; it comes from unirrigated 50-year-old indigenous Savatiano vines planted in limestone soil within spitting distance (well, 30km/19 miles) from the Acropolis. Savatiano is one of Greece's indigenous varieties; it's not usually that well regarded, because it's channelled into Retsina, which itself hasn't been well regarded.

Resin is one of the oldest ways of preserving wine. Wine in a clay jar sealed with resin was less likely to oxidize, and the resin flavour helped to disguise off-flavours, as did the herbs, spices, lead, seawater and honey that were also routinely added to wine. The herbs and spices are still with us in every bottle of vermouth; lead went out of use only surprisingly recently; honey has been supplanted by fermentations arrested by chilling, filtration or fortification to leave residual sugar. I'm not aware of any current use of seawater.

Resin comes from local pine trees and is added these days in tea-bag form, dunked in a few days after fermentation and removed when it has done its job. Here you have to imagine a crisp, citrus, herbal white wine with no more than an aura of resin. Think of proper beeswax furniture polish, of the sort still handmade by monks and sold in the shops of French abbeys on Sunday mornings; think of my beloved turpentine. But the aroma is so ethereal in this wine; it draws you in and back for more. It's irresistible.

DRINK WITH

Sardines, mackerel; Greek friends say sea urchins

BEST AGE TO DRINK

Within a couple of years

TROPHY VINTAGES

None

DECANT

No

CHILL

Yes

WHAT TO SAY IF YOU MEET THE WINEMAKER

Are there different qualities of resin?

WHAT NOT TO SAY

Do you make furniture polish as well?

PAUPER SUBSTITUTE

This is very good value

73

Cinsault Vieilles Vignes, Domaine des Tourelles

REGION
....
Bekaa Valley

COUNTRY
....
Lebanon

GRAPE
....
Cinsault

PRICE
....
*

DRINK WITH
....
A tagine, perhaps;
anything with spice
and flavour

I've always wanted to like Lebanese wines more: you have to admire the producers' doggedness in maintaining their vineyards and harvesting their grapes in the midst of war and mayhem. But this one is a revelation: a wine of freshness, complexity, grown at an altitude of 1,000m (3,280ft); flavours of tar and cherries, juicy and silky, compelling and poised – and made from a grape that until recently was being dismissed by many Lebanese growers as so lacking in prestige that it was demeaning to grow it.

Cinsault, you see, is one of those Mediterranean grapes that gained a reputation for producing vast quantities of poor quality wine. In much of southern France it was replaced by Syrah and Cabernet; in Spain by Tempranillo; in Lebanon by Syrah and Cabernet again. Yet it had been grown in Lebanon ever since Jesuits first brought it there in 1857. It doesn't mind drought (unlike Cabernet and Syrah) and thrives in Lebanese conditions. Suddenly it's being seen as Lebanon's answer to Pinot Noir: old-vine wines like this (the vines are about 50 years old) have the same limpid transparency as Pinot, the same depth. Things go wrong if it's allowed to overripen, and is then overextracted because a producer demands a dark colour, and is then put into new oak: then you get monsters. This wine, fermented with wild yeasts in old concrete tanks, and aged in old French oak barrels, keeps its balance perfectly. It feels like a ballerina *en pointe*: muscular but graceful.

BEST AGE TO DRINK

The 1976 was fantastic
in 2017, so there's
probably no hurry

TROPHY VINTAGES

None

DECANT

Could do

CHILL

No

**WHAT TO SAY IF YOU
MEET THE WINEMAKER**

Has your winemaking
changed much over
the years, apart
from details?

AND WHAT NOT TO SAY

Wouldn't you prefer to
be really high-tech?

PAUPER SUBSTITUTE

The estate's other reds
can be a bit chewy

74

Camp Meeting Ridge Chardonnay, Flowers Vineyard & Winery

REGION

Fort Ross-Seaview AVA, Sonoma Coast, California

COUNTRY

USA

GRAPE

Chardonnay

PRICE

** →***

This is the epitome of the new California: wines that have turned their back on ultra-ripeness, ultra-richness, ultra-massiveness, in favour of balance and harmony and elegance.

To get to Flowers you drive up the Pacific coast with the sea on one side and forest on the other; you drive, probably, through fog and come out above it: Flowers is 350–572m (1,150–1,875ft) up, just a couple of miles from the sea and close to the San Andreas Fault. It's a geologically complex region, with rock that includes greenstone, shale, sandstone, greywacke and schist. Topsoils are shallow and well drained. The standard adjective is "rugged". Camp Meeting Ridge vineyard takes its name from trade between the local Kashaya Indians and Russian fur traders.

But it's the climate, too, that brought Joan and Walt Flowers here in 1991. It's extreme: being above the coastal fog means that it's cool, but sunny. Grapes ripen slowly; winemaking is basically Burgundian. These wines changed how people saw California: suddenly it was possible to make savoury, flinty Chardonnay, with flavours of peaches, citrus peel and salt, in a state better known for butter, tropical fruit and a bit more butter. You get physiological ripeness here at lower sugar levels; bright, intense, focused wines.

It's not an easy place to make wine, however. Planting costs can be higher even than in Napa, and sometimes vines simply move: the geology is not completely stable. Sea breezes can be strong enough to cause problems at flowering.

DRINK WITH

Top fish: turbot, halibut, Dover sole

BEST AGE TO DRINK

Can be drunk young,
but ages well

TROPHY VINTAGES

The first vintage
was 1994

DECANT

No

CHILL

A bit; don't serve
too cold

**WHAT TO SAY IF YOU
MEET THE WINEMAKER**

Can you smell the sea
from the vineyards?

AND WHAT NOT TO SAY

Are you afraid
of earthquakes?

PAUPER SUBSTITUTE

The Sonoma Coast
Chardonnay is cheaper

75

Estate Red, Harlan

REGION
....
Napa Valley, California

COUNTRY
....
USA

GRAPES
....
Cabernet Sauvignon, Merlot, Cabernet Franc, Petit Verdot

PRICE
....
*****

If ever there was a big wine that wears its muscle lightly, that wine is Harlan. A powerful Napa Cabernet blend of great concentration that shows just how good Napa terroir can be. Because its power is tempered by freshness, it's neither tiring nor cloying – this freshening effect is familiar to every drinker of equally weighty Bordeaux.

Bill Harlan was inspired by the great Bordeaux wines and knew exactly what he wanted to make; the challenge was to make it, and to find the land to make it on. He eventually bought wooded hills above the Rutherford-Oakville bench, cleared the trees, planted vines at high density at 107–168m (351–551ft) up and released his first vintage with the 1990. By 1994 he was getting where he wanted to be, and hasn't wavered since.

The wine feels authentic. There are plenty of Napa Cabs made to a market, overpolished and overextracted. Harlan feels like the product of its intertwined vineyards and forests, its volcanic rock and its sandstone, the tension between tightness and opulence that keeps you coming back to the glass. Viticulture is biodynamic, there is no added acidity and the oak barrels are mostly new but not dominant: it walks a tightrope, and it doesn't falter. It is also wildly expensive.

It's a wine for the long term: voluptuous in youth, it then closes up for a few years, to open out again into savoury depths of balsamic herbs, sandalwood, toast, black cherries and damsons, sometimes woodsmoke, sometimes black olive. Fine and elegant, it has got fresher over the years, too: dry-farming in the vineyard, a move to natural yeasts and shorter macerations have all brought more transparency.

DRINK WITH

Guinea fowl, salt-marsh lamb

BEST AGE TO DRINK

Within the first ten years for fruit and power; after that for silkier tannins and the flavours of maturity; but it tends to close up at around seven years, so avoid it then

TROPHY VINTAGES

There are no duds, just different styles

DECANT

Yes

CHILL

No

WHAT TO SAY IF YOU MEET THE WINEMAKER

Can you make great wine without taking risks?

AND WHAT NOT TO SAY

There's nothing risky about the Napa, surely

PAUPER SUBSTITUTE

The second wine is The Maiden; don't be too much of a pauper, though

76

Geyserville, Ridge

REGION

Sonoma County, California

COUNTRY

USA

GRAPES

Zinfandel, Carignan, Petite Sirah, Alicante Bouschet

PRICE

** →***

This is a Zinfandel that is not pure Zinfandel. Recently retired Ridge winemaker Paul Draper loves old mixed vineyards: some of the Geyserville vines, those in the Old Patch vineyard, are 130 years old, and Draper points out that any Californian vineyard of that age survived Prohibition only because it was very good indeed. The original mix of vines was calculated: some give tannin, some acidity, some aroma. The whole adds up to more than the sum of its parts. Draper loves mixed vineyards so much that he even planted them: he said that if he planted Zinfandel on its own it took ten years before the grapes were good enough for Geyserville. But if he planted mixed vineyards it took six or seven years, and the wine was more complex.

Three adjacent vineyards go into Geyserville; all are on the western edge of Alexander Valley, with soil that mixes deep gravelly loam with alluvial rocks: a river once flowed through here. Vines are dry-farmed and there are no pesticides, herbicides or synthetic fertilizers. The climate is decidedly warm, though morning fogs give respite, but these are all heat-loving varieties.

It's not only in the vineyards that Ridge favours pre-industrial methods, either. Yeasts are natural, no enzymes are used and fining is with egg white. It's all as natural as possible. The wine is lush, yes, with blackberries, liquorice, pepper, savoury spices, cherry and floral notes and some sturdy meatiness, but it's also fresh and surprisingly linear, with tremendous length to balance its power. The power is actually restrained: there's nothing over the top about Geyserville.

DRINK WITH

Tagines, duck with braised red cabbage: dishes with fruity sweetness

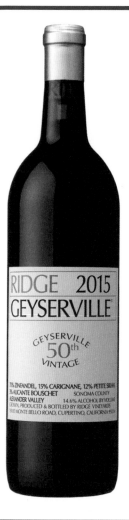

BEST AGE TO DRINK

From release, until
about ten years of age

TROPHY VINTAGES

2016, which was
the fiftieth vintage
of Geyserville

DECANT

Yes

CHILL

No

**WHAT TO SAY IF YOU
MEET THE (NEW)
WINEMAKER**

How does it feel to be
so much younger than
your vines?

AND WHAT NOT TO SAY

Will they need
replanting one day?

PAUPER SUBSTITUTE

East Bench Zinfandel
is a bit cheaper

77

Insignia,
Joseph Phelps

REGION

Napa Valley, California

COUNTRY

USA

GRAPES

Cabernet Sauvignon plus Merlot, Petit Verdot, Malbec

PRICE

**** →*****

I should make a confession here: I find it easy to admire Napa Cabernet, but much, much harder to love it. The super-ripeness, the lush, chocolatey, oaky style that Napa does so well (especially in the "luxury goods" bracket) is just not something I often want to drink. But Insignia comes into its own with age, and with food. It is not a wine to take lightly.

If California had first growths, Phelps Insignia would be one of them. It's a big, powerful, complex, structured wine, aged in generous amounts of new French oak, with flavours of coffee, pepper, black olives, cloves, damsons, chocolate; very fine-grained and long. It ages superbly. All the fruit is now estate-grown, from vineyards all over the Napa Valley – which undoubtedly helps complexity and freshness – and it is grown and made with immense care. Those vineyards are in Stags Leap District, Oak Knoll District, Saint Helena, Rutherford, Oakville and South Napa Valley, which gives some climatic and stylistic variation. The result has finesse, even restraint. There are many Cabernets from Napa that would love to imitate Insignia, yet just end up tasting of prune jam and oak. Insignia is how it should be done. The style has evolved over the years yet remained recognizably the same: one of the marks of a wine that is true to itself.

DRINK WITH

Venison, wild boar: something with plenty of flavour

BEST AGE TO DRINK

The first vintage was 1974, and it's still going strong

TROPHY VINTAGES

Any, really; there's less vintage variation than in say, Bordeaux

DECANT

Yes

CHILL

No

WHAT TO SAY IF YOU MEET THE WINEMAKER

How do you get to be a bigger perfectionist than Joseph Phelps?

AND WHAT NOT TO SAY

Do you ever think, that'll do?

PAUPER SUBSTITUTE

Phelps Napa Valley Cabernet Sauvignon is cheaper

78 Rubicon, Inglenook

REGION

Rutherford, Napa Valley, California

COUNTRY

USA

GRAPE

Cabernet Sauvignon

PRICE

*** →*****

A word of warning here. If the Napa Cabernets you admire are the big, overripe, overextracted body-builder wines that pass for "luxury goods", then don't bother with this one. You won't like it. This is for people who want finesse, elegance and balance, and want them at under 14% alcohol. Rubicon 2013 is 13.8%. It shows conclusively that the excuse of some producers, that 16% wines tasting of prune jam is what their vineyards give them, is no more than a craven chasing of 100-point scores. There is no need for any of it.

Francis Ford Coppola has owned Inglenook since 1975. By 2011, when he appointed Philippe Bascaules to make the wine, he'd already begun to move away from what had become the Napa norm of high alcohol, low acidity and overripe fruit. (The estate's wonderful white, Blancaneaux, was the first to change style.) Bascaules came from Bordeaux's Château Margaux (see page 16), and has taken the wine even further in the direction of drinkability and terroir expression. Rubicon has crossed its eponymous river and become a wine redolent of violets, with a fine-boned structure, pure, aromatic tobacco and cassis fruit, poised and limpid. It has a feeling of being at ease with itself, of not having to try too hard. It's a glorious wine.

What will happen now, though, is not yet clear. Bascaules has been lured back to Château Margaux as MD, following the death of Paul Pontallier. He will continue to direct winemaking at Inglenook, with another winemaker doing the day-to-day stuff, though how this will work remains to be seen. Perhaps Bascaules is immune to jet-lag.

DRINK WITH

Roast lamb

BEST AGE TO DRINK

At about four years, and
then for twenty or so

TROPHY VINTAGES

The 2012 and 2013 are
made in the new style

DECANT

Yes

CHILL

No

WHAT TO SAY IF YOU
MEET THE WINEMAKER

How does Rutherford
compare with Margaux?

AND WHAT NOT TO SAY

How many air miles
have you got?

PAUPER SUBSTITUTE

The 1882 Cabernet
Sauvignon, Napa Valley,
is cheaper

79

Pinot Noir Original Vines, The Eyrie Vineyards

REGION

Oregon, Pacific Northwest

COUNTRY

USA

GRAPE

Pinot Noir

PRICE

*** →****

DRINK WITH

Partridge, guinea fowl; salmon, too, preferably wild

Eyrie Vineyards, in the person of its cheerfully nonconformist founder David Lett, was what first persuaded the world that Oregon could make great Pinot Noir. Lett first planted Pinot in the Dundee Hills in 1966, and named his vineyard after the eyrie of a pair of red-tailed hawks that overlooked the site.

Many other growers, including Robert Drouhin of Burgundy, followed his lead. Fashions in Pinot changed, but Lett never succumbed to the trend for super-ripeness and high alcohol. He believed, and his son Jason, now in charge, believes in freshness, poise, tension – the things that make Pinot fascinating. So no herbicides, pesticides or irrigation are used in the vineyards, and no ploughing either – the red volcanic soil is left alone to get on with it, and manages extremely well. Picking is never too late, or at too high a level of ripeness, and fermentation is with wild yeasts; there is no artificial control of fermentation temperatures, and fermenting vessels are small enough for this to be possible. Ageing is in old oak – just one in every twenty-five barrels is new. It might sound as though this is doing things the easy way, but doing nothing can be far harder than doing something.

This special bottling is a medium-weight wine, with concentration and silky tannins. Expect delicacy and aroma: red fruits, flowers, acidity, even a note of citrus pith, to go with the savoury herbs and spices. There's raciness and grip, too. Eyrie has star quality.

BEST AGE TO DRINK

It's lovely young, but
should last 20 years
or more

TROPHY VINTAGES

1983, 1988, 1999, 2000,
2007, 2010 – it's not
made every year

DECANT

Yes, particularly
if it's got some age

CHILL

No

**WHAT TO SAY IF YOU
MEET THE WINEMAKER**

Why does Oregon
attract eccentrics?

AND WHAT NOT TO SAY

What do you think of
Californian Pinot?

PAUPER SUBSTITUTE

The basic Pinot Noir
is a bit cheaper

80

Off the Grid
Riesling, Ovum

REGION

**Illinois Valley, Oregon,
Pacific Northwest**

COUNTRY

USA

GRAPE

Riesling

PRICE

*→**

Oregon is not supposed to make Riesling, and here in the south of the state, near the Californian border, 40km (25 miles) from the Pacific, it's gold rush country. (Hence "Off the Grid".) There's magnesium, nickel and iron in the earth here, lots of stones, since only 50 years ago a creek ran here, and cold winds off the Klamath mountains compensate for the hot summer days, when the temperature can easily hit 30°C (86°F)-plus. But there's a huge difference between day and night temperatures, and it can fall to 4°C (39°F) after sunset. And the vineyard is high: 458m (1,500ft). So while you might look at the map and think "hot", actually it's surprisingly cool.

Ovum is a new winery, founded in 2011, and is focused on making wines with a sense of place. This doesn't mean that you have to infer the details of the vineyard – its soil, its sunshine and rain, its wind and shelter – from the flavour in the glass. If I were to taste this blind I would probably put it in Austria, which is a compliment, because Austria is making some of the most finely grained Rieslings in the world. This is delicate, detailed, stony and herbal, vivid yet filigree. It is intense, yet doesn't shout. It makes you listen.

Everything is low-intervention at Ovum: wild yeasts for fermentation, neutral barrels of oak and acacia and cement eggs (hence Ovum), and long lees contact of eight to nine months, for texture. Ovum say they don't want their wines to be about the winemaker but to act as a conduit for the vineyard – a philosophy you will find in Burgundy, in Austria, in Germany, in parts of Italy, but not everywhere, by any means.

DRINK WITH

Grilled fish

BEST AGE TO DRINK

At release, for ten years or so

TROPHY VINTAGES

None

DECANT

No

CHILL

Yes

WHAT TO SAY IF YOU MEET THE WINEMAKER

What does "sense of place" mean?

AND WHAT NOT TO SAY

How can I have a sense of place if I've never been there?

PAUPER SUBSTITUTE

None

81

Roseland, King Family Vineyards

REGION

Monticello, Virginia

COUNTRY

USA

GRAPES

Chardonnay, Viognier, Petit Manseng

PRICE

* →**

David and Ellen King had been looking for 12 acres of flat land for a polo field when they bought Roseland in 1996. Vines weren't even a thought; but in 1999 the first ones went in.

You might see a paradox here: a polo field needs flat land, and vines usually prefer slopes. But, says winemaker Matthieu Finot, polo fields also need good drainage, and that's where the terroir wins. It's also high up on the edge of the Blue Ridge mountains, in an area that in the time of Thomas Jefferson used to be called "Mountain Plains". Finot is from the Northern Rhône, but even so, he doesn't miss steeper slopes.

Now there are now 31 acres of the varieties that seem to suit Virginia so well: Petit Manseng, Viognier, Petit Verdot, Cabernet Franc, Malbec, plus Merlot and Chardonnay. This blend of about half Chardonnay, the rest Viognier and Petit Manseng, evolved, one gathers, because it works: Chardonnay brings weight and some apple and pear notes, Viognier brings its honeysuckle and apricots and Petit Manseng, as well as pineapple and citrus notes, brings acidity – plenty of it. Even at high sugar levels (and it was originally planted here for dessert wine) Petit Manseng has a very low pH.

It's a beautiful blend: perfectly integrated flavours of herbs, grass, hay and summer meadows, very long and complex. There's no new oak; just steel, old oak and acacia barrels. A grown-up wine with about 13% alcohol, fresh and balanced.

DRINK WITH

Scallops, trout

BEST AGE TO DRINK

At a couple of years old, for another five or so

TROPHY VINTAGES

None

DECANT

No

CHILL

Yes

WHAT TO SAY IF YOU MEET THE WINEMAKER

How about planting the polo field?

AND WHAT NOT TO SAY

Why is that horse eating the vines?

PAUPER SUBSTITUTE

None

82

Tannat, Michael Shaps

REGION

Monticello, Virginia

COUNTRY

USA

GRAPE

Tannat

PRICE

★★

Virginia is one of the most interesting winemaking states of the USA because it's able to make what we want now: bright, fresh wines of concentration and proper ripeness at under 14% alcohol. This wine comes in at about 13.7% – it depends on the year, obviously – and that's a very civilized level of alcohol. Especially considering that Tannat is massively tannic grape, and those tannins must be ripe, so it's no good trying to pick it early for low sugar: you'll just get green tannins.

Michael Shaps' Tannat comes from two sites, both pretty warm, so with good canopy management the seeds and skins get nicely ripe. The wine keeps its freshness because Tannat naturally has plenty of acidity as well; sometimes the acidity has to be adjusted in the winery, says Shaps, but much less than with the Bordeaux grapes. The wine tastes of tar and violets and black hedgerow fruit: elderberries, sloes, blackberries. It's a big wine, but with a good brisk quality that makes it moreish. The tannins are silky and everything is beautifully integrated and transparent.

Tannat is a recent arrival in Virginia, which made its name with another tannic red grape, Petit Verdot, and whites like Viognier and Petit Manseng, as well as the Cabernets. So it's difficult to say just how long it will live. Certainly at three years old it seems youthful, with more to come; that long finish promises a good future.

DRINK WITH

Roast rib of beef

BEST AGE TO DRINK

At about four years, and for another ten or so

TROPHY VINTAGES

None so far

DECANT

Could do

CHILL

No

WHAT TO SAY IF YOU MEET THE WINEMAKER

Are the grapes of Southwest France the future of Virginia?

AND WHAT NOT TO SAY

Are you making French copies?

PAUPER SUBSTITUTE

None, really

83

Malbec Argentino, Catena Zapata

REGION

Uco Valley

COUNTRY

Argentina

GRAPES

Malbec, Viognier, Cabernet Franc

PRICE

** →***

"Just the right side of flashy," sniffed a colleague when I admired this wine. Well, considering how many Argentine Malbecs are the wrong side of flashy... It's not a light wine. It also comes in the sort of annoyingly heavy bottle that deters any sensible buyer. But persevere, because it has a seamless integration that you'll find in very few top-end Argentine reds, and it has a feeling of not trying too hard. Unlike the bottle, you might say.

The slightly weird blend of grapes is because this wine is a blend of two vineyards, Adrianna and Nicosia. The Adrianna part of it is Malbec co-fermented with Viognier, and the Nicosia part is Malbec co-fermented with Cabernet Franc. Wild yeasts do their thing for both parts. The oak is French, and there's some whole-bunch fermentation, for extra aroma and grip.

Argentine terroir is mainly about soil type and altitude. Altitude (Adrianna is at 1,440m/4,725ft) gives lower temperatures and cooler nights, plus brilliant light, which mean more freshness and much silkier tannins. Adrianna was originally thought to be too cool to ripen Malbec, but Catena reckon that the long hours of sunshine, and the brightness of the light, do the trick. And the good news is that they don't need to acidify.

The subsoil of Adrianna is volcanic, with limestone and gravel over. It's the star vineyard at Catena. Nicosia is further south and less talked-about, but gives density and voluptuousness. The blend of the two is a wine of opulent blackberry fruit, redcurrants, tar, herbs, graphite and the odd floral note, all perfectly tucked in, and with a beautiful silky texture. It's quite showy, so keep it for when you feel like that sort of thing.

DRINK WITH

A hunk of steak, preferably cooked rare

BEST AGE TO DRINK

From release for about
15 years

TROPHY VINTAGES

Not really

DECANT

Yes

CHILL

No

**WHAT TO SAY IF YOU
MEET THE WINEMAKER**

Were you really the
first to plant that high
up in Argentina?

AND WHAT NOT TO SAY

Can Argentine Malbec
ever be unshowy?

PAUPER SUBSTITUTE

There's an entry-level
Malbec, which has some
high-altitude fruit in it

84

Pencopolitano, P. Parra y Familia

REGION

Itata and Cauquenes

COUNTRY

Chile

GRAPES

Malbec, Syrah, Carmenère, Carignan, Cinsault, País

PRICE

*

This is the new Chile: vibrant, balanced, poised. The old Chile, being a little unsure of itself, strove for authority via overoaking and overextraction. The new Chile doesn't need any of that. It's not afraid to take risks, and it seeks acidity in the way that old Chile sought softness. It is so secure and confident it feels as though it doesn't have to try.

Enough poetry. The first thing (person, actually) to talk about is Pedro Parra. He's a terroir consultant (not a career likely to feature in a school careers office) with clients from Sonoma to Burgundy, and he's obsessed with finding the very best terroirs for wine. "A lot of my job is making people change their mind," he has said. He has joined forces with Louis-Michel Liger-Belair (see page 30) in a Chilean project called Aristos, but this is his very own project, the grapes sourced from a handful of different vineyards of ungrafted vines of up a hundred years old, some of them field blends, right down in the cool south of the country.

Marginal climates are something Parra likes very much. What he also likes is the red granite soils here, which he says give a nervous tension to the wine and lots of upfront flavour on the palate. There is also some schist in these vineyards: schist, he says, brings a more horizontal structure and powerful tannins.

The winemaking uses indigenous yeasts, and there's great purity to the wine, along with vivid black fruit, a stony, mineral character, floral, red-berried notes, medium body and immense moreishness. The tasting sample I have at my elbow while writing this has been followed by a second tasting sample. It's an exhilarating wine.

DRINK WITH

My tasting sample was rather good with some old Parmesan

BEST AGE TO DRINK

From release for five
or six years

TROPHY VINTAGES

None

DECANT

No

CHILL

Keep it on the cool side

**WHAT TO SAY IF YOU
MEET THE WINEMAKER**

Can you recognize soil
types in wine, blind?

AND WHAT NOT TO SAY

I can't even tell red
from white, blind

PAUPER SUBSTITUTE

This is the
entry-level wine

85 Tannat B6, Bouza

REGION
....
Canelones

COUNTRY
....
Uruguay

GRAPE
....
Tannat

PRICE
....
**

Uruguay is heaven for people who like old cars – sometimes quite old. Bouza, founded in 2000 in the undulating hills north and northwest of Montevideo, has a remarkable collection of them; a museum, in fact. What with that and a rather good restaurant, the bodega is worth a visit if you happen to be in Uruguay.

If you are, you'll be struck by the clarity of light – almost sea light, because neither the Atlantic nor the broad Rio de la Plata are far away – but also the temperate warmth. It's not that hot here, and there's cloud cover, and humidity. All these things are perfect if you want to make ripe reds with moderate alcohol – and isn't that what almost everybody wants these days?

So the late-ripening, tannic Tannat grapes can stay on the vine until they're properly ripe – which means no greenness, no rusticity. The bottle is slightly unfortunate because its weight and square-shouldered shape leads you to expect something oaky and extracted, and this isn't; instead it's a burly but fresh glassful of blackberry fruit and spice, extremely easy to drink and a lesson to anyone who thinks that the answer to Tannat lies in oak and chewiness. The wine is fermented in steel tanks, and then aged in new French oak barrels for 16 months, and it simply soaks up the oak, leaving no feeling of oakiness. It's not an incredibly complex wine but it is hugely enjoyable, and it's a most accomplished wine, sensitively handled, from a young wine country. It is one of those instances where a grape variety can seem most at home a long way away.

DRINK WITH

Roast meat, or the local barbecues; punchy vegetables; flavoursome fish dishes

Young; Tannat doesn't really seem to improve beyond about five years

None

No

No

Your combination of humidity and moderate temperatures works wonders

Please can I drive one of those cars? Please?

The Sin Barrica is cheaper, and (as the name suggests) is not aged in barrique

86

Sangreal Pinot Noir, By Farr

REGION

Geelong, Victoria

COUNTRY

Australia

GRAPE

Pinot Noir

PRICE

** →***

It's the name that's so wonderful, with its connotations of Arthurian legend transposed to the plains of Victoria. By Farr is in the Moorabool Valley – a name that one could imagine in Malory. Sir Moorabool took his lance...

But I'm rambling. The Farrs, Gary and son Nick, show how Pinot should be made in Victoria. Gary's label is By Farr; son Nick's is Farr Rising. Sangreal is their oldest vineyard, a north-facing slope of bluestone, red ironstone and limestone; it's an early ripening site that makes wonderfully perfumed, silky wines. Sangreal is so perfectly integrated, so full of finesse and concentration, and amazing perfumes of red fruits, a touch of roses, smoke, raspberry, wild herbs and a touch of the *garrigue* flavours that Victorian Pinots often have – all tucked into a fine-boned structure. Gary Farr worked ten vintages at Domaine Dujac in Burgundy, so it's not surprising that he's a fan of whole-bunch fermentation, which lifts the aroma and gives weight on the palate. About 60 per cent of the oak is new, and this is by no means too much. There's no fining or filtration; everything is meticulous and detailed. It's a powerful wine, but it wears it gracefully; it is the most elegant of the Farr single-vineyard Pinots.

Moorabool Valley is close enough to the sea to catch the sea breezes, and near enough to the flat western plains of Victoria to get the blustery winds from inland. It's a dry, harsh climate, and not a spot where you'd choose to make high volumes because those strong winds affect fruit set and keep yields down. It's not a bit like the Côte d'Or, but Burgundy is in Gary Farr's blood – which brings us back to Sangreal.

DRINK WITH

Roast beef

BEST AGE TO DRINK

On release, for eight to ten years

TROPHY VINTAGES

Geelong is a really consistent region for Pinot

DECANT

Yes

CHILL

No

WHAT TO SAY IF YOU MEET THE WINEMAKER

What advice would you give to other Victorian Pinot-growers?

AND WHAT NOT TO SAY

What's your Holy Grail?

PAUPER SUBSTITUTE

Farrside Pinot is cheaper, though not cheap

87

Polish Hill Riesling, Grosset

REGION

Clare Valley, South Australia

COUNTRY

Australia

GRAPE

Riesling

PRICE

**

It seems difficult to imagine now, but there was a time, not long ago, when Australian Riesling was in danger of having no legal protection; a time when it could be used to describe any generic white wine made from any commonplace, bulk-producing grape. That Riesling is now on the list of grapes in Australia that are subject to the same stringent labelling regulations as say, Shiraz or Cabernet – that a wine labelled "Riesling" must be made from Riesling – is due to Jeffrey Grosset. It took him seven years to win the battle.

For all that time, and before, and since, he has been making Riesling that has proved to the world that the Clare Valley is one of the great Riesling sites, and that he is one of its greatest producers. Grosset himself divides terroirs into "hard rock" sites and "soft rock" sites: Polish Hill is one of the former, with slate underlying clay marl and a layer of shallow shale; the vines struggle and the berries are small, the wine concentrated. The Springvale vineyard, by contrast, is a "soft rock" site, red loam over sandstone, which allows the roots to reach more water and more nutrients. Springvale wines are more generous; Polish Hill tighter, more austere.

I've talked elsewhere (see page 100) about the importance of tension in Riesling. Polish Hill has tension in excelsis. The lime-cordial flavours that are typical of Australian Riesling are there, but elegantly so; the wine is intensely mineral, with some floral notes and tight linearity. The word "austere" shouldn't put you off; the wine is compelling, and just needs a while to open up. It has huge depth and length, and a mouthwatering palate; it's a wine of clarity and purity.

DRINK WITH

Crab would be good

BEST AGE TO DRINK

Between ten and
fifteen years

TROPHY VINTAGES

2002, 2008, 2009, 2010,
2012, 2013, 2015

DECANT

No

CHILL

Yes

**WHAT TO SAY IF YOU
MEET THE WINEMAKER**

Are these the wines you
intended to make when
you started in 1981?

AND WHAT NOT TO SAY

Do you mind other
people using the Polish
Hill name?

PAUPER SUBSTITUTE

Springvale is slightly
cheaper

88

Hill of Grace
Shiraz, Henschke

It's an instantly memorable name. It comes from the little Gnadenberg church near the vineyard, named after a region in Silesia, and translated as Hill of Grace. The alternative would have been to name it after the village that was at the other side of the vineyard back in 1860 when it was planted. But Parrot Hill just doesn't have the same gravitas.

This is a wine of great gravitas. Power, too, and weight, but also grace and harmony. The oldest vines are those same ones planted in 1860; they're known as the Grandfathers – from cuttings taken from Europe before phylloxera destroyed European vineyards. Younger vines are from cuttings from the Grandfathers. The vineyard is much higher than the nearby (and hotter) Barossa Valley: about 400m (1,312ft), and with colder nights; most of the vineyard is unirrigated. The soil is quite rich, and holds moisture.

Hill of Grace is a magical wine: massive, but poised and harmonious; super-ripe, but fresh. The flavours are of chocolate and mocha, vanilla and toast, pepper, mint, spices; gloriously complex, and bursting with energy. It drives forward on the palate like a train. It ages to notes of forest floor, perfumed leather and roast meat; the tannins become melting. It is probably better now than it has ever been. The first vintage was 1958; Prue and Stephen Henschke took over Hill of Grace in 1990 and have brought ever greater detail to vineyard and wine: the vineyard is run organically and biodynamically, the choice of (largely French) oak is subtle, the judging of ripeness precise and the tannin extraction gentle. They have brought, in a word, grace.

DRINK WITH

Very well-flavoured
beef

BEST AGE TO DRINK

Start drinking it from eight to ten years. Great years will last thirty years-plus

TROPHY VINTAGES

1986, 1990, 1994, 2002, 2005, 2010

DECANT

Yes

CHILL

No

WHAT TO SAY IF YOU MEET THE WINEMAKER

Do very old vines give better tannins?

AND WHAT NOT TO SAY

Will they die soon?

PAUPER SUBSTITUTE

Henry's Seven will give a taste of Henschke energy

89

Art Series Chardonnay, Leeuwin Estate

REGION

Margaret River, Western Australia

COUNTRY

Australia

GRAPE

Chardonnay

PRICE

***

DRINK WITH

Rich fish or chicken dishes

It was Robert Mondavi who recommended to Denis and Tricia Horgan, back in 1972, that they plant vines on their new cattle farm. They were not great wine-lovers then, but they did as he suggested, hired Mondavi as a consultant and released their first Chardonnay in 1979, at double the price of its rivals. The accolades started coming in, and haven't stopped since. For many, this is the best Chardonnay in Australia.

It's evolved over the years. It's always been in the cashew-and-oatmeal camp rather than the overflowing-tropical-fruit camp; the style seems to have become steelier, the richness more compact and restrained, but the changes have not been dramatic. There is mango, toast, crème brûlée, citrus peel, spice, hazelnuts and almonds; the wine is layered and precise, rich and driven.

The estate has 62 acres of Chardonnay, supplying different levels of wine. Block 20, known as the "Front Gate", is always the heart of the Art Series Chardonnay, with gravelly, well-drained soil, cooled by breezes from the Southern Ocean, which in turn cause *millerandage* at flowering. Leeuwin turns a problem into an advantage, and gains greater complexity and acidity in the wine. It's called Art Series because of the pictures on the label: it was the first Australian wine to do this. Horgan got the idea from Mouton Rothschild. The Horgans' art collection is now considerable, and can be visited at the winery; there are also concerts there in the summer, and there's a good restaurant, too.

BEST AGE TO DRINK

From about five years,
for another twenty

TROPHY VINTAGES

The quality is
remarkably consistent

DECANT

No

CHILL

Yes

**WHAT TO SAY IF YOU
MEET THE WINEMAKER**

Would you describe
this as fruit-driven or
terroir-driven?

AND WHAT NOT TO SAY

Do you miss the cattle?

PAUPER SUBSTITUTE

Prelude Chardonnay is
cheaper and very good;
a bargain

90

McLaren Vale Grenache, S.C. Pannell

REGION

McLaren Vale, South Australia

COUNTRY

Australia

GRAPE

Grenache

PRICE

**

One moment Steven Pannell is a Young Turk; the next he's a Grand Old Man. (Not old at all – sorry, Steve.) One moment Australian Grenache is trying to be Shiraz, with overripeness, masses of extraction; the next it's the warm-climate answer to Pinot, with delicacy, lightness, freshness and a mission to reflect every terroir that comes its way.

That Aussie Grenache has blossomed into this extraordinary delicacy is in large measure due to Pannell. His wines have always had a lightness of touch; before he set up his own winery he was chief red winemaker at Hardy's for ten years, and before that he went round Europe working vintages (Aldo Vajra, Barolo; Domaines Dujac and Pousse d'Or, Burgundy): Nebbiolo and Pinot and now Grenache – you see the pattern.

He works with old, dry-farmed vines, picks early for freshness and keeps everything simple, with reductive winemaking and early bottling. The result is Grenache with raspberry and Turkish-delight flavours, floral and aromatic with violets, roses and dried herbs. The texture is silky, but with an enlivening edge of tannin. He says he doesn't know why his wines turn out so well; this might not be the whole truth.

The even better news is that he's one of many McLaren Vale winemakers doing great things with Grenache. If I can mention other names: Bekkers, D'Arenberg, Marmont, Ochota Barrels, Yangarra Estate. If you want transparency, lightness and freshness in Australian Grenache, McLaren Vale is where to look.

DRINK WITH

Fish, vegetable dishes, partridge; almost anything, really

BEST AGE TO DRINK

From about three years
for another fifteen-plus

TROPHY VINTAGES

None

DECANT

If you want

CHILL

No

**WHAT TO SAY IF YOU
MEET THE WINEMAKER**

What did Pinot Noir
teach you about
Grenache?

AND WHAT NOT TO SAY

I'll bet you'd really rather
be making burgundy

PAUPER SUBSTITUTE

None; splash out

91 Grange, Penfolds

REGION

Multi-regional blend

COUNTRY

Australia

GRAPES

**Shiraz,
Cabernet Sauvignon**

PRICE

*****

DRINK WITH

Beef of good flavour
and sublime texture,
or venison

The story of how Grange came to be is well
known, but still worth retelling. Max Schubert,
chief winemaker at Penfolds, visited Bordeaux
in 1950 and came away inspired. He became
determined to make something just as great
in Australia; not just with Cabernet Sauvignon,
since there wasn't enough in Australia at that
time, but with what he had to hand, which was
Shiraz. He bought some barriques, and made
his first experimental Grange Hermitage in 1951.
In 1957 he allowed the management of Penfolds
to taste what he'd made so far – and they hated it.
He was told to stop production.

He made a couple more vintages in secret,
however. The board decided to have another
look at those early attempts, and this time they
liked them: production was to restart. During
the 1960s Grange Hermitage established a
reputation for being Australia's grandest red,
a badge that it has kept ever since. You might
prefer the elegance of Penfolds St Henri, but
there's no doubting the importance of Grange.

Current winemaker Peter Gago has brought
extra refinement to Grange (it dropped the
"Hermitage" with the 1990 vintage), and he
seeks out cooler vineyards in warmer years. A
typical mix today might be 2010's Barossa, Clare,
Adelaide Hills, McLaren Vale and McGill Estate.
There's usually an admixture of Cabernet; only
1951, 1962, 1963, 1999, 2000 didn't have any. In
youth it is intense and powerful, with black fruits,
spices, notes of the American oak in which it is
aged, and with great silkiness and integration.
With time it ages to mocha-scented leather,
graphite and liquorice, meat and exotic spice.

BEST AGE TO DRINK

Give it ten years at least, and then for another ten, or twenty, or thirty

TROPHY VINTAGES

1951 for its rarity, 1953, 1962, 1963, 1966, 1971, 1983, 1986, 1990, 1991, 1996, 1998, 2002, 2004, 2006

DECANT

Yes

CHILL

No

WHAT TO SAY IF YOU MEET THE WINEMAKER

How does your Grange differ from Max Schubert's?

AND WHAT NOT TO SAY

Can I buy a bottle of the 1951?

PAUPER SUBSTITUTE

Kalimna Bin 28 is a good place to start

92

Vat 1 Hunter Semillon, Tyrrell's Wines

REGION
....

**Hunter Valley,
New South Wales**

COUNTRY
....

Australia

GRAPE
....

Semillon

PRICE
....

**

DRINK WITH

Crab or scallops

If you wanted to make great dry white you would never plant Semillon in the Hunter Valley. Never. It's too humid, too hot. Semillon is a low-acid grape that thrives – for sweet wines – in the cooler maritime climate of Sauternes. And yet Hunter Semillon is one of the world's classic wine styles, and one that owes nothing to any other country – except for the vines, of course.

Partly it's the cloud cover in the Hunter that helps keep sugar levels down in spite of the heat – Semillon is often picked at around 10% potential alcohol here. The humidity also helps to keep the acidity up.

Semillon was planted, like most grapes in the early winemaking history of Australia, as an all-purpose workhorse. Its dry wines used to be labelled "Hunter River Riesling", and I remember, in the 1980s, tasting some from the 1960s. They were glorious: honeyed, toasty, fresh, deep. It is still making the same styles now, and they still need ageing: bone-dry Semillon, picked early at 10% alcohol, often in a rainy year and without any oak ageing, can taste remarkably like battery acid when very young.

Tyrrell's makes several Semillons (having been growing it since at least 1870), and this one is the tops. With a few years on the clock it's tight, vigorous and tastes of celestial honey and lemon, seasoned with fennel and rosemary. As the years pass the honey becomes more pronounced and the wine becomes toasty, so you'd swear it has been aged in oak – but it hasn't.

BEST AGE TO DRINK

Give it six years before
you open it, but it'll keep
for decades

TROPHY VINTAGES

Most years seem to be
good or very good

DECANT

No

CHILL

Yes

WHAT TO SAY IF YOU
MEET THE WINEMAKER

Are you really descended
from Walter Tyrrell, who
came over with William
the Conqueror?

AND WHAT NOT TO SAY

Isn't there a murderer
called Tyrrell in
Shakespeare? (Actually,
do ask that; Bruce T has
a good story, too long
to tell here)

PAUPER SUBSTITUTE

The straight Hunter
Valley Semillon

93

Reserve Sauvignon Blanc, Elephant Hill

REGION

Hawke's Bay, North Island

COUNTRY

New Zealand

GRAPE

Sauvignon Blanc

PRICE

*

There are a clutch of New Zealand Sauvignon Blanc producers, you may be glad to hear, who are turning their backs on the Marlborough paradigm of green beans, gooseberries, asparagus, box and all those other unripe flavours that attack the palate so stridently.

The Sauvignon Blanc at Elephant Hill has a nose of round white fruits and a palate of melon, ripe citrus and confit lemon, tight and taut. It's bone-dry, fermented with natural yeast half in stainless steel and half in old oak barrels, with richness from ageing on the lees. The acidity has a beautiful linear elegance and the alcohol is just 12.5%. It's proper Sauvignon Blanc; Sauvignon Blanc as it should be.

It comes from the shingle soil of the Te Awanga vineyard, a cool site near the ocean. The vines were planted in 2003 – Elephant Hill is a newish estate, created with plenty of resources behind it – by Reydan and Roger Weiss, who arrived on a visit in 2001, fell in love with the place and set about creating a thoroughly modern winery with striking architecture (patinated copper cladding on the outside) and a commitment to sustainability. Roger died in 2016 and son Andreas has taken over; the winemaker is Steve Skinner, who has a talent for detail and subtlety.

They set out from the beginning to make world-class wines. If you don't like Sauvignon, try their complex, silky Syrah, which holds its own with top Côte-Rôties in tastings. There's a rather good restaurant, too, if you happen to be passing.

DRINK WITH

Crab, mackerel

94

Block 5 Pinot Noir, Felton Road

REGION

Central Otago, South Island

COUNTRY

New Zealand

GRAPE

Pinot Noir

PRICE

***

Nigel Greening is a self-taught winemaker, self-taught cook, self-taught mathematician and a dead ringer for Richard Branson. He started off studying biochemistry, dropped out to play the guitar, set up a design company, became a bit of a petrolhead, went to work for BMW in the Pacific Rim and fell in love with New Zealand Pinot Noir. So naturally he bought a vineyard in the back-of-beyond bit of nowhere the locals refer to as Central. He ended up by selling everything he owned except his house to buy Felton Road.

Central Otago has the only semi-continental climate in New Zealand: hotter, colder and drier than most other places. Block 5 comes from block 5 of the 14.4-hectare Elms vineyard, in a north-facing valley in the Bannockburn Hills. There's a bit more clay in the soil here, for more weight in the wine, and the vines were planted in 1993, so are of a respectable age.

Felton Road has been certified biodynamic since 2006. Greening doesn't necessarily believe in the biodynamic preparations, though he makes them and uses them, and says that biodynamism is, in essence, "learning that your relationship with the land is negotiation, not dictatorship". He adds, "we have the best-qualified, most-motivated viticultural team on the planet. It tops a stag's bladder any day for benefits from biodynamism."

Block 5 tastes like burgundy from a relatively warm year: red-fruited but succulent, spicy, precise, sleek, with plenty of depth. It's a bit fleshier than burgundy, a bit more about primary fruit and all about pure pleasure. Very hedonistic.

DRINK WITH

Hot smoked gammon or ham

BEST AGE TO DRINK

At a couple of years onwards, for probably 15

TROPHY VINTAGES

2004, 2007, 2009, 2012, 2014, 2015

DECANT

If you want

CHILL

Yes

WHAT TO SAY IF YOU MEET THE WINEMAKER

Can you apply Heisenberg's Uncertainty Principle to wine?

AND WHAT NOT TO SAY

Do you make natural wine?

PAUPER SUBSTITUTE

The Bannockburn Pinot Noir is a bit cheaper

95

Coleraine, Te Mata

REGION

**Hawke's Bay,
North Island**

COUNTRY

New Zealand

GRAPES

**Cabernet Sauvignon,
Merlot, Cabernet Franc**

PRICE

** →***

A Bordeaux blend from New Zealand: why?
Simply because it's superlative. Coleraine
is a wine of authority and resonance from one
of the most intriguing corners of a country that
is discovering that red wines might be what it
does best of all.

Hawke's Bay, tucked into a curve of the
coast, has 25 different soil types. The Te Mata
vines are on gentle, north-facing slopes in
three subregions: Havelock Hills, Woodthorpe
Terraces and Bridge Pa Triangle. At blending
time there'll be 50 or 60 samples lined up, all
blind. "We don't blend by variety at all," says
Nick Buck. "It takes over a month, tasting twice
a day, and there are about five of us. We all make
up our own blend. Then we come back after the
summer holidays, taste all five, and pick one.
The 2013 blend is mine." There might be a lot
of Cabernet Sauvignon in the blend, or hardly
any: it's the most variable part of the blend,
and depends on the year.

Blending is a delicate and skilful art. You
want the wine to express what the vineyard
is telling you, but you want to guide it, as well.
John Buck, Nick's father, has always preferred
aroma over palate weight, which is why
Coleraine has such wonderful aromas of roses,
garrigue, herbs, summer dust... Nick smiles at
this point. "Blackberry and summer dust to me
is the smell of Hawke's Bay. I go for a run between
bay hedges, and I smell summer dust and bay."
All this plus density, ripe tannins, good acidity:
it's a beauty.

DRINK WITH

The best salt-marsh
lamb you can find

Coleraine is a 20-year-old wine, but you can drink it earlier

TROPHY VINTAGES

It keeps getting better, so buy young and keep; the 1990s weren't the best period

DECANT

Yes

CHILL

No

WHAT TO SAY IF YOU MEET THE OWNER

What does Te Mata mean in Spanish? (Answer: "It kills you")

AND WHAT NOT TO SAY

And does it?

PAUPER SUBSTITUTE

The second wine is Awatea, and is also expressive of Hawke's Bay

96

Red Blend, A.A. Badenhorst Family Wines

REGION

Swartland

COUNTRY

South Africa

GRAPES

Shiraz, Grenache, Cinsault, Tinta Barocca and/or others

PRICE

* →**

Hein and Adi Badenhorst came from Constantia to make wine from 28 hectares of old dry-farmed bush vines in Swartland, found a slightly tumbledown old cellar and set about making wines with as little intervention as possible.

The soil is granite of three different kinds, facing north, south and east, so already that's quite a variety of styles. There's no crushing or destemming, there's some foot-treading, fermentation is in big old wood casks or concrete tanks, and there's a long maceration. The grapes – I forgot to mention the grapes – are Cinsault, Grenache and others; traditional SA varieties capable of giving wines of tremendous character. Anything they don't grow they buy in.

In other words it's a hotbed of doing nothing; of picking great grapes and seeing what they give you. This wine has some bought-in grapes, as you'll have guessed (the blend varies from year to year), and those tannins give a robust, even chewy centre to the wine. The flavours are savoury, meaty, bright and dense; there are lovely dark aromas of black cherry and liquorice, and layers of complexity. Elegance, too. It's an energetic, even wild wine, but it has good manners.

A word about Swartland: the old bush vines of this region way north of Cape Town have redefined what SA wine can be. Some of the most innovative wines are found here; many of the best are blends, demonstrating again that wine doesn't have to be about varietal flavours. A good blend is more than the sum of its parts.

DRINK WITH

Slow-cooked ox cheek would be good

BEST AGE TO DRINK

From five years to
probably fifteen

TROPHY VINTAGES

None

DECANT

Yes

CHILL

No

WHAT TO SAY IF YOU
MEET THE WINEMAKER

Can you be fashionable
and counter-cultural at
the same time?

AND WHAT NOT TO SAY

Do you wash your feet
before you tread grapes?

PAUPER SUBSTITUTE

The estate's
Secateurs Red

97

Chenin Blanc Reserve, De Morgenzon

REGION

Stellenbosch

COUNTRY

South Africa

GRAPE

Chenin Blanc

PRICE

*

Chenin Blanc has long been vaunted as SA's speciality grape, making wines with the complexity of the best of the Loire. This wine is brilliant. The vines are 40-years-plus, which gives proper depth to the wines, planted in decomposed granite at about 250–300m (820–984ft) near False Bay, so the sea breezes help to keep things cooler. You can see Cape Town from here, and the Table Mountain, and Simonsberg – and of course the sea. The name De Morgenzon means "morning sun": it is high, so is the first part of Stellenbosch to see the sunrise. And it is an old property; it was part of Uiterwyk, which is recorded as having been let to an early settler in 1682. Since 2003, De Morgenzon has been owned by Wendy and Hylton Applebaum. The winemaker is Carl van der Merwe.

This Chenin Blanc is an opulent wine held in check by acidity. There's a pithy edge, which helps to focus the apricot and quince fruit, sweet spice and underlying salt and the white flower, mandarin peel and honey notes. It's complex and taut. And it's weighty; fermentation is with natural yeasts in French oak barrels, a quarter of which are new, and then it gets another 11 months or so in those barrels, on the lees. It also gets a constant diet of baroque music.

Yes, they play music to their wines 24/7. They're not alone in this, though it's not usual. They are convinced that sound waves affect physical matter. It's all about proportion and formal mathematical patterns.

DRINK WITH

Pork with lemon or quince

98 Rubicon, Meerlust

REGION

Stellenbosch

COUNTRY

South Africa

GRAPES

Cabernet Sauvignon, Merlot, Cabernet Franc, Petit Verdot

PRICE

* →**

This is not the only wine called Rubicon in this book, which proves not so much the importance of rivers to wine but the importance of radical change. The change here was making a blend, which in the 1980s was revolutionary in SA. As so often, the inspiration was Bordeaux.

South African wine has come a long way since then, but Rubicon has kept its place at the top for its grace and elegance, its supple tannins and its black-fruited complexity: think of blackberries, elderberries, black plums, tar and soot, black truffles. Savoury spices, too; cumin and nutmeg, and a stony, gravelly touch which makes one think of the Graves.

The estate is not a new one: its first owner settled here in 1693. The name he gave it means "pleasure of the sea"; it's only 5km (3 miles) from False Bay and catches the sea breezes. Now the whitewashed Cape Dutch house with its magnificent tree-lined avenue, oaks alternating with palms, is a National Monument, and the Myburghs have been here since 1756. Hannes Myburgh is the eighth generation.

What gives the wine its style? A temperate climate, certainly, mists and dew, winter rains and those winds off the sea; and also very varied soils – gravel for the Cabernets, clay for the Merlot (all of which is perfectly Bordelais) and everywhere a seasoning of granite and a black laterite known locally as koffie klip. The wines are big and rich but always fresh, always restrained, firmly in the classical mould. The price is moderate because plenty is made: this is no *garagiste* rarity.

DRINK WITH

Go Bordelais with lamb, or South African with lamb on the braai

BEST AGE TO DRINK

It's released at four years of age, and another couple of years will improve it; then for twenty years

TROPHY VINTAGES

2001, 2003, 2007, 2008, 2009, 2010, 2011, 2012

DECANT

Yes

CHILL

No

WHAT TO SAY IF YOU MEET THE WINEMAKER

Who was first with the name, you or Inglenook?

AND WHAT NOT TO SAY

Is there a trademark issue here?

PAUPER SUBSTITUTE

The Estate Red is made from younger vines and the barrels that didn't make the Rubicon blend

Seadragon Pinot Noir, Newton Johnson Family Vineyards

99

REGION

Upper Hemel-en-Aarde Valley

COUNTRY

South Africa

GRAPE

Pinot Noir

PRICE

***

DRINK WITH

Côte de boeuf, rare

Gordon Newton Johnson describes this wine as "a drawing of my favourite vineyard". That phrase tells you about his intention – that of transmitting the terroir to the glass – but to me it's notable that he uses the word "drawing". A drawing is more delicate, more transparent, more revealing than a painting. There's nowhere to hide in a drawing.

All of which is exactly what Pinot Noir should be like: transparent, exact, expressive, but only in the right hands and in the right place can it achieve that. Hemel-en-Aarde ("Heaven and Earth") is a particularly favoured spot for Pinot, near the coast in Walker Bay; it's cool and catches the southern winds off the Atlantic. Gordon's parents founded the winery in 2001 when it was virgin land, planted the granite soils with Chardonnay and Pinot, and set about getting a reputation for wines of finesse and character. The next generation is continuing the work.

This wine is going to be hard to track down, however. Just 108 cases were made, because the vineyard is just one hectare – though in fact that's bigger than many Burgundians' parcels of vines. The family describe the terroir as "a narrow contour of broken-up claystone in the granitic soil"; the grapes are carefully selected and fermented without sulphur – risky, but rewarding when it works. It's a toasty, structured, firm wine with plenty of weight in the middle surrounded by succulent red fruit seasoned with spice and pepper; taut, tight, focused, long. It's beautiful.

BEST AGE TO DRINK

From three or four
years onwards, for
probably ten

TROPHY VINTAGES

None

DECANT

Yes

CHILL

No

**WHAT TO SAY IF YOU
MEET THE WINEMAKER**

Can you see whales
from your vineyards?

AND WHAT NOT TO SAY

Are salt winds
a problem?

PAUPER SUBSTITUTE

Newton Johnson
Walker Bay Pinot Noir

REGION

Swartland

COUNTRY

South Africa

GRAPES

Chenin Blanc, Grenache Blanc, Clairette, Viognier, Verdelho, Roussanne, Marsanne, Semillon, Palomino, Colombard

PRICE

** →***

You might wonder, reading the list here, how many grape varieties you actually need in a wine. Surely the more colours you mix the more you get mud? But this blend isn't just thrown together. It's not about varietal flavours: it's about expressing a place, achieving something that is precise and rich, tight and complex, subtle and giving – all the contradictions you find in great wine. Imagine a fruit salad of melon and pear, yellow plum, peach and salt, fennel and herbs – and then imagine a polished, shiny, steel-coiled spring giving structure and edge to all those flavours. It has got weight, a bit of grip, a streak of lime pith, all held together in a crystalline structure of tension and balance.

It's from Swartland, where some of SA's finest and most surprising wines from Mediterranean varieties are found, and it's made by Eben Sadie, who set up on his own in 2000, having travelled widely in Europe and become obsessed with the idea of terroir. He made only red to begin with (Columella is the one to look for; that's Columella as in *De Re Rustica*, the famous account of Ancient Roman viticulture) and when he started with white he started with Viognier. Then came Chenin Blanc and Grenache Blanc to balance the richness of Viognier. He has found pockets of old vines all over the place, works them as gently as possible (he bought a horse to help with the ploughing) and does as little as possible to the grapes in the winery. It's the sort of approach that sounds simple but relies on obsessiveness.

DRINK WITH

Fish, shellfish, maybe pork; the older the wine the richer the flavours can be

BEST AGE TO DRINK

From a couple of years,
certainly up to ten

TROPHY VINTAGES

There are no bad years

DECANT

Yes, if it's young

CHILL

Yes

**WHAT TO SAY IF YOU
MEET THE WINEMAKER**

Do you think you'll
ever make two vintages
the same?

AND WHAT NOT TO SAY

Do I have to remember
all these grapes?

PAUPER SUBSTITUTE

This is the only white,
so far

101

G.V.B. White, Vergelegen

GVB could stand for Grand Vin de Bordeaux (or, if you prefer, Grown, Vinified and Bottled), and that would tell you pretty well everything you need to know. Yes, it is something of a homage to the great whites of Bordeaux, fermented and aged in new French oak. Yes, it is a classic Graves-style blend of Sauvignon Blanc and Semillon. And it's made by a producer whose name means "situated far away"; quite appropriate, really.

Vergelegen is an old estate, first planted with vines by its founder, Willem Adriaan van der Stel, in the early years of the 18th century. Nowadays it's owned by Anglo American, which has invested a ton of money in restoring the landscape and eradicating leaf-roll virus, the scourge of SA wine. It sits high up, about 6km (4 miles) from the sea, with 15 different soil types in its vineyards, all giving different flavours, and has always focused on freshness and acidity – on drinkability, even when fashion favoured the opposite. Picking is on aromas rather than super-ripeness and this wine is ripe and toasty but also mouthwateringly mineral and citrus; long, tense and elegant, herbal and pithy, cool and salty.

Given that the winery is corporate-owned it always comes as a bit of a surprise to meet the winemaker, André van Rensburg, who has the sort of outspokenness that generally goes with owning the place yourself. He's mellowed a bit over the years, it's true, but his wines continue to have character. As a rule of thumb, boring winemakers make boring wines. André is never boring.

DRINK WITH

Crayfish, prawns, fish

BEST AGE TO DRINK

On release, for up
to ten years

TROPHY VINTAGES

It's consistently
very good

DECANT

No

CHILL

Yes

WHAT TO SAY IF YOU
MEET THE WINEMAKER

Why is white Pessac-
Léognan so seldom as
good as this?

AND WHAT NOT TO SAY

Say anything you like,
but be prepared for
an answer

PAUPER SUBSTITUTE

Semillon Reserve,
crisp and focused

Glossary

Acidity A crucial part of wine, giving freshness and liveliness. Without acidity wine is cloying.

Acidify/acidification In hot climates acidity might be "adjusted", usually by a discreet addition.

Amarone The richest and deepest wine of Valpolicella, made by drying healthy grapes for a hundred days or more before fermentation.

Amphorae The Classical world used big clay jars for everything; now they're fashionable again for fermenting wine.

Appellation A legally defined wine-producing area.

Ares An are is a tenth of a hectare.

Aszú The shrivelled, botrytis-affected berries used in Tokaj to make the sweet wine of the same name.

Battonage Stirring the lees in a barrel of newly fermented wine. It adds weight and texture.

Biodynamic A system of agriculture based on the phases of the moon and the movements of the planets, which instead of chemicals uses infusions of natural products in homeopathic quantities.

Blind tasting Tasting without knowing the identity of the wine.

Botrytis cinerea (noble rot) A fungus which, on ripe grapes, concentrates sugars and acids to give intense and complex sweet wines.

Botti Italian barrels, usually large.

Chai A French wine cellar.

Chef de cave Head winemaker, usually in a large French operation, especially in Champagne.

Clavelin 62-cl bottle used in Jura, France, for Vin Jaune.

Cold-settled If wine or juice is turbid, the solids need to be allowed to settle to make it clear. Chilling is one method.

Consorzio In Italy, a body running a Denominazione di Orgine Controllata.

Crushing Grapes may be crushed in the winery before fermentation.

Cuvée A blend.

Destemmed Red grapes may be partly or wholly destemmed, or not at all, before fermentation.

Direct pressing Rosé is made by direct pressing if the grapes are taken from the vineyard, pressed and fermented. The alternative method is *saignée*, or bleeding vats of red wine at an early stage of colour.

Disgorgement A stage in the making of traditional-method sparkling wine by which the dead yeasts are swiftly removed from the bottle.

DOC/G Denominazione di Origine Controllata/e Garantita. In Italy, an appellation, equivalent of France's AC.

Dosage A stage in the making of traditional-method sparkling wine: straight after disgorgement the bottle is topped up with a mixture of wine and sugar, to adjust the sweetness of the final wine.

Dry extract Everything in the wine except water and alcohol. More dry extract means more weight and body.

En foule Vines grown higgledy-piggledy in a vineyard and on their own roots. Rarely found.

Enoteca Wine shop and tasting centre in Italy, usually run by the local tourist board.

Enzymes Employed in fermentation, often to extract colour or aroma. Natural winemakers avoid them.

Fermentation The transformation of grape juice into wine by the action of yeasts, producing alcohol and CO_2.

Filtration A way of clarifying wine and removing any trace of yeast to ensure stability in bottle.

Fining The clarification of wine using a range of substances, including egg white. Strips out less than filtration.

First growth Premier Cru in France: an official title given to wines in Bordeaux, and vineyards in Burgundy and Alsace. Indicates high quality.

Flor A yeast layer that grows on Fino Sherry in barrel, and on a few other wines including Vin Jaune. Protects the wine against oxidation, and gives it a fresh, pungent flavour.

Foot-treading Only a few wines are foot-trodden before fermentation nowadays, but vintage Port still may be. Mechanical crushing is more usual for other wines.

Fortification Fortified wines have had an addition of pure grape spirit, either to stop the fermentation (Port) or to increase the alcohol after fermentation (Sherry).

Glycerol Found in wine; gives a feeling of body in the mouth.

Grand Cru Like Premier Cru, an official designation of quality applied to top vineyards (Burgundy) or wines (Grand Cru

Classé in Bordeaux). Sometimes used informally of aspirational wines elsewhere.

Green tannins If tannins in black grapes are not properly ripe they are said to taste "green". A fault.

Leaf-roll virus The plague of vineyards in South Africa, also found elsewhere. Stops the vine ripening its grapes properly, thus leading to green tannins – though not the only cause.

Lees Dead yeast cells. If kept in contact with maturing wines in barrel can give more weight and texture to wine, and help to prevent oxidation.

Lieux-dits Vineyards, especially in Burgundy, which have a recognized specific character. A *lieu-dit* on a label is below Premier and Grand Cru level.

Liqueur de dosage The mixture of wine and sugar added to sparkling wine at dosage to adjust sweetness.

Malic acid A type of acid found in wine, sharp-tasting. See malolactic fermentation.

Malolactic fermentation A bacterial fermentation that transforms sharp-tasting malic acid to milder-tasting lactic acid.

Médoc A region of Bordeaux; also an appellation that contains many smaller and usually finer appellations.

Minerality A much disputed and overused term. Correctly should only be applied to the feeling of stoniness or chalkiness found in certain wines of high quality, eg. Chablis.

Moelleux In French wine, sweet, though less sweet than *liquoreux*.

Nervosité A sense of zestiness and energy in a wine; a refreshing quality.

New oak Barrels made of new oak are widely used for ageing wine, though mercifully the actual flavour of new oak in wine is no longer so desirable. The ideal is for the wood flavours to meld into the wine and be detectable only as extra weight and structure rather than as the flavour of vanilla or whatever.

Organic All wine is organic in the sense that it is based on carbon. Definitions of "organic" vary from country to country and indeed between one certification body and another. "Wine made from organically grown grapes" has been produced without the use of artificial fertilizers, fungicides or pesticides; "organic wine" is made without the use of sulphur dioxide as a preservative in the cellar. Not in itself an indication of quality.

Oxidation/premox The effect of oxygen on wine; ultimately leads to spoilage, but slow and gentle oxidation is part of the maturing process and a valuable aspect of barrel-ageing. An oxidized wine has gone too far and is faulty. Premox, or premature oxidation, has been the bane of white burgundy and other wines since the mid-1990s: many great bottles have oxidized and died at a young age. It appears to have more than one cause, and while leading oenologists generally have a firm opinion on its cause, they seldom agree. Many advances have been made in its prevention, but don't celebrate too early.

Phylloxera A disease spread by a tiny insect, *Phylloxera vastatrix*, which destroyed vineyards across Europe in the late 19th and early 20th centuries. Also found in other continents. There's no cure, but prevention lies in grafting young vines onto immune rootstocks.

Prestige cuvée Used of Champagne and other sparkling wines: an extra-special and very expensive bottling.

Pumping over During fermentation of red wines the "cap" of skins and pips rises to the top. Since it contains many substances, including tannins, which need to be extracted, the juice needs to kept in contact with it. Pumping over is one method: juice is pumped from the bottom of the vat and sprayed over the top of the cap.

Racking Maturing wine in barrel may be kept on its lees, or it may be racked off. To do the latter the lees are allowed to settle at the bottom and the wine is run off, usually into another barrel. Racking also aerates the young wine, which can stop it becoming reductive (see below).

Rancio A pungent flavour found in some old fortified wines, notably Banyuls and other Vins Doux Naturels from the south of France, Sherry and Madeira. It's a flavour of oxidation but does not indicate spoilage; in fact this acidic, almost cheesy note is desirable.

Reductive The opposite of oxidative; what happens to wine in the absence of oxygen. A touch of reductiveness can give the smoky or nose so beloved in some white burgundy, and "reductive winemaking", avoiding contact with oxygen, produces tight, super-fresh wines. But too much reduction gives rise to unpleasant volatile sulphur compounds, at which point it becomes a fault. Mild reduction can be dispelled by aerating a wine in a decanter. Reduction can be recognized by a smell of struck match (often nice), but too much gives smells of bad eggs or rubber.

Ripasso A technique used in Valpolicella, of adding the skins of Amarone, after pressing, to standard Valpolicella to induce a small second fermentation. The wine thus has extra body and flavour, and a little extra alcohol. Ripasso has become so fashionable, however, that from 2017 it may be made by blending Amarone with standard Valpolicella.

Second wine A blend of those lots not quite good enough, or different in style from, the main wine (*grand vin* in France). Often from young vines.

Seed tannins Tannins that are extracted from the pips. Other tannins come from the skins and from the stems.

Solera A system of fractional ageing used for Sherry. A solera will have several scales or stages. Mature wine is taken out from the 218

final scale and bottled, and replaced by wine from the scale before. New wine is put into the first scale. It gives a balance of maturity and freshness in the finished wine.

Sulphur Used as a shorthand for (usually) sulphur dioxide, winemaking's all-purpose preservative and antioxidant. Some is included in bottled wine to carry on its work. Too much is unpleasant, and even low levels can be dangerous to those with an allergy – hence the warning "contains sulfites" on US labels. Organic wines or natural wines may have very low levels of sulphur or none, thus running a risk of oxidation, which is also unpleasant.

Sur lie Wine aged on its lees. A sign of quality in eg. Muscadet.

Tannins Polyphenols found in the skins, stems and pips of grapes, giving colour and structure. High tannin levels give a drying sensation in the mouth, like that of strong black tea. Ripe tannins are silky; green tannins are harsh and raw. Ageing in oak barrels, especially new oak, gives more tannins.

Tartaric acid One of several acids found in grapes. Tartaric acid is found in ripe grapes, but is also the acid of choice for hot-climate winemakers bent on acid adjustment.

Terroir The combination of geology, aspect, altitude, climate and human intervention that makes one vineyard different to another. Great wines should have a sense of place. In industrial wines the place of which they have a sense is probably an anonymous factory.

Vertical tasting A tasting of several vintages of the same wine.

Vieilles vignes Old vines. An overused term. Should mean at least 40-plus years old, but sometimes applied to striplings of 25.

Volatile acidity What you get as wine, usually red, turns to vinegar. At very low levels its savoury, balsamic note can add complexity, though very stringent winemakers consider it a fault at any level. At high levels it tastes acetic.

Wind-machine Propellers expensively installed in vineyards as a frost protection measure.

Whole-bunch fermentation Fermentation without crushing or destemming: a popular technique for Pinot Noir, and Syrah too, because of the spicy notes, extra

aroma, greater structure, silkier tannins and freshness it imparts. Ripe tannins are essential. If overdone, the "whole-cluster" character can dominate the wine.

Yeast, wild/natural/indigenous or laboratory By using a selected yeast produced by a laboratory you can have a reliable fermentation that will give a reliable, predictable result. First you have to kill any natural wild yeasts with sulphur, to ensure your lab yeast has no competition. If, however, you wait for fermentation to start spontaneously you will allow a variety of yeasts to be involved, some of which will be active early and then die, and some of which will finish the fermentation. It's riskier because you might get off-flavours, or the fermentation might stop before all the sugar has been fermented. (A stuck fermentation is a winemaker's nightmare.) But those who favour wild/indigenous/natural yeasts or spontaneous fermentation love the more subtle, complex flavours it brings and believe that those wild yeasts are a part of their terroir. Many great wines use lab yeasts, but the desire to use natural yeasts is no longer the preserve of those who wear socks with their sandals.

Grape Index

Acknowledgements

Author Acknowledgements

My thanks to all those producers and merchants who provided samples and information for this book, and my apologies to all those whose wines I wasn't able to include. Thanks also to my excellent editors and long-suffering colleagues Hilary Lumsden and Pauline Bache, and to Denise Bates, whose idea it was.

Picture Credits

Mitchell Beazley would like to acknowledge and thank all the wineries and their agents who have kindly provided images for use in this book.

Additional photographic credits: page 17, 21 Deepix; 27, 29 Vincent Rougeau, Marigny L'Eglise; 31 Flore Deronzier; 33 Xavier Lavictoire, Agence Chic; 77, 79 Bruno Bruchi; 81 Lisa Anselmi; 95 Riccardo Bucci; 115 Herbert Lehmann; 119 Marçal Font; 133 Paco Barroso; 137 Pedro Lobo; 141 Fabrice Demoulin; 145 Rob Jewell; 147 Francois Poinçet; 155 Constantino Pittas; 161 Robert Bruno; 163 Kelly McManus; 173 Aaron Watson; 191 Emily Shepherd; 197 Lee Warren; 205 Peter Rimmel; 207 Riehan Bakkes; 209 Catea Sincaire

Alamy Stock Photo: 2 Jan Wlodarczyk; 4 LOOK Die Bildagentur der Fotografen; 9 Lynne Otter

We would also like to thank wine merchants Berry Bros & Rudd, bbr.com for the images on pages 49, 53, 55, 56, 65, 67, 75 and 135; Wine is Terroir, wine-is-terroir.com, page 85; and The Madeira Wine Company, madeirawinecompany.com, page 143.

The Secret World of
Polly Flint

ALSO BY
HELEN CRESSWELL

Dear Shrink
The Piemakers
Bagthorpes v. the World
Bagthorpes Unlimited
Absolute Zero
Ordinary Jack
A Game of Catch
The Winter of the Birds
The Bongleweed
The Beachcombers
Up the Pier
The Night Watchmen

Helen Cresswell

THE
SECRET WORLD
OF
POLLY FLINT

Illustrated by Shirley Felts

Macmillan Publishing Company • New York

Macmillan Publishing Company
866 Third Avenue, New York, N.Y. 10022
First American edition 1984
Printed in the United States of America

10   9   8   7   6   5   4   3   2   1

Library of Congress Cataloging in Publication Data
Cresswell, Helen.
The secret world of Polly Flint.
Summary: Polly Flint, a girl who sees things other
people can't, finds herself involved with the "time
gypsies" of Grimstone, inhabitants of a lost village
who have become trapped in a time not their own.
[1. Fantasy.   2. Space and time—Fiction]
I. Felts, Shirley, ill.   II. Title.
PZ7.C8645Se 1984   [Fic]   83-24861
ISBN 0-02-725400-3

*For Lewis Rudd, who unearthed,
and gave me, Grimstone*

The Secret World of
Polly Flint

No one was in the fields
But me and Polly Flint,
When, like a giant across the grass,
The flaming angel went.

— From "Tom's Angel" by Walter de la Mare,
quoted by permission of the Literary Trustees of
Walter de la Mare and The Society of Authors as
their representative

Chapter One

Once upon a time – and I mean last week, or last year – there was a girl called Polly Flint, and one day she saw an angel. It was the strangest thing. She had gone into the field to pick flowers, and was quite alone. Then she tired of this, and instead, started to spin. Round and round she whirled with her arms out-spread. Soon she was dizzy and fell sideways into the long grass. And she lay there, face upturned to the sky and a queer roaring in her head, and that was when she saw the angel.

He was tall as a giant and tongued with flame and he went swiftly, so that his hair streamed. He went along close by like a rushing wind. Polly came up on her elbows to watch him go with wings bristling and bare feet that touched the grasses but did not stir them.

"Oh my!" said Polly Flint softly to herself. "Oh, my good gracious!"

The whole world was a brilliant, singing green and amongst all that green went that bright angel. The shine of him was too much for her to bear so she closed her eyes, and when she opened them again, he had gone. Back she lay again with her eyes closed and wondered what it all meant. She had never in her life dreamed that she might see an angel in the fields, but now she had, and she wondered why.

She went straight home and told them.

11

"I saw an angel in the field – just this minute ago!"

"What's that?" said Alice, who was making bread with plenty of noise and thumping.

"An angel, Mam! I saw one in the field, tall and flaming – and ooh, beautiful he was!"

"Now come along, Polly," said Alice. "You know you never did."

"I did! I saw an angel!"

"Now don't you go saying things like that!"

"Why, why mustn't I say it?"

"Because you just don't *see* angels, Polly."

"Why?"

"Because there's no such – because you don't!"

"I did, I did! I was just lying there, after I'd been twizzling, and he came striding right past me – I could see the ruffling of his hem and his bare feet and – "

"Twizzling?" said Alice. "*Twizzling?* You can't see a deal straight when you've been twizzling, that I *do* know."

"Could've been the sun shafting through the grasses, Polly," said Tom. "Rum tricks, the sun can play."

"Well, I know it wasn't," said Polly, kicking her feet against the table.

"And the less twizzling you do, the better," Alice told her. "Dizzy enough, without that. Polly, *don't!*"

Polly stopped kicking her feet.

"I'm going right back," she told them. "See if he's still there."

"And that's very likely!" called Alice after her. The door banged. "Polly – *don't!*"

"You're always Polly don't-ing her," Tom said. "Let her *have* her angel."

"Oh, *you*, Tom Flint!" Alice was kneading the dough now, slapping and pulling with a will. "Bad as she is, you are. Where she gets it from, I daresay. Not from my side, that is a fact. You'll be saying next that *you* believe in her blessed angel."

"I do believe that she believes she saw it," Tom said carefully.

"There you are then!" said Alice. "Mazed as cuckoos, the pair of you!"

"I'll go on after her," Tom said. "Do with stretching my legs."

He went out and saw that one of his pigeons was just flying back to her roost, and stopped to give her water.

"There, my pretty." He stroked her soft neck. "There's a clever lass!"

Down in the field Polly was looking in vain for her angel.

"I'll try twizzling again," she thought.

Round and round she spun, fast as before, and down she fell. But all she saw was a blur of green and gold, and twice more she twirled and then felt sick. This time when she opened her eyes, she did see a tall figure, and squealed.

"Dad! You gave me a real fright!"

"Thought you'd 've seen me coming," he said. "But too busy twizzling. Never took *me* for an angel, did you?"

Polly sat up, her head still reeling.

"Oh Dad!" she said. "Don't *you* start!"

"Here, let's give you a hand up," and he pulled her to her feet.

"Do you believe that anything can happen in the

world?" she asked. "Because I do, after today. Anything at all."

"Aye, I believe that, I suppose," he said.

"I bet you'd have made one of your rhymes about it."

"I believe I should," he agreed.

"Well then," said Polly, "that's what *I* shall do. That way, I'll keep him for ever."

"That's the way," Tom said. "Good."

"So shall you help me with some rhymes, to start me off?"

"Come on, then," he said. "Let's see . . . flame, came . . . yes, and scene, green. . . ."

"Pass . . . grass," supplied Polly.

And so the pair of them walked on back home, happily exchanging rhymes, as they often did. Tom was a coal miner but he was also a poet. He said that the two jobs fitted together very well. When he read out his finished poems Alice would sometimes sniff, and say it was the first time *she'd* heard of a rhyming miner, but secretly she was proud of him, and so was Polly. His other great loves were his pigeons and his fishing.

He kept the pigeons, eight of them, in a special wooden house he had made in the back yard. He knew them all by name, and they would fly to his call. He was out there with them when Polly came to show him her finished rhyme. She'd been sitting upstairs on her bed sucking her pencil for nearly an hour.

"Dad! I've done it!"

"Good lass. Hear it, can I?"

She drew a deep breath.

"It's not very good," she told him. "Nothing,

really. And nobody could *ever* tell how tall and bright and startling that angel was to me. But anyway . . .

> *"As I lay in the green green grass*
> *I saw a tall white angel pass.*
> *Rushing like the wind he came*
> *With feet of snow and hair of flame."*

"Good!" cried Tom. "Good!"

"There's one more line," she told him:

> *"And the world will never be the same."*

There was a pause, filled only by the soft purr of contented pigeons.

"Well, I reckon that's something, our Poll," Tom said at last. "I reckon that's really something."

"Are they all in?" Polly asked, meaning the pigeons.

He nodded.

"You love them old birds, don't you, Dad?"

He nodded again.

"It's something pr'aps you wouldn't understand. But I reckon there's a reason why we go in for birds, round these parts. When you're down there under the ground, hours without a glimpse of daylight, and working sometimes in tunnels that narrow you can hardly stretch – well, the thought of them birds, winging and flying and making patterns in that great huge sky somewhere up there – well, that's a good thought. One you can hold on to down there."

"I think I *can* see," said Polly. "Even if I've never been down there. What's it *like* in a coal mine, Dad?"

"Shut off from the world," he said, "and with a warm wind blowing."

"A wind?" Polly was amazed. "A *warm* wind?"

"Hot, and dry, and dusty," he said. "You'd know you was down there, even if you was blindfold."

His face was hidden. He was all the while mending the netting on a door frame. Polly watched him, and thought,

"I'm glad he's my Dad. He's as brave as a lion because he goes down into the depths of the earth. *And he makes rhymes, and he believes in angels.*"

Then Alice came to the back door.

"Just look at the pair of you!" she said. "Mooning over them dratted birds! Are you wanting any tea, or aren't you?"

Tom turned and gave his slow, wide grin.

"We're wanting," he said.

In the days that followed Polly Flint did not see another angel, and nor did she ever again, for that matter. But when she had written that last line of her rhyme, "And the world will never be the same," she was right. She now knew, for absolutely certain, that the world was more mysterious than she had ever supposed it. She felt all the time as if she were on the very fringes of another world, a wider one, and would catch glimpses of it – only fleeting, perhaps only for a few seconds, but glimpses all the same. She began to spend even more of her time in the fields and woods beyond the little town. She would sit and string daisies by the hour and time would pass in a dream. And then sometimes, when she lifted her eyes, the world would seem to blur, as if it were only a reflection, and strangest of all, one day the town beyond seemed to melt away and leave an empty landscape, fields, trees, sky. But even as she stared, the town began to come again, and she rubbed her eyes hard.

"Haven't been twizzling *this* time," she thought. "Threading daisies ain't like twizzling. Can make you dizzy, though, in a way. Sick of it, anyhow!"

Then she got up and ran to the little wood beyond, where sometimes she would think she heard distant voices echoing, threading the clear whistling of the birds. And the echoes seemed to be calling her name – "Polly! Polly!" Not a word did she say of this to Alice and Tom.

And then something happened that was to change their whole lives. It was a day in April, a day of daffodil yellow sun and the first calls of cuckoos, and never a day you would expect to end in a terrible darkness.

Polly came running down to the kitchen where Alice was giving Tom breakfast. He was a big man, and he ate heartily.

"Mam, Dad – just heard the first cuckoo!"

"You spend much more time mooning in them fields, and *you'll* end up cuckoo," Alice told her. "Nip and fetch the milk in, there's a good girl."

"Fishing weather," Tom said, as she came back in. "Perfect."

"Oh Dad! Can I come, can I?"

"Can you what?" Alice whipped round from the sink. "Can you *what*, Polly Flint? School, my girl, is where you're going. I never heard of such a thing!"

"A *morning* don't make much difference," Polly said. "Don't learn much in just a morning."

"Hmph!" Alice tossed her head. "And that depends who you are. Learn plenty in a morning, if you put your mind to it."

Polly poured a golden shower of cornflakes and kicked her feet against the table.

"I daresay the odd morning here or there don't make *that* much difference, Alice," said Tom.

"That child ain't going fishing, she's going to school, and there's an end to it!" said Alice. "Polly – *don't!*"

Polly poured milk on her cornflakes, and thought, "Might as well be *called* Polly Don't, number of times it gets said. Not Polly Flint at all – Polly Don't."

"You on nights, Dad?" she asked out loud.

"Afternoons," he told her.

"Might as well say goodnight to you now, then," she said. "You'll be gone when I get back from school."

"Why, then, goodnight, Polly," he said gravely.

"Goodnight, Dad," replied Polly, and they both began to laugh, while Alice cried, "Well, if now I haven't heard it all – goodnight at breakfast!"

But in the end she laughed, too, which was good, because it was to be a long time before they were all to laugh together again.

That night when Alice came up to say goodnight to Polly, she said, "I do believe I forgot to say goodnight to you at breakfast, so I thought I'd best come up and say it now, if it's not too late!" and they both laughed again.

"I don't like it when Dad's on nights," said Polly. "I never get read to."

"I have offered," said Alice, "and I can't do more."

"I'm sorry to say, Mam, it's not the same," Polly told her. She giggled.

"Little madam!" Alice told her, and stooped to kiss her.

"Don't like to think of Dad down there in the dark, either," Polly said.

"Little goose! Makes no difference day *or* night, down there – nor winter or summer either, come to that!"

"*Seems* different," said Polly obstinately. "To me it does."

"Off with that light now." Alice leaned over to it and spotted tell tale crumbs on the table. "Here – I see you've had biscuits up here again. I've told you before, Polly – don't!"

"Sorry," said Polly. "I'll try to remember. 'Night then, Mam."

"'Night, Polly. Sleep tight."

She went out and Polly turned over on her side.

"Polly don't from morning till night," she thought. "First thing in the morning and last thing at night. Polly don't!"

She closed her eyes and thought of Tom working away down there under the ground.

"Might be under this very house at this very minute," she thought. "How did he say it was down there. . . . ? Shut off from the world, with a warm wind blowing . . . queer . . . *cold* I should've thought it would've been . . . "

Her thoughts faded into a haze of silently unfolding pictures and then they, too, faded. And in her sleep she may or may not have heard the unaccustomed wail of the pit siren, but afterwards she thought she had.

She woke with a start to the sound of voices in the kitchen below. Something about those voices frightened her. They were urgent and raised in a way she had never heard before. Still dazed, she thought, "But it's dark – it's still night time! What's happening?"

She stretched out to turn on the bedside lamp and looked at the clock. Nearly eleven o'clock. Downstairs, someone was crying.

Swaying a little, half asleep, Polly went down the stairs and into the kitchen. It seemed to be full of people. Then there was absolute silence. She stood in the doorway and looked at the faces of George and Betty Garret from over the road, and Ted and Doris King from next door, Bill Stevens, and a man whose face she knew but could not put a name to.

Everyone was looking at her with such strange expressions – looks of fear, sorrow and pity – that for a moment they all seemed strangers, even her own mother.

"Oh Polly!" It was Alice, white-faced and scared-looking. "Come along, my pet!"

She moved swiftly forwards and put her arms round Polly, holding her tight. Then she stroked her hair, very hard and fast.

"What, Mam?" Polly was bewildered. "What's the matter?"

"Polly, you've got to be very brave. You see – "

Polly screamed, "Dad, dad!" She *must* have heard that wailing siren, or must have dreamed it.

"Hush now, hush my darling. We don't know yet."

"What's happened? Is he down there still? Oh Dad!"

She wailed, and held on tight to Alice, smelling the starch of her apron. (Alice rarely took off her apron, until she went to bed.) People were talking again now, all at once.

21

"Now you must be brave, Polly, you hear me? I'm going now, with George and Betty, to the pit head. I'll be there, then, when they bring him up."

"I'm coming, Mam, I am!"

"No, Polly. It's late at night – and no place for you, anyhow."

"But Mam – "

"I want you to be a good girl, as your Dad would want you to be. I want you to go back to bed, and try to go to sleep. Doris'll stay down here till I get back."

"I can't sleep! I shall never sleep!"

"Come along, love. I'll take you up now."

She took Polly's hand and they went together up the stairs and back to her tumbled bed.

"I'll ask Doris to fetch you up some warm milk," Alice promised before she went.

Polly very meekly climbed into bed, and allowed herself to be tucked back in. But the moment Alice had reached the foot of the stairs, Polly was out again. Nimbly and silently she dressed, hardly noticing the tears that were running down her cheeks and splashing down.

Down the stairs she tiptoed, glad of the hubbub in the kitchen. The front door was directly opposite her. Carefully she clicked back the latch, gently eased open the door. Then she was outside, in the shock of the cold air, and pulled the door gently to behind her.

Then began the long run through the night, through the narrow, terraced streets to the pit head. The pavements were empty, the windows of the houses blank, but that meant nothing to Polly Flint. She saw only a picture of her father's face, black with coal dust (though she had never seen it so) and heard only her own gasping breath and the sound of her feet thudding on the cobbles.

She paused at the top of Parson Hill for breath, and a car came by, and she caught a glimpse of her mother's pale face. Her eyes were fixed and sightless, and Polly guessed that Alice, too, was seeing Tom's face instead of the world.

Now it was downhill all the way to the pit, she could see the floodlights below and the flashing blue lights in the pit yard. And now her thoughts ran fast to the pattern of her feet, "Let him be all right, let him be all right, let him not be dead, let him not be dead . . ."

She saw Alice at once in the pit yard, standing in a huddle of others under a pool of light. Straight to her Polly ran and for a second time was caught and held tightly.

"Mam, mam, I had to come!"

"Hush, my darling, it's all right. Of course you did."

"Is he safe? Have you heard?"

"There are three of them hurt. They're bringing them up now."

Polly would remember that wait all her life long. She'd remember the wide yard and the sharp, criss-crossing shadows under the flood lights and beyond the darkness, moon and stars invisible. She'd remember, too, her father being brought at last on a stretcher. Alice and she leant over him. Polly had never before seen her father with the dust of the pit on him. His face was blackened, and the hands that lay limply on the blankets.

"Tom!" Alice put out one of her own hands to clasp his. "Tom, love – it's me, Alice!"

23

"He'll not hear you, love," said one of the men. "The doctor's been and injected him, see."

"Oh! Oh!" Tears of disappointment squeezed from her eyes. "How bad is he?"

It was then that Doris and Ted arrived, in a terrible taking.

"There she is!" they cried, seeing Polly.

And then there was confusion as Alice asked leave to go with Tom to the hospital, and Polly was sent sobbing home again.

It was a sad night's work, though not so bad as it might have been. Tom would live, though he was the worst hurt of the three. At the moment he could not move his legs at all. This might come right, they said, in time.

"It will!" said Polly fiercely, when she was told. "It will, it will!"

She would not believe that Tom, who was tall and strong and went with a long, lank stride, might never have the use of his legs again.

She went to see him as he lay there and his long slow grin had altered not a bit, and she tried not to think of his legs lying useless under that iron cage. He made her promise to look after Alice.

"For you know how she is," he said. "Try to stop her from getting low, shall you?"

Polly agreed, and did her best in the days that followed. She ran errands, laid a table without being asked, and helped look after Tom's pigeons, with Ted next door. The familiar sight of them tumbling out of the sky, and the sheer comfortableness of them as they blinked and purred in their warm straw, somehow made the world as it should be again for Polly, and she spent hours talking to them.

"My Dad's going to get well, you know," she would tell them. "He'll be back to throw you your corn, never you fear. You won't catch my Dad spending his life flat on his back. Mam says so, too. Says it's not in his nature. 'T'ain't, either!"

The pigeons would gaze roundly at her, and seem to nod their heads. At any rate, Polly knew they understood. It was one day when she was out talking to them that she met the coal miner. It was the strangest thing. One minute he was not there and then, when she looked, he was. She smiled at him and he smiled back, and his teeth and eyes flashed white out of his sooty face.

"Fond of these old birds, ain't you, lass?" he said, and Polly nodded.

"And so'm I." He reached and very gently lifted one and held it cradled between his two hands. "Good, when you're down there underground, to think of 'em up here. Go through that huge sky as if they'd their own map, inside their heads."

"That's just what my Dad says," Polly told him.

"Then your Dad's right," the coal miner told her. "And I reckon it must do him good, and all, to think on 'em now. I reckon he dreams on these birds as a prisoner dreams on freedom."

"Oooh, I'd give anything to be able to fly," Polly said. "Think – swooping and soaring, all the quietness up there, and the space!"

"Well, then, and so we all *can* fly," said the coal miner.

"What do you mean?" Polly asked.

"Inside of our heads," he told her. "Fly wherever we've a mind to. Could tell your Dad that. He'll know what you mean, like enough."

"Oh, he will," Polly assured him. "There's a lot goes on inside my Dad's head. He can make rhymes, you know."

"Well, can he now?" said the miner. "That's good, then. That's very good."

At that moment Alice's voice came from the scullery.

"Polly? You out there?"

Polly turned.

"Here, Mam!"

"Come along, will you? You're not near ready, and we shall miss the bus."

"Coming!" Polly turned back to explain to the coal miner that she and Alice were going to visit Tom, but he had gone.

"Well!" said Polly Flint. "*That's* rum!" and she walked slowly back into the house, shaking her head.

"You do spend a deal of time with them birds," said Alice. "Get your hair brushed, will you, and your other shoes on."

"I was just talking to a coal miner," Polly said.

"Oh yes? Who was that, then?"

"Well, that's the funny thing. I don't know. I *felt* as if I knew him, but I didn't. Not to know his name, anyhow."

Alice was not really listening. She was checking her basket, in case she had forgotten something.

"Soap . . . clean pyjamas . . . library books . . . mints . . . butterscotch . . ."

So Polly saved the rest of her story until she could tell the pair of them. Tom's first question was nearly always after his birds.

"Oh, they're smashing," Polly told him.

"She spends more time talking to them birds than she does to me," said Alice. "There's some'd take offence."

But she smiled as she said it, to indicate that she herself did not fall into any such category.

"And listen, Dad, I met a coal miner today!"

"Well, I'll go to the foot of our stairs!" said Tom. "A coal miner! Imagine!"

"No, Dad, listen. I call him that because I didn't know his name."

"Then how d'you know he *was* a miner?" Alice demanded. "Got a badge on his front, had he, with 'coal miner' wrote on it?"

"Well, that was the queer thing," Polly admitted. "The more I've thought of it, the queerer it seems. You see . . ."

She looked backwards and forwards from Alice's face to Tom's, and then back again. Should she tell them? She had told about the angel, and look what had happened. But you couldn't bracket a coal miner with an *angel*. . . .

"Come on, then, love," said Tom.

"We – ell . . . he had a helmet on, see. Yes, and sort of overalls – oh, and funny pad things on his knees."

"In his pit gear," said Tom, looking at Alice.

"I suppose . . . and – and his face was all black and grimy, but it gave him the nicest look, because his eyes were so white, and his teeth!"

"Oh, *I* see!" said Alice. "We're in the same category as that blessed angel, a while back!"

"Oh, I *knew* you'd say that!" Polly was close to tears.

"Hold on," said Tom. "What else were you going to tell us about your miner?"

"What he said. What he said about the birds."

"And what was that?"

"Well – first he said nearly exactly what you said, Dad. You know – about being good to think about the birds swooping and flying when you're cooped up down there in the mine."

"Aye. I remember."

"And then he said that *you* could fly, as well, Dad."

"Very likely!" sniffed Alice. "Walk'd satisfy me, let alone fly!"

"He meant inside your head, Dad. And he said it'd do you good while you're lying here, and that you could fly wherever you've a mind to."

"Then he was right, Polly. I can. And I do."

"There's not a word either of you says makes sense to me," said Alice. "I sometimes wonder if I belong in this family."

"You belong," Tom told her. "The likes of Polly and me, we need the likes of you, to keep us right ends up."

"Haven't made a deal of a job keeping *you* right ends up," Alice said.

"Now, Alice love, that's daft. That's plain daft, and you know it is."

Alice heaved a deep sigh.

"Am I to tell her what we've decided, then?" she asked.

"We'll tell her now," Tom said.

Polly saw a kind of shadow pass over his pale face, and cried, "What? What is it?"

"It's a big thing," said Tom slowly. "But not too big."

"We're to move, Polly," said Alice.

"Move? Move house?" She saw by their faces she was right, and in the moment felt her world shiver and rock and splinter.

They were to leave home and go and stop with Aunt Em at Wellow.

"But you don't *like* Aunt Em!" cried Polly.

"Rubbish!" said Alice flatly. "She's family, and it's family you need at times like this."

They went on to explain matters to her, and Polly could see that they had hatched a good deal without letting her in on things. It seemed that Tom would never again be able to work down the pit, however things worked out. The doctors had said that he could come out of hospital if he could be looked after at home.

"And that'll mean a deal of lifting," Alice said. "And that's where Em comes in."

Polly could see that to go to Wellow and have Tom at home was better than to stop, and have him in hospital. But what she really wanted was neither of those things. What she wanted was to stop, and for Tom not only to be home, but walking, as well.

"I've forgotten what your face looks like, the right way up," she told him.

"What's it like, at Wellow?" she asked Alice that night.

"Right enough," she said. "There's a big park, with a lake. Oh – and a maypole. A maypole twice as high as a house, and striped like a barber's pole. And a golden weathercock on top."

"Oh!" Polly gave a little gasp. "I think I've seen it! Have I?"

"Did go there with us, once," Alice told her. "But you were ever so little. I should hardly think you'd have remembered."

"I can see it," Polly said, "in my mind's eye. If I *don't* remember, then I must have dreamt it. Will they dance round it? It's nearly May Day now!"

"Oh, they'll do that, I should think," said Alice. "Fancy to be Queen of the May, do you?"

Polly was intent on her own thoughts, frowning a little. Then her face lightened.

> *"A maypole in the month of May*
> *Is magical – or so they say!"*

Alice shook her head.

"Just made that up, have you?"

Polly nodded.

"Just a phase you're going through, it's to be hoped," said Alice. "One in the family already, thank you. Can be doing without two."

"I like doing it," said Polly, on her dignity now. "I might do it forever, for as long as I live. And I might get better and better at it, till I'm the top poet in England. Except Dad, of course. Is Aunt Em *much* older than you?"

"Ten years," Alice told her. "Bossed me terrible, when I was little."

She started to talk about the old days, just as Polly had meant her to. She was still at it when Polly went to bed.

"Not to mention the time she boxed my ears, because I'd lost my glove..."

"And then you *found* it again," supplied Polly with delight. "Found it by the laurels, by the front gate..."

"...and then Mam boxed *her* ears," finished Alice, not without satisfaction even now, after nearly forty years.

"Will she try to boss you now, d'you think?" asked Polly, as she drew the bedclothes up to her chin.

"She certainly won't be boxing my ears," said Alice.

"You've never boxed mine, have you, Mam?"

"People don't, not these days," said Alice. "Had your bottom smacked plenty of times."

Polly giggled.

"Light straight out, now," said Alice. "And tomorrow you'll have to set about sorting this room out. We could have a jumble sale of our own, the stuff you've got."

"What – you mean throw things *out?*" Polly was aghast.

"There's stuff in this room you've had since you were a baby," Alice said.

When she had gone, Polly gazed about the room by the light that shafted in from the landing.

"It's you she means," she said to the row of faces watching from the top of her wardrobe and bookshelves. "You, old fox, and you, giraffe, and you, old one-eyed Lucy!"

She felt coming the tears she had been fighting back ever since they had told her.

"Don't want to go to Wellow!" she thought. "Or hateful old Aunt Em!"

And so she sobbed a little for the old faces and the old places, for everything she would leave behind and perhaps never see again. The back yard, with its criss-crossing pigeons and their lovely, day-long purr, the willow at the river where Tom and she would fish, and the field where she had seen the angel.

But then, when she finally turned on her side, ready for sleep, she thought,

"But it's for Dad's sake, so it's worth it." And then, "That maypole . . . what was that rhyme. . . . ?

A maypole in the month of May
Is magical – or so they say. . . ."

And she sighed and shivered at the strong sense of magic, and slept and dreamed all night of maypoles ringed by dancing children, almost as if part of her already knew what was to come, and what strange adventures would befall her and into what secret world she would go, all because of a maypole.

Chapter Two

Aunt Em's was a house of old furniture, embroidered mats and cushions, half drawn curtains and, at times, a thick, funereal silence. This was broken only by the heavy ticking of a grandfather clock that stood in the hall. That tick reached every furthest cranny of the house, it followed Polly even in her dreams. The sampler that hung above the sideboard in the best room observed that Cleanliness is Next To Godliness, though it had not, surprisingly enough, been stitched by Aunt Em herself, or even one of her ancestors. She had seen it in the W. I. Bring and Buy, she told them, and been instantly taken by it.

Polly reflected that, if asked, she herself would have associated darkness with dirt, and cleanliness with light, and that it was astonishing that Aunt Em had managed to make cleanliness and dark go hand in hand. Within hours of arriving at Forge Cottage Polly had found herself rhyming, and the rhymes that floated to the surface most were "gloom" and "doom".

Polly's first sight of her aunt had been when the taxi drew up outside the cottage. As the driver and Alice heaved out the luggage, Polly stood staring up at the nearby maypole on the green. It was twice as high as she had imagined it, and in the instant of seeing it, she knew that she had been right. Even now, in broad daylight, bare of ribbons and bright garlands and rings of weaving dancers, it spelled utter and certain magic. She felt her bones melting with it, and went into a trance where she could almost see it circled by dancing children all in white, as she had in her dreams, and hear faint voices singing:

> Come lasses and lads
> Take leave of your dads
> And away to the maypole hie! . . .

"Oh!" she gasped softly. "You *are* a magic sort of a thing!"

"Polly. *Polly!*"

Polly turned slowly and came out of her dream.

"Say how d'you do to your aunt!" Alice hissed.

Polly turned her gaze, still quite blank, towards the open door of the house.

"So you'll be Polly," said Aunt Em.

"Sticks and stones," Polly thought. "She's got bones like sticks and stones."

Out loud she said, "How d'you do, Aunt Em. I'm glad to meet you."

She was, of course, nothing of the sort. Polly had pictured her aunt in the last few days, but it now became clear had been far too hopeful. Aunt Em was tall and bony, which might not have been her fault, but her face was sour and her eyes were cold – and that, undoubtedly, was.

"You'd better fetch that luggage inside, if you please," Aunt Em told the taxi driver.

"I daresay he charged you twice over," she told Alice, as the door shut behind him. "They all do."

Polly was surprised to find her aunt so knowledge-able on the subject of taxis. When did she ever ride in one, she wondered? She was later to discover that Aunt Em was an expert on a great number of subjects, from bed-making to weather-forecasting.

"You'll be tired, Alice," she said now. "You'd best go and lie on your bed while I get tea."

"Best – what?"

Alice obviously could not believe her ears. Polly could remember only a handful of occasions when her mother had taken to her bed in the daytime.

"Lie on your bed. Rest," said Aunt Em. "Do you good."

"But I don't feel like lying down, Em," said poor Alice. "I'm only ever so little tired. I could help you to get the tea."

"That," said Aunt Em, folding her arms across her wrap-around pinny, "is exactly what I don't want, Alice."

"But I *must* help, Em!" cried Alice. "You can't be waiting on us all hand and foot! And besides – "

She broke off, but Polly thought that what she was about to say was that she, Alice Flint, would go clear out of her mind without a job to do. Her inability to waste a single moment was a joke between Polly and Tom at home.

"If ever your mother does run short of summat to do," he would say, "she'll be out there measuring up them pigeons for waistcoats, and baking mincepies for 'em!"

And he was not exactly joking. Alice loved to work, especially with her hands, and as she worked she sang.

"Now look you here, Alice," began Em, "there's one thing to be straightened out between us before we even start. Sit you down and listen, for it must be said."

Alice and Polly both sat down on the extreme edges of their chairs, and listened, and stared up into her face.

"You've come here to stop for a while, and I'm glad to have you," she said. "I'd do as much for anyone, I hope, let alone my own flesh and blood."

"Oh, I *know*, Em!" cried Alice, "and we're – "

"But!" Aunt Em held up a hand. Evidently a tremendous "but" was to follow. "*But* – this is my house. Home. And especially, Alice, it is my kitchen. And that's why I mean to start as I mean to go on. There is only room for one woman in a kitchen, Alice. Once we understand that, I'm sure we shall get along a treat."

"But surely sometimes. . . ?" pleaded Alice. "Just to make a few scones, perhaps, or bread, or – "

Up went the hand again.

"No. The running of this house is up to me, and me alone. I've been here thirty years, near on, and have my own way of doing things. I don't like fuss, and I don't like change."

"No, Em," said Alice weakly.

Polly's heart went out to her cheerful, busy mother – sentenced now, it seemed, to a future of dreary inactivity.

"Does that mean I shan't have to make my bed, Aunt Em?" she inquired sweetly, but with intent to infuriate.

"You'll make your bed," said Aunt Em, "and then I

shall look at it. If you don't make it right, then I'll *teach* you to make it right."

"Oh. Thank you." Polly was now as neatly reduced as Alice. The pair of them sat helplessly staring up at Em.

"So," said Aunt Em, closing the matter, "I'll show you to your rooms."

She turned, and they obediently followed.

"Now, these *are* nice," said Alice to Polly, as Aunt Em's footsteps retreated. She was whispering.

"Mine's lovely!" Polly whispered back. "Fancy looking right out at the maypole!"

"And look at the pretty bedspread – all patchwork! D'you know, I half believe I remembered it, from when *I* was your age!"

"Why are we whispering?" asked Polly suddenly in her normal voice. It sounded so loud that they stared pop-eyed at one another for a moment, and then burst into uncontrollable giggles. Alice fetched out her handkerchief and dabbed at her eyes and gasped "Oh dear! Oh dear!" and Polly threw herself down on the bed and stuffed the bedspread into her mouth to smother laughter. Back and forth they rocked until at last Alice started to recover.

"Oh dear! Oh deary me!" she said again, wiping her eyes. "Do be careful with that cover, Polly. Here – use this!"

Polly sat up, dabbing her own streaming eyes.

"If you don't make it right," she gasped, mimicking Aunt Em, "then I'll teach you to make it right!"

"Now give over, Polly, do. You'll set me right off again. Hush!"

Slowly their mirth subsided.

"Anyway, it *is* nice," Alice said, looking about her. "Plain white walls and nice old beams – don't you like them beams? And I've got a nice view, as well. It is *prettier* here, Polly, than at home. That you must admit."

"Come and have another look at my room."

Back they went over the landing and into the little room overlooking the village green.

"Oh, it is lovely!" exclaimed Alice. "We're ever so lucky, you know, Polly. When you think of the trouble we're in, with Tom . . . and then . . . oh . . ." she broke off, now nearer to tears than giggles. "We must try to fit in, Polly. You will try, won't you? Your aunt means well, I do know that. It's a big upset, us all coming into her house after all those years on her own. I can understand that. Do try, there's a good girl."

"Yes, Mam."

But Polly was not listening at all. She was looking out on to the green and at that towering maypole and again catching glimpses and hearing snatches of song, and thinking, "There's a whole other world out there, I know there is. Side by side with this, there's a secret world, and I'm going to find it, I am!"

She and Alice unpacked their things. They enjoyed putting their neatly laundered clothes into the empty (but nonetheless mothballed) drawers. Polly set a selection of her favourite toys and pictures about the room, and looked about with satisfaction.

"It *does* seem like home, a bit," she decided.

Then came Aunt Em's call from the foot of the stairs and Polly and Alice dutifully descended, daring each other to giggle.

The three of them sat around the gateleg table with its embroidered linen cloth and plates of ham salad. Aunt Em poured thick brown tea from a teapot dressed in a green woolly waistcoat, and urged her visitors to eat up.

"That's right!" she exclaimed as Alice put down her knife and fork. "That's what I like to see, a nice clean plate."

"That's what you used to say when we were little. When *I* was little."

Aunt Em seemed temporarily taken aback.

"Did I? Well, fancy. Come along, Polly, finish up. Then we can go on to the trifle."

"I don't think I can eat any more, Aunt Em," Polly said.

"It'll be all the excitement," said Alice swiftly. "She's usually ever such a good little eater."

"There's no need for her to have the trifle – it's the one I used to make – your favourite, Alice. But she's to finish what she's got on her plate. You shouldn't take what you can't eat."

"But the salad was already laid out on the plate!" protested Polly.

Aunt Em was floored for a moment by this truth.

"Now stop fussing," she said, "and eat up!"

Polly speared a piece of pinkish, rubbery ham and looked at it.

"Ugh!" she thought, "I'll be sick!" And then, "Bet Aunt *Em* don't eat what she don't want!"

She put the fork down again.

"I can't," she said. "I'm sorry."

Alice swiftly reached for Polly's plate, scraped its contents on to her own, and stacked them. Aunt

Em eyed this manoeuvre with patent disapproval.

"I hope you know what you're encouraging, Alice."

Polly sat there, listening to the ruthless ticking of the clock in the hall, and longing for bedtime.

"She *is* kind," said Alice to Polly later, as she saw her to bed for the first time in this strange place. "That trifle of hers always was my favourite – and she'd remembered it all these years! D'you know, I feel half guilty now that we haven't seen more of her. I mean, it must be lonely for her here on her own."

"I think she likes it," said Polly.

"Likes what?"

"Being alone. I think we're going to be a bother to her."

"Now don't say that!" cried Alice in consternation. "We shall be here for weeks and weeks – perhaps months and months!"

"I'm only saying what I think, Mam," Polly said. "Dad says I should always say what I think. And oh – tomorrow he'll be here! Oh – won't he think it wonderful, after hospital."

"Your father," said Alice slowly, "inclines to see everything wonderful, if he can. Even when he's laid flat and can't stir a step. Sees everything wonderful."

"Oh, I know, Mam!" and now they clung together in tears as before they had clung in helpless laughter, and eyes had to be dried again.

"Sleep well, then," Alice said. She stood by the window. "It is nice for you, this view. Em says that maypole's one of the oldest in England. Been there centuries, she says."

"Yes," said Polly, and not a word more. She knew

40

– or felt – more about that maypole already than ever Aunt Em could tell her, but kept her lips tightly buttoned.

"My secret," she thought. "Mine."

"Ah well!" Alice drew both curtains together at once. "Tomorrow's another day . . ."

Polly giggled weakly.

"Oh Mam, you are *daft*. Of course tomorrow's another day!"

"Just a manner of speaking," said Alice. "And like you, Polly Flint, to take me up on it. Goodnight."

She bent to kiss her and Polly could smell her hair, newly washed last night for this great adventure, and on an impulse threw up her arms and hugged her.

"Goodnight! I *like* it here, I do."

"Little lamb." Alice had not called her this for ages. "Good girl. God bless."

And then she was gone. Gone to cry for a while in her own room, Polly guessed, before going down again to spend the evening with Aunt Em. And she wept a little herself for her brave mother, who over-night had left her own home and become a visitor in a strange place, all her roots pulled up.

"But it's all for a *reason*!" Polly told herself fiercely. "Dad will get better, he will, he will!"

And then, after a time, she knelt up on her bed and parted the curtains. There it still was in the twilight, the green and its maypole. And for the first time she noticed, right opposite, The Red Lion, brightly lit and with voices floating out into the quiet evening.

"Oh!" she said softly to the maypole. "I know that you and I are to meet. I know that you have a secret, and I shall find it."

She was about to let the curtains fall, and lie back again, when she saw a movement. It was a figure lit from behind by the lights of the inn, and with a long shadow falling almost to the foot of the maypole. What she saw was a gigantic shadow with its arms raised.

"Strange . . ." thought Polly. "What it reminds me of, is a magician making a spell."

She stared and stared, but in the end the pattern made by the pole and the giant shadow and the figure itself went into a kind of blur. She blinked and rubbed at her eyes, and when she looked again, the pattern had dissolved. All she saw was the maypole, and beyond it a tall shadowy figure moving away and towards the inn. She shook her head, and sank back on to the pillows.

Next day, Tom was to be brought.

"You'd best not go far," Alice told Polly, who was itching to explore her new world. "Not if you want to be here when he comes."

Polly wandered out into the sunlight and on to the dewy green to greet her maypole – for already she thought of it as hers. It had been there centuries, she thought, and knew a thousand secrets.

"Who're you?"

Polly turned and saw that the voice belonged to a boy of about her own age.

"Who're you?" she countered.

"You're new here," he said. "I'm not. Everybody knows who *I* am. Did you come out of old hag Ridler's house?"

"My aunt Em lives there," said Polly, "and she is *not* a hag."

"Stopping with her, are you?"

"I might be."

Polly had hoped to make friends in her new world,

but knew already that this boy would not be one of them.

"Pity you, then," he said. "Old hag!"

She began to walk away, annoyed that he had interrupted her conversation with the maypole. At the other side of the green she saw a man sitting on a bench outside the Red Lion. He was looking straight at her.

"Morning!" he called.

"Good morning," Polly replied, and he made a gesture beckoning her to cross over to him, and unthinkingly she obeyed.

"Well, now," he said, "you'll be new."

Polly thought to herself, "Well, now, you'll be old!"

His face was mapped with a thousand lines, and browned by wind and weather. One hand curved over a gnarled stick, the other lay on his knee like a piece of bark. Polly looked right into his bright and wicked eyes.

"I'm Polly Flint," she told him.

"Well, now . . ."

"And I'm stopping with my Aunt Em. Miss Ridler, over the road."

"Emily Ridler, is it," he murmured. "And shall you be stopping long, Polly Flint?"

"Could be," said Polly. "It depends. My father's poorly, you see."

"All summer?"

"I should think all summer," she replied, and wondered why he should ask.

"You'll be here for the May Dancing."

"Oh, I shall! I'm longing for it!"

"They'll deck that pole with garlands," he said.

44

"Garlands, and brave ribbons, and dance the old dances . . ."

A little silence fell. Polly cast round for something to say to this strange man. But it was he who spoke first.

"Have they told you?" His voice was lowered now, he was speaking of secrets to be told.

"Told me? What?"

"Of the lost village . . ."

Polly felt a little cold thrill at the nape of her neck. Slowly, her eyes locked to his, she shook her head.

"Aaaah!" He let out a long breath. "They not all believe it, see. They think it's nobbut a tale to tell by the fireside. But me, I know it to be true. Tell you, shall I?"

Slowly Polly nodded.

"Hundreds of years ago, hundreds and hundreds, there was a village standing where we are now . . . right here, on this very spot . . ."

"What can he mean?" Polly wondered. "There still *is* a village."

"And the name of that village," he went on, "was Grimstone. And it wasn't very big – oh no, not at all, and in fact it had hardly the number of children it needed to dance the May Dances."

There was a silence.

"And then – " he paused, "and then – it vanished!"

Polly swallowed hard.

"Vanished?" Her voice came out very high and thin.

"It vanished – right off the face of the earth! Or rather – as some believe – was swallowed right *into* the earth! What do you say to that?"

45

Polly shook her head dumbly. He was watching her with something like triumph.

"Legend goes," he went on, "that if you kneel and put your ear to the ground on Christmas Day, you can hear the church bells still, ringing away down there."

Again she shook her head and stared into his eyes.

"Away down there – under all this – " he waved a long arm about him – "the church bells ringing! That's what the legend says. What *I* say," he leaned towards her again, his voice down almost to a whisper, "is that you can hear them bells *any* Sabbath, if you will."

"Really hear them? Through the ground?"

"Lay your ear to the turf and listen," he said. "You'll hear 'em ringing, sweet and true. And that ain't all . . ."

"What?"

"Ah . . . signs for those with ears to hear and eyes to see. Voices. Flitting shapes and shadows . . . faint music . . . reflections. . . ."

"*Reflections?*"

"In the lake. You get by that lake, and you'll be but a fingertip away. Water . . . Water always finds its own level . . ."

"You *mean*," said Polly Flint, deciding to state the case in her own words, since he was so full of enigma and glancing meanings, "you mean, that there's a village down there *still*?"

"I say," he replied, "that when the earth opened to swallow it up, in that very instant – it slipped the net of time!"

"Slipped the net of time . . ." Polly pondered. "Still there, then. But if it *is* still there, where. . . ?"

46

"Polly! Polly!"

It was Alice, calling from beyond the green.

"Come on back, will you? I want you!"

"Yes, Mam!" she called back, and then told him, "My mother. I'll have to go. But thank you for telling me the story. Goodbye!"

And she was off, running, not out of any particular desire to please Alice, but because she had had as much magic as she could stand, for the time being.

It turned out that the stranger was the reason for her being called back. Aunt Em had spotted them from a window as she took down some curtains.

"You keep away from that Old Mazy," she said. "Same as everybody else."

"Is that his name? Old Mazy?"

"What we call him. Mazed in the head, of course."

"How long has he lived here?" Polly was not quite sure what she hoped to hear – centuries, perhaps?

"Lived? He don't *live* here, for a good job. Just turns up, round about this time of year. Stops a few weeks, then gone again till next year. You let him well alone, d'you hear me?"

"He told me a story," Polly said. "About a village that vanished. That was swallowed, right into the earth, in the twinkling of an eye – houses, fields, people and all! Is it *true*?"

"Now what do *you* think!" Aunt Em sounded disgusted. She was not a believer in magic, nor even mysteries. "Now – from under my feet, if you please!"

She made a sweeping movement with a long cobweb brush, seriously endangering a potted fern, and Polly noticed that she was wearing a scarf swathed turban-wise around her head.

"To sweep the cobwebs out of the sky!" thought Polly, and almost giggled.

"Your aunt's having a springclean," said Alice, somewhat desperately. She was pulling some kind of face at Polly over Aunt Em's shoulder.

"A thorough springclean," affirmed Aunt Em, with grim satisfaction.

"But – Dad's coming!"

"Room already done," she said. "Ready and waiting."

"But – "

Alice's grimace intensified, and Polly stopped short.

"Can I help?" she asked, half-heartedly.

Neither Alice nor Polly could help, it seemed. Aunt Em alone could carry out the attack. She alone knew the crevices where dust could gather, spiders lurk. She alone knew why she should pick this particular day, out of three hundred and sixty four others, to tackle the enemy – the very day Tom was to come.

Alice thought she could guess.

"It's to show us all it's *her* house," she explained to Polly later. "It must seem like – well, like a kind of threat, us all coming. As if we were invaders. She's just keeping her end up, that's all."

"This house is too clean already," Polly said, and Alice laughed. And then the door knocker banged, and it was Tom, coming home at last – or at least, to a kind of home.

He was installed in a big high bed specially put up in a downstairs room, and when the men had gone away, Polly ran in to see him there.

"Oh Dad, Dad!" She bent to kiss him, and then

stood back, and then laughed. "Oh, it does seem funny! You should see yourself!"

"Oh yes," said Tom. "Laughing at me now, are you?"

"It's just that – well, all this – " sweeping her arm to indicate the room which contained, besides Tom's bed, an old-fashioned sofa and chairs, a cabinet of china, numerous covers and cushions and gilt framed pictures, and even an old upright piano. "And Dad – you should just see what's hanging over your head!"

Obligingly he rolled up his eyes towards the stitched sampler in its mahogany frame.

"Sampler, I can see that. No – can't read it. Go on – tell."

"Cleanliness is next to Godliness!"

They both laughed.

From where he lay, Tom could see the top part of the maypole with its golden weathercock.

"It's magic, Dad," Polly told him, "so you'd best keep your eye on it. And you'll never guess what *else*!"

And she told him about Old Mazy, and the legend of the vanished village.

"And then he said, 'It slipped the net of time.' What does it mean, Dad?"

"I don't know," Tom admitted at last. "But it's surely a beautiful picture it makes in your head. Beautiful."

"You can lie there and think about it," Polly told him, "and maybe write a rhyme about it. And me – I'll go and find that village, if it's there!"

"That's my lass!" Tom said. "Like it here, do you?"

Polly shook her head.

"Not yet," she said. "But I expect I shall, in the end.

49

Especially now you've come. But I just wish Aunt Em wasn't so *clean*."

"That her banging away out there, is it?"

"Springcleaning!" said Polly scornfully. "This house'll vanish, if she doesn't watch out. Swept clear away, it'll be!"

"Ah well. Her house, remember. You've got to let her be queen in her own kingdom, Polly."

Aunt Em was certainly being as bossy as any queen. And wherever Polly turned to tuck herself away, she found herself under Aunt Em's feet. There were regular cries of "Polly – don't!" from Alice, who sat frantically knitting even though summer was coming, and kept dropping stitches in her frequent moves from place to place to be out of her sister's way.

Straight after dinner Polly left the house. She ran straight past the maypole and on toward Rufford Park.

"There's plenty to see there," Aunt Em had said, "but watch out for the lake, and don't get into any mischief."

"If I could *think* of any mischief, I'd get up to it, all right," she thought as she ran. "I would, for certain definite."

She slowed as she saw the ford ahead, a shallow stream crossing the road. She stepped to its edge. What she really wanted was to paddle over, though she knew there was no need. She saw the little footbridge Aunt Em had told her about. She looked toward the left, and saw the sun glancing through the leaves and striking spears of light into the water. The stream was shallow, clear in the sunlight, and thickly green in the shade.

"Tadpoles," thought Polly longingly. "Minnows, tiddlers, sticklebacks and – wheee!"

She was drenched from head to foot with icy water. She turned and glared after the retreating car. The grinning face of a boy looked back from the rear window.

"And mustard tarts to you, too!" she screamed. She shook herself and looked down at her splattered front.

"Found some mischief to get into, I s'pose," she thought. "Only good thing about it."

Over the footbridge she went, and towards a little clearing, where she hesitated. Little paths ran away through the trees on all sides. Which to take? Birds whistled about her and she listened, already approving the place, pleased with the feel of it.

"Left," she decided, for no real reason, and took that path, and the next minute was looking out over a wide, shining lake and was astonished by the suddenness of it.

"Oh!" she gasped. "Oh moon and stars! Ain't it just . . ."

She was dumbstruck. She stood and took it all in. It was the widest stretch of water she had ever seen – inland water, not counting the sea. There was not another person in sight. Even the sky seemed bigger and emptier than usual.

"And birds!" she exclaimed. "And ducks, and geese and – things!"

Flotillas of them there were, some swimming or gliding, others stalking the wooden planks of a kind of platform, or deck, at the near end of the lake.

Polly Flint, who knew what she liked when she saw

Polly Flint's Kingdom

Ice House

Bluebell Wood

Anim
Grav

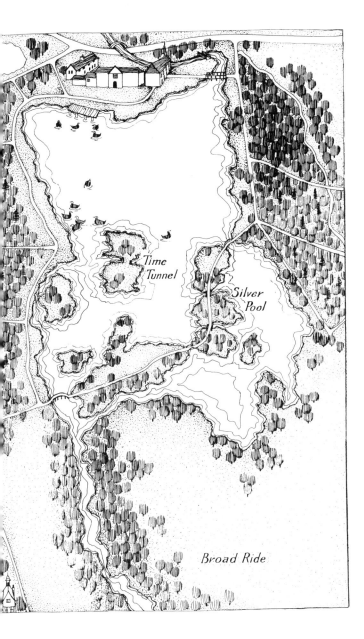

Time
Tunnel

Silver
Pool

Broad Ride

it, was almost mad with delight. She flung out her arms, and cried,

"*My* kingdom! This is my kingdom, and I am the queen!"

She ran forward and the birds all went into storm and the ducks came swimming swiftly towards her as if to a summons, and quacked in chorus, as if to greet her. (They were expecting bread to be thrown, but Polly was not to know that.)

"They heard!" she gasped, hardly able to believe it herself, though she was very good at believing in almost anything.

She marched on then through her new kingdom, taking it all in and bestowing names, left and right. She passed an island, with a low arched tunnel passing right under it.

"You are the Secret Tunnel!" she proclaimed.

She paused to regard a passing family of ducks.

"Swans, royal birds should be, really," she thought. "But I don't care. I'm the queen, and you are my royal ducks!"

They swam on as carelessly as ducks do in the early spring when the air is warm and the water calm.

She came to a smaller pool, where silver birches on the far side went reaching down into the green depths.

"You are the Silver Pool!" she cried. "I am queen, and I name you – Silver Pool!"

And then, quite suddenly, she was aware of echoes, of whisperings, of hints, inklings, reflections. And she heard again the words of Old Mazy:

"Water always finds its own level . . ."

Polly Flint, feeling herself but a fingertip away from magic, shivered.

Chapter Three

And so from that time onward Polly Flint began to live in two separate worlds. There was the world of every day, of clocks ticking and rain falling and the polish-smelling kingdom of Aunt Em. And there was her own, secret world, where she reigned over her own kingdom and even time seemed to stand still for her.

The very next day she returned to the lake, and this time she went all the way round it, counting the little overgrown islands, giving names to the smaller pools that led off on the further side. And as she walked, it seemed to her that now and again, faintly, she heard children's voices, and laughter. Then she would stop and listen intently, but always was left with the feeling that she *might* have heard something – or she might not.

She told Tom about her kingdom. She described to him the different birds, the pool with the reflection of five silver birches, the curious arched tunnel that went under one of the islands.

"I can see it as clear as with my own eyes," he told her.

"And one day you'll see it for yourself," said Polly. "*And* I bet there's fish in there!"

Then she went for the first time to the village

school, and came running home for dinner with her news.

"They're practising the May Dances!" she cried, "and I can't join in!"

"Now that *is* a shame," said Alice, "you being so keen on the maypole, and all."

"It's not fair! It's not fair!"

"Only to be expected," said Aunt Em. "Very complicated, them dances. I've seen them. In and out and up and down, and plaiting the ribbons as they go. Takes *months* to learn them, I daresay."

"And another thing!" cried Polly. "They're not *doing* it on May Day! May Day's on Tuesday, and they're doing it on the Saturday after."

"Always do," said Aunt Em infuriatingly. "Got to do it on a Saturday, so that folk can come and watch. No use doing dances for the birds."

"It *is*!" Polly almost screamed. "You don't understand! It's magic! You have to do it at the break of day, on May Day."

"I never heard such rubbish," said Aunt Em. "And lower your voice, if you please. Fine audience they'd get at crack of dawn!"

"But it isn't *meant* for an audience!"

Polly despaired of making them understand. Those dances, she well knew, should be danced in the mysterious half light of dawn, barefoot in the dew wet grass. They should be danced solemnly, a celebration of life, of all greenness and growth, of all the mystery of the world.

But she did not tell them this. Nor did she tell them of her secret knowledge that the maypole was the key to another even greater mystery, and another world.

"And there's another thing," she contented herself with saying, "they don't even have a May Queen!"

"And I suppose you were fancying yourself as that!" said Aunt Em waspishly.

"They have a *gypsy* king and queen! Whoever heard of *that*?"

"Always have." Aunt Em was maddeningly in the know. "It's a tradition, round here. There's always been a boy and a girl picked, gypsy king and queen."

Polly eyed her coldly.

"Thinks she knows it all," she thought. "And she don't know *owt*!"

From that moment she decided that she would celebrate her own May Day. Over the next few days she hatched her plan. She would see May in on her own. She would set her alarm clock for five o'clock, and go out on to the green and herself dance round the maypole.

"No one'll see me," she thought. "No one about, that early."

And this secret scheme took her happily through the next few days. She now watched the other children practising their steps, without in the least wanting to join in. She watched only to learn some of the steps that she might copy. Then she would run to the lake and practise them there. She wove the steps back and forth and round a silver birch that she had cast as pole.

She never saw anyone else there until the last evening in April. She was practising her steps, and humming "Polly Put the Kettle On", because this was one of the tunes the children danced to, in a dance called "The Gypsy's Tent." All at once, as she skipped and bobbed, she was again aware of magic at work.

"My name," she thought. "My very own name – and the main dance! Must mean something, that must!"

Breathless she came to a halt, and bowed to her invisible partner. Then, above the sound of her own breathing she heard a rustling and snapping of twigs, and looked into the copse beyond and saw a figure go striding by. It was there and gone in a trice, hidden by the trees, but Polly saw it for long enough to know that this was no ordinary visitor, come to feed the birds or walk the dog.

The man (for she saw that it was a man) went with long bounding strides – scissoring through the bracken – and yet there was a curious dreamlike slowness to his movements, as in a film show in slow motion. He might have been treading on air. And raised in his right arm was a long rod and a – "Net?" Polly shook her head to settle it. Who would go striding through the woods at evening with a huge net, as if to catch some mysterious quarry?

"Not for butterflies," she thought, "nor even birds. Much too big."

Again she shook her head.

"Must've dreamed it," she thought. "All that twizzling."

On this occasion, even Polly Flint herself could not believe her own eyes.

She wandered home in the blue steepling shadows and from time to time she shivered. It was the eve of May Day, and already magic was abroad in the air. The grass was sprinkled with daisies, half closed now.

"'Tisn't spring till you can plant your foot on

twelve daisies," she thought dreamily. "That's what Mam says. *Tomorrow* it'll be spring!"

And the thought came to her that she would make a chaplet of daisies to wear on her head next day. She sat straight down on the cold grass and began to pick and thread them.

"I shall wear this," she thought, "and I shall keep my nightie on – at any rate it's white, and long, and near the proper thing!"

A few minutes, and the thing was done. She tried the garland for size, nodded, satisfied, and started again for home. She turned the corner on to the green.

"It's Polly Flint!" she heard. "Oooh – look at that!"

Davey Cole was there with his friends, and she realized too late why they were pointing and laughing. She snatched the daisy chain from her head and began to run.

"Wake me early, mother dear," they chanted after her, "for I'm to be Queen of the May!" and again, "Wake me early, Mother dear, for I'm to be Queen of the May!"

She dashed into the house and slammed the door behind her.

"Polly – *don't!*" she heard Alice's voice. "Come along here, I want you."

She was knitting, somewhat desperately, as usual. Aunt Em was embroidering yet another cloth.

"I don't like doors slammed," she observed. "Not in this house, thank you."

"Do remember, Polly," begged Alice.

"I'm sorry," said Polly, but only for her mother's sake.

"What's that you've got?" Alice asked.

61

Polly opened up her palm.

"Oh – a daisy chain!"

"Those that've got time to stitch daisies," remarked Aunt Em, "could as well be stitching something useful."

"What I should really like," thought Polly, "would be to stitch your mouth up, for good and all!"

"Go and say goodnight to your father," said Alice. "You're late. We were beginning to wonder. I'll bring you up some milk."

Polly gladly went out and across the passage and past the dictatorial clock to where Tom lay, quite still in the half light.

"Asleep, Dad?" she whispered.

"Not asleep," came the answer, "but dreaming."

"Flying, were you?"

"Aye. Flying." He drew a long breath, a sigh.

"Just come to say goodnight. Been down by the lake. All silver it was, when I left. Wish you could've seen it."

A sudden thought struck her.

"Why not? Dad, it's May Day tomorrow!"

"And so it is, Poll," he said.

"And I just *wonder*," she went on swiftly, "if, with it being a *magic* sort of a time – you know, like Midsummer Eve or Hallowe'en, and that – why not – why not make a *wish*?"

"A wish ... why, there's never any harm in wishing, Poll."

"I know that. I spend half my *life* wishing. What I mean is, it might be one of the times when wishes actually come *true*!"

"It might, at that," he agreed. "Try, shall we?"

"Oh let's, Dad! But neither of us to tell, for fear it breaks the spell!"

She laughed.

"Rhymed without even meaning to! But neither of us to tell, for fear it breaks the spell!"

She leant over the bed to kiss him, and was half tempted to tell him her secret. But this was so private a thing that not even Tom could know.

"Afterwards," she thought. "Perhaps."

Then she went up, set her alarm clock for five o'clock and put it just under the bed, with the daisy chain. She fetched out her long white nightdress instead of the one that was under her pillow. That one was not at all suitable for a serious occasion, being of bright pink with rabbits and buttercups right across the chest. When Alice came up to say goodnight Polly pulled the bedclothes up to her chin, in case the exchange was noticed, and remarked upon.

And when the curtains were drawn and Alice gone, Polly turned on her side and fell asleep almost straight away, and she slept all night without a single dream, as if she knew that the dreams were yet to come.

And so the night passed swiftly, as dreamless nights do, and when the alarm rang Polly was wide awake in the instant. She stretched out a hand to stop the bell and sat up and stared at the curtains, where only the faintest light seemed to show. She knelt on the bed and parted them.

There lay the green, the cottages, the church tower beyond, all strangely bleached of colour and robbed of outline in the dawn half light. The sky itself was blank and grey with not a hint or tinge of the coming sunrise. But the sunrise was certain, that Polly did know – and she raised her arm in salute to the maypole before dropping the curtains again. It stood intent, as if it were waiting. Polly shivered. Her teeth started to chatter.

Softly she opened the door of the room, and stole tiptoe down the telltale stairs. The grandfather clock was relentlessly telling the time – tick tock tick tock. There was a chink of chain, the turn of a key – and Polly was out.

She stood and looked about her, all alone in that vast dawn hush. Far away she heard a cock crow, and the thought crossed her mind that it might come from the farm beyond the inn, or it might be calling from some hidden stack in the buried village of Grimstone down below.

And no sooner had she thought this, than she heard faint voices singing, and strange music. The voices were those of children, and all the children of Wellow, Polly well knew, were still fast in their beds and sleeping. She stared at the greyish, dewed green, and half expected it to open up under her eyes. Now the voices were closer. They were singing a song that she knew well.

> "*Come lasses and lads*
> *Take leave of your dads*
> *And away to the maypole hie!*"

"They're coming! They're dancing the Spider's Web!"

Polly's heart thudded hard. She strained into that milky half light and saw shapes making themselves, shadows blossoming. The May Dancers were

64

coming, they were slipping into the upper world, running free in time!

At first they were merely faint and ghostly, and then they took on a sepia tinge as in an old print, and she saw that the girls wore dresses all of white and garlands on their heads, and each was weaving a pattern; heel and toe they went about the boys, who stood staring straight ahead and motionless as statues. And all the while the bright ribbon that now miraculously crowned the pole was crissing and crossing to form the mazy pattern of a spider's web.

Polly started forward. Her bare feet were heedless of the icy dew.

Now a troop of tiny children ran forward under the ribbons with squeals of delight, and the fiddles struck up a different tune, and another dance began.

Polly's thoughts were very strange and slow.

"They are all in the Spider's Web," she thought. "Web . . . net . . . slipped the net of time . . ."

All the time the dawn was inexorably breaking and the scene was lit with a thin wash of gold. The net of streamers glowed and the grass was all at once on fire and dazzling. And as Polly Flint stood all alone stock-still and staring, she saw now that the dancers had no shadows!

She shut her eyes and shook her head, stunned.

And then they fled. They went, not running, but dancing their way out of time again. The bright figures dissolved, first to shadows, then to air. The music dwindled to a pale echo.

Silence. The sun struck fire from dew and leaf and blade. Dumbstruck, Polly Flint wheeled about for hint or sign, and saw none. Slowly she advanced and looked down at the turf as she went. The dew lay innocent and undisturbed where lately dancers went. Polly sighed a deep sigh and half turned away and then turned back and saw – footprints!

"Oh!" gasped Polly Flint. "Oh my moon and stars!"

She peered and saw a narrow darkened streak running through the silver. She started to follow it, planting her own feet exactly on the line, heel to toe. She did not explain to herself why she did this. It simply seemed to be at the same time a very magic and very natural thing to do. She might even have half hoped that she, too, would be sent reeling out of time.

At any rate she solemnly trod that teasing line, watching her own feet go heel to toe with ritual care. She had not the least idea what she hoped to see, but it was certainly not the abrupt end of the trail where grass met tarmac, and she let out a cry of disappointment. Left and right she scanned the road, but knew as she did so that the scent was lost. She turned and looked back over the deserted green.

"I shouldn't have *trod* it," she thought, dismayed. "Now all I can see are *my* footsteps."

It even fleetingly crossed her mind that she might not have seen human footprints in the first place, that she might have seen only what she wanted to see, and had been following the harmless path of a cat, or rabbit.

Slowly and thoughtfully Polly Flint followed her own path back toward home.

That evening, as she was walking along one of the woodland paths, watching the sun shaft down to light the silver stems of the birches, and tarnish the brilliant green of the new bracken, she heard, beyond the whistling of birds, clear echoing laughter. She stopped and listened, and this time it did not fade, and she glanced half fearfully about her.

"Oh my!" she thought. "Hold fast, Polly! There *is* someone there!"

On impulse she dropped to her knees.

"If there is," she thought, "I'll see *them* before they see me!"

The echoing voices were all around her, it seemed at first, but gradually the hollowness faded and she heard them, quite distinctly, to her left. Without thinking she jumped back on to her feet, and there they were. She saw them plainly, a boy and a girl, about her own age, wading knee high in the bracken.

She cried, "Oh!" out loud, and clapped her hand to her mouth as the pair stopped dead still and looked toward her. Her eyes met theirs for a few seconds, all three of them stood frozen, and then they were off, darting swiftly between the trees and soon cut off from sight behind the foliage. Polly was too startled to give chase until it was too late. She made her way to the spot where they had disappeared. Nothing. No voices, no laughter, not even the rustle of grass or fern or telltale snap of a twig.

"Hello!" she called. And then again, "Hello!"

Only the faint roar of traffic from the road beyond, and the evening whistling of birds.

Very slowly Polly turned and retraced her steps. She did not put into words the reason why she did not go further into the woods. She did not admit that she was afraid. As she went, she tried to recall that brief sighting.

"The strangest thing *is*. . . ." she thought, ". . . no, I must be wrong. Can't have seen that. . . ."

And yet at the back of her mind she was perfectly certain that as they ran she had seen that the girl had been holding something round, and to Polly it had looked like –

"A tambourine!" she said out loud.

Her mistake was to tell about what had happened.

"I saw a boy and a girl in the woods just now. And would you believe, the girl was wearing a *bonnet*?"

"Oh yes?" said Alice. "Was your eyes open or shut at the time?"

"And holding a tambourine," went on Polly. "It was the queerest thing. And I even thought I heard it jangle."

Alice shook her head.

"Just one of her fancies," she explained to Aunt Em. "Thinks she sees things. Bit of a dreamer, like her father."

"I wasn't dreaming! It was real!"

"Real to you, I daresay," said Alice. "But what anyone else would call daydreams."

Polly was furious.

"How do you know what's real and what's not? How do you know I'm not dreaming *you* – 'cos I saw those two as plain as I see you! How d'you know *you're* not dreams? Just you tell me that!"

She stared back at their open-mouthed faces, pushed back her chair and fled. She slammed the door behind her.

"Polly—don't!" came Alice's voice from the other side.

69

Polly wandered away from the house, kicking at the turf of the green, glaring at her feet.

"That settles it!" she thought. "Once for all. Never believe anything I say, they don't!"

She became aware of a long shadow moving ahead, and raised her eyes. She was looking straight into the low sun and had to shield her eyes with a hand, and at first saw only an outline, long and lank and moving with a curious loping stride, as if perpetually tumbling forward. Then the silhouette resolved itself into a person, and that person was Old Mazy. She had not thought him so tall.

"Evening!" she called, heedless of Aunt Em's warning, indeed, in deliberate defiance of it.

He stopped and turned.

"Why, good evening," he replied.

Polly was seized by an urge to tell him what she had seen.

"He'll believe me," she thought.

"You know what you were telling me the other day," she began. "About the vanished village, and about the . . ."

She did not quite know how to put it.

"Go on," he said. "You've seen something, then. Seen? Heard?"

She nodded. He moved closer.

"Going to tell, are you?" he said softly.

"Saw," she said. "Today. In the wood by the lake."

"Ah. By the lake."

"I think – I think I'd heard them before. Kind of echoing. But today they came nearer, and they didn't echo . . ."

70

"Slipped the net of time," he murmured, as though to himself.

"It was a boy and a girl," she went on with a rush. She had started to tell, and now must finish, get it over with. "And they saw me as well, and then they ran off, and – "

"And?" he prompted.

"Something that stuck in my mind. Something I noticed when they ran. They were holding something, both of them, and the girl – she had a tambourine, I'm sure she had!"

He did look at her now.

"Time gypsies," he said at last.

"Time gypsies?"

"Wanderers," he said. "Not like ordinary gypsies, from place to place. From time to time."

A car went by just then and Polly shook herself, as if awakening from a sleep. Her eyes travelled from the moving car to Old Mazy's face and then to the maypole.

"Not a May Queen," she said slowly. "A gypsy king and queen . . . of course . . ."

She looked back at him. She was not sure that she liked him, though she wanted to, to spite her aunt. He wore a curious expression of satisfaction, even gloating.

"Shall you listen?" he asked her suddenly. "Shall you?"

"Listen?"

"For the bells!"

"Ah! Yes, yes, I shall!"

And she did, too. It was not an easy matter. Polly supposed that the church bells of Grimstone away down below would ring at the same time as those of the church above. It seemed likely. She, Alice and Aunt Em set off to the church over the green. Just as they reached the porch Polly nudged Alice, and whispered, "Forgotten my hanky! Back in a minute!"

She darted away. She had already decided where to put her ear to the ground. The best place of all would be by the maypole, she was sure of that, because that was where the magic seemed to gather. But she did not wish to be seen, and so she went swiftly round to the far side of the church.

She was quite alone among the leaning tombstones. She hesitated. Was it really possible that away down there under that innocent turf there was a village snatched out of time? Were there cottages with high hollyhocks and chimneys with smoke rising and smells of dinner wafting through open doors? Was there really a church down there, with weathercock turning in timeless winds and bells ringing out at this very moment, while the people came walking in their Sunday best?

"Only one way to find out," she thought. "Nothing to be scared of, either. Wish my heart would stop banging!"

She dropped to her knees. She could see every blade of grass distinct and separate and the smell was strong and green. Above her the church bells tumbled in the tower. But was there an answer from below, were bells ringing far away down and centuries ago? She strained to catch that peal, because she was certain of it, and certain, too, that she was meant to hear. Now her ear was right to the ground and her heart lurched. She heard them! Faint and sweet she heard those other bells in that other place ringing out from who knew what wild acres lost in time and space?

She listened in a dream and her head was filled with bells, and when they stopped, abruptly, the sudden quiet was huge. She let out a long, shuddering breath and raised herself slowly. So dizzied was she, that at first she forgot that she was out here, in the graveyard, but her mother and Aunt Em would be nudging one another and fidgeting in their pew. It was only the singing that roused her:

> *Morning has broken*
> *Like the first morning,*
> *Blackbird has spoken*
> *Like the first bird . . .*

"Oooh!" she gave a little shriek. "First hymn! Oooh!"

She began to stumble silly-kneed back round the church and went almost headlong into Davey Cole and shrieked again with surprise.

He laughed right in her face.

"Daft thing!" he told her. "*I* saw you! Wait till I tell 'em!"

"You shut up!" she hissed, keeping her voice churchy as if she were already inside. "You just shut up – and get out of my road!"

She tilted her chin and marched on, but Davey Cole's foot went out and next minute Polly was flat on her face, down in the daisies again. When she had picked herself up he was half way over the green, and she dared not shout after him, as she wanted to. She looked ruefully down and saw that the front of her dress was damp and stained, and hoped that the others would be too busy praying to notice.

It was roast lamb for dinner. This was Polly's favourite and perhaps that was why they decided it would be a good time to tell her. The three of them sat round the table and Tom's door was left open so that he could join in the talking. Polly felt very light and elated. She hugged to herself the sound, the secret sound, of those faraway-down bells.

"Could hear the singing from where I am!" Tom called through. "You did very nicely."

"We were short of a baritone, I thought!" called back Alice smartly.

"Are you going to tell," asked Aunt Em, "or aren't you?"

"What?" asked Polly instantly.

"You tell her, love," came Tom's voice.

"*What?*" demanded Polly again.

"It's about Tom," Alice began. "You see, he won't be stopping here as long as we thought."

"It's *good* news!" Tom roared.

"*What?*" Polly was desperate.

"Me and your Dad are leaving in a day or two, Polly," said Alice. "But you'll be stopping on a bit, with your aunt."

Polly stared.

"Why?"

"He's going to another hospital," Alice told her. "A special one, down in the south. And they think . . ." her voice shook a little, and Polly saw that her cheeks were brightly flushed, "they think that they might make him better!

"*Will* make me better!" came Tom's roar. "*Will!*"

Polly was torn between delight and despair. Was her father *really* to walk again – and did she really have to stop alone with Aunt Em?

"What do you say to that?" Tom's voice demanded.

Polly flung down her knife and fork and rushed out of the room and over the passage to where he lay. His plate of roast lamb was balanced on his chest and a napkin tucked under his chin.

"Oh Dad!" She was both laughing and crying. "Oh Dad! It's wonderful."

The most important part of the news *was* about him.

"Right way up again," he said. "What do you say to that?"

And for once, Polly Flint could think of nothing to say at all.

Later, Alice said, "I'm sorry, love, I really am. That you'll be left."

"That's all right, Mam," Polly lied.

"She'll maybe soften up a bit, when we're gone," said Alice – meaning Em.

"Yes," said Polly bleakly. Then, "Oh, Mam, *why* did I have to be an only?"

"Now, Polly, *don't!*" said Alice. "We've been through all that, hundreds of times."

"If only I had just one other person – just one brother or one sister – or even a baby – or even a *grandma!*"

"You'd not necessarily be any better off at all," said Alice firmly. "You look at Em and me!"

"That's different," said Polly.

"That isn't different at all," replied Alice. "You'd be fighting cat and dog from morning till night. And anyhow, you know it wasn't to be."

Polly wished then that she had kept quiet. She knew very well that Tom and Alice had wanted a houseful of children. But she was scared of the silence that would surely fall when the front door shut behind her mother and father.

And when that time came, only two days later, the silence did fall. Tick-tick-tick-tock – the grandfather clock in the hall came into its own, and it seemed to Polly as she lay in bed and listened to it that first night, that the ticking of the clock was making a prisoner of time. Caging it in.

"And making me a prisoner, too," she thought. And then, "Didn't make prisoners of time of *them*, though. Slipped the net of time, that's what he said. And them dancers – spinning round that pole they were, free as birds!"

And thinking of birds brought her mind full circle again, to Tom, and she wept for a while into her pillow.

With Tom and Alice gone, Polly spent more and more time escaping from Aunt Em's kingdom and into her own. The very next day she went, and when she reached the lake stood and gazed out at it with a kind of desperation. It was busy and alive enough, with its ducks and geese, and here and there broods of tiny bobbing chicks, but Polly vaguely knew that this was not enough. She wanted something more.

"Wonder if it might have a monster, like Loch Ness?" she thought. "*That'd* liven things up!"

But she knew this to be unlikely, and so went wandering further into the woodland, treading paths that were new to her. And as she went the voices came again, and the laughter, and children singing, and she began to run, because it felt as if they – whoever they were – were playing hide and seek. They were tantalising her, daring her to follow. In the end she had to stop for lack of breath. She decided to try something else.

"Come out!" she called loudly. "Come out! I am the Queen of this kingdom, and I command you!"

After that she heard no more voices. She was left feeling not only alone, but also rather silly. And feeling silly made her mad.

"I'll wake you up!" she shouted, and began to stamp furiously on the ground. "I'll wake you up, down there!"

"Am I stamping on their sky?" she wondered. "Am I being thunder?"

She set off.

"Stamp stamp wake up! Stamp stamp wake up!" she chanted as she went. "Stamp stamp w – !"

A man and woman were sitting on a bench nearby and watching her with astonishment. She felt her face burn. Then the woman nudged the man and laughed. Polly fled. She ran deep, deeper into the woods, and so it was that she came upon the bluebells. She stopped dead.

They stretched as far as she could see, acres of them it seemed, just on the point of breaking into flower. They lay as a faint blue mist under the trees, marvellously blue, the distilled essence of blueness itself.

"Beautiful!" gasped Polly out loud. "Oh, if only Dad could see them!"

She stared entranced, the voices forgotten. Then she stooped and began to pick.

"Take 'em to Aunt Em," she thought. "Even *she*'ll see they're beautiful."

She straightened up and took one last look at the expanse of blue. She vowed to herself to come back every single day as long as they were in flower.

"Might never see so many again," she thought. "Not so long as I live."

Just then a cuckoo called, and to Polly the moment was made perfect.

She wandered dreamily away, taking the path she thought would lead her back to the lake. All at once she turned a corner, and saw to her left a number of flat stone slabs, each fenced in by iron railings.

"Whatever...?" she wondered out loud.

She went over and read the inscription on the first tablet:

"Snuffy, The Pet Dog of Miss L. Saville Lumley, died December 23rd 1893."

"They're animal graves!" said Polly. "Well – that *is* posh!"

She passed on, reading each inscription aloud.

"'Boris. Faithful friends are hard to find.' Hmmm. *That's* true, right enough. Boris... That's a funny name for a dog. Wonder what he was like...?"

Polly Flint stood and wondered and as she did so raised her eyes and saw, watching her from a few feet away, a dog. He was black, except for a white bib and shoes. Polly gaped at the dog and he sat and gazed back – or so far as she could tell. He was so shaggy that his eyes were almost hidden. All the time her mind was racing.

"Could it be ... could it ... ? Can't! You can't have ghosts of *dogs*!"

They held their gaze, the pair of them, while the cuckoos called about them.

'Boris!" said Polly softly at last.

He came then. He was at her feet wagging his tail, and she was patting him and saying, "Good boy, good boy!" and there was no possibility of his being a ghost because he was warm and soft and solid, and she felt his breath on her hands.

He ran off a little way. Then he stopped and looked back as if expecting her to follow. So she did, and then called again, "Boris!" and again he came to the call, as if knowing the name as his own.

This time she knelt and felt in the fur at his neck for a collar, but her fingers encountered not leather, but a large-linked chain, slightly rusty.

"No name!" she exclaimed, light-headed with relief. "No name and address!"

She hugged him, and scratched under his chin as you would a cat, and he rolled over on his back, all four paws waving in the air, and Polly knew that he must be hers.

She stopped scratching, and he rolled back on to his feet again and sat looking at her, waiting.

"Listen, Boris," she said, and was surprised to find her voice trembling. "I'm going to keep you, I am, no matter what! D'you want to stop with me? Do you?"

His tail moved. He watched her intently.

"You can tell every word I'm saying," she said. "I know you can. But the thing is, you see, I've got this Aunt Em, and I'm stopping with her. Not for ever, but for a bit. And the thing is, I bet you my last currant bun she don't like dogs!"

He looked up at her – expectantly, it seemed.

"Come along with me," she said, getting to her feet again. "And what we'll do, when we get there, you stop outside while I sneak in and get a brush and comb. She might just like *clean* dogs, I suppose!"

Polly sounded more hopeful than she felt. She marched very straight along the path toward the lake, and the dog trotted beside her like a little black shadow.

"Bit of a funny old name, Boris," she said thoughtfully. "Sounds a bit foreign, if you don't mind me saying."

He made no response, one way or the other.

"Could shorten it. I wonder...?" she turned the matter over. "Boz!"

The dog stopped. He looked up.

"Good old boy, Boz!" He wagged his tail. "Come on, Boz!"

She started off again and so did he.

"Isn't it a wonder," said Polly Flint aloud and to nobody in particular, "how the world can change from one minute to the next!"

When they reached Forge Cottage she stopped.

"Stay!" she commanded in a loud whisper. The dog sat. "Good old Boz!" she whispered. "Shan't be long!"

Very gently she turned the knob and pushed open the door. She was greeted by the heavily ticking clock. She listened a moment. All was quiet.

"In the garden, round the back," she decided.

She stole upstairs, took her brush and comb from the dressing table and peered down from the window. There Boz sat exactly as she had left him. She felt like shouting aloud. She crept down again.

"Good boy!" she told him. The tail thumped. "Going to smarten you up a bit. Bit of a scallywag you look."

He stood patiently while she brushed and combed his tousled coat. His look seemed reproachful.

"It's only for Aunt Em," she told him. "Fussy. Much too clean. Eat your dinner off the floor. Now stop there, and I'll go and fetch her."

She picked up the bluebells from the table. Aunt Em was hoeing her weedless garden.

"Wonder is she doesn't dust it," Polly thought. "And vacuum the lawn. And polish the pansies."

She giggled. Aunt Em turned. Polly straightened her face. This was not a good beginning.

"I've got you these, Aunt Em," she said, holding out the bluebells.

"What? Oh! Bluebells! You've never got them out the park?"

Polly nodded.

"Then you shouldn't. There's notices everywhere telling you not to pick things. Look well if you'd have been caught! Whatever would the neighbours've said!"

"I didn't notice," Polly stammered. "I'm sorry!"

This particular bunch of flowers was not going to make anything easier.

"Aunt Em . . ." Polly said. "I've something to show you."

"Oh yes?"

"Well, not exactly some *thing*."

There was no reply.

"Will you come and look, then?"

"Won't it wait?"

"I'm not sure if it will or not!" said poor Polly. What if he ran off? What if he saw a cat, or a rabbit? "*Please* come!"

Aunt Em stepped back on to the path and sighed.

"It's out at the front," Polly told her.

Aunt Em was extremely startled when confronted with Boz.

"What*ever*?" she exclaimed.

"He's a stray. I found him in the wood and he's got no collar and no address so I brought him home," Polly gabbled. "He's ever so good and he does everything you tell him, and – "

"Stop!" Aunt Em held up a hand and stared down at Boz with unconcealed distaste.

"*That* ain't a deal of a dog," she observed at last. "Whatever make is it? Nothing *I've* ever seen before!"

"I don't know," admitted Polly. "But he's got a nice face."

"If you could see it!" said Aunt Em tartly, but not without justification.

"He's ever so friendly," said Polly quickly. "Aren't you, Boz old boy?"

He got up then and advanced, wagging his tail. Aunt Em rapidly dropped back several paces.

"He likes you!" cried Polly.

"*What*'s his name? *What* was that you called him?"

"Boz," said Polly. She left out the part about Boris. She had the feeling that ghosts and foreigners would be suspect alike. "It just came into my head. Can I keep him, Aunt Em? Can I, please?"

"You certainly cannot," replied Aunt Em promptly. "I never heard of such a thing!"

"But can't he stop till we've found him a home? He was lost – he's a stray. We can't just turn him back loose in the woods. Besides," she added with cunning, "somebody might report us to the R.S.P.C.A."

"I hold no truck with animals in the house," said Aunt Em. "But now you've brought him, you'd better get him off the doorstep. Are his feet clean?"

And so Boz gained a foothold in Aunt Em's kingdom, against all likelihood, because of her fear of what the neighbours might say. And once he had sniffed about him and was satisfied, he settled himself down with his nose between his paws and there was nothing at all in his behaviour for Aunt Em to take exception to.

That night Alice telephoned and Polly told her about the dog, and then Alice asked to speak to Aunt Em, and the upshot of it all was that Boz was to be allowed to stay, for the time being.

"We shall have to advertise, of course," she said. "In the Lost and Found. Only thing is – what to *describe* him as."

That night Boz slept on a blanket by Polly's bed. Aunt Em had objected very strongly to this at first, but when she had run through the list of other possibilities, which were *her* kitchen, *her* sitting and dining room and *her* landing, the thing was inevitable.

"It's unhygienic, of course," she told Polly, when she came up to say goodnight. "It's to be hoped you don't catch anything. Enough trouble in the family, as it is."

When she had gone Polly began to tell Boz in a low whisper about the magic. She told him about the maypole and that secret dawn when the May Dancers had come, about the voices and echoes, the glimpses of figures in the woods.

"And this weekend," she concluded, "we'll go there, we will, and you'll sniff 'em out for me!"

She wondered fleetingly whether ghosts – daydreams – Time Gypsies – *had* scents, but thrust the thought away.

"In any case," she thought, "Boz could be a Time *Dog*."

Before settling herself to sleep she took her usual last look at the maypole. She did not really expect to see anything. Light streamed from The Red Lion opposite, and cars came and went, momentarily flooding the green with light. But this had become a ritual, that on waking, and again last thing at night, she held tryst with whatever magic it was that haunted this place.

A solitary figure passed over a lighted patch of the green, seeming gigantic, footlinked with his own shadow. Old Mazy.

"And *he* fits in somewhere," she thought, as she let the curtains fall.

Chapter Four

When she woke next morning Polly looked straight away to see if Boz was still there. He had, after all, appeared under very strange circumstances.

"He is!" Her relief was enormous.

He came over and put his two front paws on the bed, and she told him,

"We're going hunting today, you and me!"

She gave his blanket a good shake out of the window, tidied her own bed with extra care, and went down, light hearted as she had not been for ages. Even the ticking of the grandfather clock seemed less ominous today.

When she had run errands for Aunt Em and fetched dog food from the shop, she and Boz set off for the lake. She went first, as queen, to the wooden landing stage, where she threw crusts for her courtier ducks.

"I know why they've let me keep you," she told Boz. "It's to keep me company. I can read 'em like an open book. And so you are – company, I mean. But of course, a dog ain't a Dad, Boris old lad. Hey – that rhymed! A dog ain't a Dad, Boz old lad! Not a brother or sister, either. Always wanted one. But Mam couldn't, see. One of those things, she says – whatever that means."

She stood up and brushed off the crumbs.

"Ah well! Come on! We're hunting, remember!"

Polly deliberately avoided the path that led to the animal graves. She did not exactly believe that Boz would vanish there just as he had appeared, but it seemed wise not to take any risks. She wandered along the path by the lakeside and looked yet again at the island that had a curious, arched tunnel running from one side to the other.

"What's *that* for?" she wondered out loud.

She gazed for a while, and was about to walk on when she turned back with a gasp. There – in the water – a reflection! She stood absolutely still, hardly daring to breathe. She craned forward to see the better, and made out that it was a boy – water rippled, of course, because of the swimming ducks – but a boy, right enough, and doing something with his hands . . . holding something. . . .

There it was! Very faint and far away, the sound of a fiddle. "Polly put the kettle on, Polly put the kettle on."

Slowly, very slowly, trying not to move her head, but swivelling her eyes as far as she could to her left, she sought the original of the reflection. Nothing! She looked down again at the water. Gone.

At her side sat Boz, patiently waiting. Had *he* seen, she wondered? Dogs were supposed to have a sixth sense, to see things invisible to human eyes.

"Did *you* see, Boz?" she asked.

He looked up at her, and his tail moved ever so slightly, but Polly could make neither a "yes" nor a "no" of his answer.

She took a final long look into the lake, but the image had gone, and the music faded, and she was left yet again clutching at straws. What was it that Old Mazy had said about the lake...?

"Water always finds its own level..."

What could he *mean*?

She happened to look up at that moment, and caught sight of a stationary figure at the far side of the lake. As she watched, an arm was raised in greeting. It was Old Mazy himself. She waved back, but she did not want his company. The park was big enough to lose fifty people in, let alone one, and she quickened her step and soon took one of the little paths that led away from the lake and into Broad Ride, the wide grassy avenue that in the old days had led to the great Abbey beyond. She crossed that, too, and was soon meandering along a narrow track with trees on either hand, lacing their boughs overhead.

"Won't find me *here*!" she thought.

When she first saw the bluebell haze again through the trees, she was again flooded by an astonishing sense of sheer blueness. The very air above them was so thickly blue that she almost felt that she could touch it.

"Though I expect it'd be like a rainbow," she thought. "When you get up to it – gone!"

And like the Time Gypsies, too, for that matter. Elusively there at a distance, but always ahead no matter how hard you ran.

Polly stopped. Boz looked up enquiringly.

"I've tried chasing," she said. "But I've never tried *calling*. I reckon the time has come to call."

She wheeled about, scanning for hints, whispers, signs.

"Hallo!" she called. And then again, "Hallo! I'm Polly Flint, and I want to be your friend!"

She listened, and heard only the usual small noises of a wood.

"And also," she called, "I am Queen, and this is my kingdom!"

Boz began to veer off to the right of the path, his nose close to the ground.

"Tracking!" she thought. "He's got a scent!"

She followed him then as fast as she could, and saw that he had stopped among the bluebells. His plumy tail was waving above them. She wove her way through to him, and whatever it was she had expected to see it was not what she saw now. It lay wrapped in a bundle of bluish cloth and its eyes were wide open and tiny fists opening and closing as if plucking at something invisible in the air.

"A baby!" gasped Polly. Then, "Whose? Whatever. . . ?"

It began to make little gurgling noises. Boz had finished his exploratory sniffing, and now sat squared and fixed by the baby's head, as if a self-appointed guardian. His chain, hanging medallion-like down his front, added to the impression that his position was official.

Polly dropped to her knees. She did not quite know what to say to a baby – particularly a baby that might be at least five hundred years old. There was no way of telling, she thought. Bundled up babies must have all looked more or less the same since the world began.

"Been left," she said out loud. "Like Moses in the bulrushes."

The baby gazed up at her. Polly liked its wide bright

eyes, its friendliness. Hesitantly she held out her hand and it was held, quite tightly, by the tiny grubby fingers. A marvellous thought came to her.

"First Boz," she said, "and now you. Perhaps – perhaps *you're* meant for me, as well!"

Her mind reeled and raced at the thought. She had just got to the point where she tried to think how she would introduce the baby to Aunt Em, when she heard a call behind her. To her amazement, Boz stiffened, stood for a moment with his head cocked, then raced away. She leapt to her feet, and heard a second call.

"Baggins! Baggins!"

And now at last Polly Flint saw them plain. After all the shadows, echoes and reflections, after all the vain pursuits, there, at last, they were. She could not see their faces yet, because they were bending over Boz, patting and praising him, and seeing this she was torn between exultation and annoyance.

"Just as if they owned him!" she thought.

"Boz!" she called. "Come on – come on, boy!"

To her delight he came, and so did the boy, lit in flashes as the sunlight struck him. A man followed more slowly behind him. They stopped a few yards away. Boz was back at his post by the baby again.

"It's no use your doing that now, you heathen!" The boy was wagging a finger at him. "Set to *guard* him, you were. Where've you been?"

"He's been with me," said Polly boldly. "I'm Polly Flint and he's *my* dog."

The pair of them looked at her now, up and down.

"Stuff!" the boy said. "He's ours. Ain't you, Baggins?"

"Boz – come on Boz, good boy!"

He rose and trotted to her outstretched hand.

"See?" she cried triumphantly.

"See nothing!" the boy said. "Baggins – here, come on!"

He trotted towards the outstretched hand.

"See?" he mocked.

Polly's mind was racing. *Was* he their dog? He was, after all, a stray – though whether in space or time she could not know.

"All right," she said, "if he's yours, how long've you had him? And where did you get him?"

"We found him," the boy said. "Finders keepers. And never mind how long. We don't care about how long – time's nothing."

Polly looked at him, taking in the ragged shirt and breeches that looked several sizes too big for him. In one hand he held a fiddle and a bow. His feet were bare.

"Time mightn't mean anything to *you*," she said deliberately. "Because you're Time Gypsies."

There was no reply. They gazed at her, hard and long. The boy's expression changed to one of suspicion – even fear.

"She's on to us," he said at last.

"She sees us," said the man, "*and* hears us."

"Just our luck! *Two* of 'em now, stalking and hunting!"

"She's been on to us from the start. She was there at the May Dancing."

"*And* The Catcher!"

Polly was not pleased to be discussed as if she were

not there.

"I am *here*, you know," she said. "I can see you and I can hear you."

"That's just it," said the boy glumly. He looked hard at Polly.

"You called us Time Gypsies," he said. "How did you know?"

"Someone told me."

The pair exchanged glances.

"The Catcher!" said the man. "There's only him could've told her."

"P'raps she's in with him!" The boy looked swiftly about him. "Could've sent her to trap us!"

They were frightened now, both man and boy, and Polly found it unbearable to think that it was because of her.

"Don't be frightened!" she cried. "Please! I'm not in with anybody, honest I'm not. I want to be friends."

They stood there uncertainly, all three of them, and Polly wondered desperately what she might do to make them believe her. Then, beyond them, she saw figures approaching.

"Look out!" she cried. "Hide! Somebody's coming!"

They did not even turn their heads.

"There's a whole family!" she cried.

"Better pick *him* up, I s'pose," said the boy, jerking his head towards the baby. "Don't want him trod on."

He bent and picked up the grubby bundle.

"I warned you," Polly said.

"Now listen here," the boy said, "*we* don't need to hide. We see them, but they don't see us."

93

"There's only you *can*," said the man, "so far as we know. You and The Catcher, maybe."

"Of course!" This she had quite forgotten. Now that she at last could see them, the notion that the Time Gypsies were invisible seemed absurd – impossible, almost.

The figures were now scattered and picking bluebells, except for one, a boy, who was still advancing.

"It's Polly Flint!" She saw that it was Davey Cole. "Who was you talking to, just now?"

"I was talking to Boz," Polly said.

"That your dog?"

"Yes, it is, as a matter of fact."

"Can it see where it's going?" He sniggered.

"As a matter of fact he can. As a matter of fact, he can see better than *you* can."

"*Very* likely," said Davey, "through all that fur!"

"*And* hear better," said Polly. "Hear that baby crying, can you?"

"What baby?" He looked about him. "There ain't one."

Polly smiled sweetly.

"Funny. I could swear I hear one crying."

"You're barmy. Daft."

"One of us is," said Polly. "Come on, Boz!"

She started to walk away, but kept a sidelong eye on the Time Gypsies as she went. She supposed they could slip out of sight as suddenly as they had appeared – for all she knew they would vanish – melt into thin air before her very eyes.

They were following her. As soon as she was out of earshot of Davey Cole she stopped, and waited for them.

"What did you say your name was?" the boy asked.

"Polly Flint. What's yours?"

"Don't tell!" said the boy quickly.

"Why not?" Polly was indignant. "I told mine."

"It'll give her power over us," he told the man.

"She already has," he returned. "She sees and hears us."

"I don't *want* power over you!" Polly was quite desperate. "I want us to be friends."

"We'll tell," the man said. "Not a deal more harm to be done, now. I'm Gil."

She looked enquiringly at the boy.

"Sam," he muttered at last, reluctantly.

"And what about the baby?" Polly asked.

"Ain't got a name, not yet," Gil said. "Hasn't been named yet, by parson. Babby Porter, that's what he gets called."

"And he's a great fat nuisance," Sam said. "One of these days he'll get trod on. But you can't lug *that* lump round all day."

"Gil! Gil! Sam! Sam!" A thin cracked voice floated through the trees.

"It's Granny Porter," said Gil. He raised his voice. "Here!"

The oddest figure was approaching. At first Polly could not make it out, and even when she did, it seemed more like a bush or a shrub that had suddenly sprouted feet, than like a human being. The shape advanced with a curious hobbling gait, and seemed to be moving both sideways and forwards at once. As it approached, a low mutter was to be heard.

"In and out up and down day to night dawn to dusk!"

"She ain't going to be none too pleased about *her!*"
said Sam, meaning Polly.

The figure was dressed in stitched tatters of a
thousand mucky rags, that looked like the plumage of
a particularly frowsty large bird. The face was at first
invisible on account of a large and bedraggled bonnet.

"Up and down in and out," came the mutter again.

"Here we are, then, Granny!" exclaimed Gil, with
an attempt at cheerfulness.

"Here?" snapped the bonnet. "Where's here? Up
down in and out, here there and everywhere!"

"Now then, Granny," said Gil soothingly.
"World's still spinning!"

"World? World? *Me* that's spinning. My poor old
head, round and round in and out up and down here
and – "

"Look you what's here, Granny," interrupted Gil
to prevent a further flow.

The bonnet lifted. Polly saw the oldest, most criss-
crossed and wrinkled face she had ever seen.

"She must be a *hundred!*" she thought. "At least!"

And yet the eyes were not old. The eyes were amaz-
ingly bright and quick and birdlike. They looked at
Polly long and hard.

"Who's that?" she snapped. "That ain't one of
ours!"

"No, Granny," agreed Gil.

"Oooh! I knew there'd be ill luck!" she wailed.
"We're not spotted! Never say we're spotted!"

She glared at Polly with such intensity that she fell
back a couple of paces.

"Give that Babby Porter here to me!" she said,
snatching the baby from Sam. "Wicked it is, a little

babby being risked up here. How do we know there's not wolves?"

"Oh, there aren't any wolves," said Polly, pleased to have something to add to the conversation. "You don't get wolves, not in England."

Silence. The old lady fixed Polly with yet another glowering look.

"So she *does* see us, does she?" she said slowly and terribly. "And hears us. *She's* our ill luck!"

"Now go easy, Granny," said Gil. "She's nobbut a little lass."

"And I'm not bad luck!" said Polly passionately. "I'm not, I'm *not!*"

"Then why does she see us?" demanded Granny Porter. "And hear us?"

"I do see things," Polly told her. She added, proudly, "One day, I saw an angel."

They stared at her, all three.

"You saw *what?*" hissed the old woman.

"An *angel?*" repeated Gil incredulously.

Polly nodded.

"Not that they believed me," she said, "any more than they would if I told 'em about *you!*"

"And why not, *pray?*" The raggy plumage was all a-twitch and a-quiver. "We're *here*, ain't we? Which is more than angels is."

"All I mean is," said poor Polly, "that if I *do* see you, and nobody else does, they'll think you aren't real."

Granny Porter advanced.

"Here – you take this!" She thrust the baby at Gil. "We – ain't – *what?*"

"Oh – I don't know!" wailed Polly. "I'm all mixed

up. But there's a real world over there – " she waved an arm vaguely about her – "a world with cars and buses and TV and my Aunt Em and – and – fish fingers! And none of *you* – "

She faltered.

"Go on," said the old lady dangerously. "None of us – what?"

"Oh, it's not fair!" Polly burst out. "You think it's you that's real and me that's not, just because there's more of you. You're three to one!"

She looked at the baby.

"Four to one!"

"Four to two," corrected Sam. "You've got our Baggins."

"She's what?" Granny Porter sounded dangerous again.

"Got Baggins, Granny. Must've fed him."

There was a long pause. Granny Porter shook her head and hissed softly between her teeth.

"I don't understand," said Polly, "I honestly don't. Of course I fed him. What difference does that make?"

Another silence. Polly was aware of secret looks exchanged, a mystery.

"Never mind," said Gil at last. "It does."

"She gives me the creeps," said Sam. "Ain't used to being seen."

"It's you that ought to give *me* the creeps!" said Polly indignantly. "At least I'm here – properly here, I mean!"

She was back on the old dangerous ground. Granny Porter held up a hand and wagged a finger.

"Never you cross me, girl," she said, and there was a hint of menace in her looks, so that Polly suddenly

99

shivered. "You beware of me – just as I must beware of you!"

Polly shook her head dumbly.

"You have powers," Granny Porter went on, "just as I have powers."

"Come on," said Sam then, tugging at Gil's sleeve. His face was pinched and scared. "Let's go! She's got our Baggins – how do we know she won't get us?"

"Best to go, yes," Gil agreed. "Let things be now, Granny. There's no harm done."

"No harm done but harm to come," the soft voice crooned. Then she turned, and Polly saw only the bonnet and the raggedy figure was shuffling off without another word to say.

"Farewell," said Gil, and turned to follow.

"And you look after our Baggins!" Sam said, and darted after them.

Polly watched them go, that strange trio under the slanting shafts of sunlight.

"*Where* will they go?" she wondered. "And what will they do?"

"Will you come again?" she called after them.

All she had in reply was a slow raising of an arm from Gil, his back still turned.

"Could mean *owt*, that could," she said. She looked down at Boz who sat watching them too. "Least you didn't follow them. Mine, you are. Have *you* been under earth?" He looked up at her. "Pity dogs can't talk. Pity . . ."

She sighed. They were out of sight now.

"Come on!" said Polly. "We'll follow 'em!"

But the Time Gypsies had gone, there was neither sight nor sound of them.

"Could they have gone invisible again?" she wondered. "Or back under earth. And if they do go under earth – how do they get down there? Secret tunnel . . . or lift, like at pit . . ." She laughed then. "And that's a funny thing . . . If there *is* a village down there, with people living in houses, and that, why don't the coal miners see them . . ?"

She shook her head. It was all beyond her. Polly Flint wandered on through her kingdom, marvelling at the thought that under her very feet, beneath the bracken, the moss and the bluebells, was another world and, most amazing, another time.

"It's a puzzle!" she said out loud.

She was now by the pool she named The Silver Pool because of the birches reflected in its waters.

"It ain't much fun being a queen if there's nobody to command," she told Boz. "Excepting you, of course. I wish – oh *how* I wish them Time Gypsies had stopped!"

And then the wood was suddenly peopled. It was the strangest thing. One minute she was standing there alone gazing at the pool and its quiet reflections, and the next there was thin, echoing laughter, voices, music – and there, flitting from tree to tree, children, fast and slippery as quicksilver and quite certainly and beyond question brought there by magic.

Then the small figure of a boy advanced to the very edge of the pool, and he raised a fiddle and started to play. His eyes met Polly's, and she saw that it was her boy – Sam.

"Not gone!" she breathed.

The tune he played floated over to where she stood.

Polly put the kettle on
Polly put the kettle on,
Polly put the kettle on
We'll all have tea!

"For me!" she thought. "He's playing it for me!" and stood straight and proud as any queen.

"All those children," she thought, "a *maypoleful* of children, and all singing for me!"

The song came to an end and the children ran forward and bowed and Polly clapped her hands.

"Hurray!" she cried.

The fiddle struck up again, and this time it was "Ring a Ring o' Roses". The children ran together to join hands but all at once a cry went up from one of them,

"The Catcher! The Catcher!"

They screamed and scattered, crying "The Catcher! The Catcher!" as they fled. The tune came to an abrupt end. Bewildered and scared, Polly scanned about her and saw, through the trees, that same striding figure she had glimpsed before in the woods. He went with slow huge strides as he had gone before, and in one hand brandished a long stick curved like a shepherd's crook, and in the other a giant net.

"The Catcher!" shrieked Polly, and began to run as fast as she could, because although the pool lay between her and that awful shape it seemed to her that he might come striding on right over the water, and she herself become enmeshed in that terrible net.

She ran pell mell and not caring where she went, and stopped only when she felt a sharp stitch in her side. Under a low, widely branched tree she crouched, and tried to listen, above her own heavy breathing, for sounds of pursuit. Limply she dropped to the ground.

"Can't run any more!" she gasped, and took hold of Boz's chain to stop him running out and betraying her hiding place.

"Oh dear! I don't know *when* I'll dare to come out from here!" she told him. "We'll have to stop here *ages*. And then I'll be late for dinner, and Aunt Em'll be mad at me!"

She was, too. When she finally emerged she ran all the way back, because she did not know where that figure might be striding now, or whether at any moment a giant net might drop from nowhere over her head.

For once, Forge Cottage almost seemed like home.

"Lucky it's nothing that'd spoil," said Aunt Em, ladling stew on to the plates. "Didn't you *know* what time it was?"

"Haven't got a watch!" gasped Polly, still trying to get her breath.

"Then you should have!" she retorted, and then, as an afterthought, "Though even if you had, you'd lose it, I suppose."

Polly thought for a little.

"Aunt Em," she said, "do you believe in time?"

"Do I. . . ? Now what kind of a ridiculous question is that? Of course I believe in time."

"Why?" asked Polly.

"Because – because time's time, that's why!" replied Aunt Em lamely.

"Ah, but what if it *wasn't*?" said Polly. "Suppose it wasn't?"

"I shall suppose no such silly thing!" snapped Aunt

Em. "I don't know where you get your ideas from I really don't."

Polly was making a pattern in her stew with her fork.

"Polly – *don't!*"

"Polly Don't, again," thought Polly. "*Should* be my name, and that's a fact."

She munched a little and went on thinking.

"Aunt Em," she said, "you know my park..."

"Do I know what? It's Rufford you mean, I suppose."

"Well – have you ever heard ... any stories about it?"

"Stories? What kind of stories?"

"I don't exactly know," said Polly. She thought, "I can't tell her. Mustn't. Wouldn't believe me in any case." Out loud she said, "*Legend* kind of stories."

"I've heard nothing," said Aunt Em. "There's nothing *to* hear."

"Oh, but there is," thought Polly Flint. "I could tell you a story, a *true* story, that'd make you *goggle!*"

"I don't know what you find to do there all day," Aunt Em told her. "I hope you don't go getting near that lake."

"Not near enough to fall in," said Polly. "And even if I did, I should soon swim out again. This is very nice stew, Aunt Em."

"Oh!" she said. She was almost, but not quite, sidetracked. "The day you drop in that lake," she observed, "will be the last day you ever go near it."

"Yes, Aunt Em," said Polly meekly.

There was a silence – or at any rate as near a silence as was possible in that particular house.

104

"That grandfather clock's got a very loud tick," said Polly.

"It was my mother's," said Aunt Em, as if that accounted for the matter. "And her mother's, before that. It's never lost a single second."

Polly looked at her aunt and gave a little sigh.

"I don't expect it *dare*," she thought. "Not in *this* house!"

After dinner she went up to her room to write a letter to Tom. She spent a long time sucking her pencil before she decided.

"Shall I, or shan't I...?" she wondered. She pictured Tom in his high hospital bed, staring at the ceiling and seeing his own private skyful of birds.

"All day long, just lying there..." she thought. "I *shall* tell him!"

And so she began, "Dear Dad, I hope you are well and feeling better, and here is what has been happening to me. You know that lake I told you about, with all the birds..."

And she went on and described it all, exactly as it had happened, she told of the echoing laughter and silvery voices, and then of her meeting with the Time Gypsies, and she named them, Gil, Sam, and Granny Porter.

"And then there's Babby Porter," she added, "and they only *call* him Babby Porter, can you believe!"

Then she wrote of the scene by the Silver Pool, and how The Catcher came striding by with net and crook; her own heart thudded as she remembered it. When she read it over, she decided that Alice might be frightened by it, so she added, "But you mustn't worry, because I have Boz and I expect he would guard me."

She looked down at Boz where he lay slumped, nose between paws, and wondered about this.

"He certainly don't *look* like a guarding kind of a dog," she thought. "And come to think, he didn't make much of a job of guarding Babby Porter!"

She turned back to the letter, and added, "I miss you, Mam and Dad, I really do."

She sucked again on her pencil and tried to think up a rhyme for Tom.

"And now I'm ending with a rhyme, to say I don't believe in time!"

She put the letter in its envelope.

"Don't, either!" she thought, and went downstairs to ask for a stamp. "You sent my love, I hope," said Aunt Em as she fished in her purse.

"Oh yes," said Polly. But it was not true.

"Hadn't thought of love, in connection with her," she thought.

"You weren't thinking of going down Rufford again this afternoon, I hope?" said Aunt Em.

"Oh yes!" said Polly, dismayed.

"Then you'll need to think again," said Aunt Em. "You can come along of me, collecting."

"Collecting?" echoed Polly.

"For the Jumble," Aunt Em nodded. "W.I. Jumble, today week. We'll go knocking round and see what there is. I shall need you to help carry."

"Yes Aunt Em," said Polly. She did not really mind, when she thought about it. "Might not have *dared* to go back there," she thought. "Not with The Catcher about."

Besides, she liked Jumble. She had often helped Alice collect it, and liked to rummage through it, seeing things that other people threw away, and sometimes fishing bits and pieces out for herself, before other people got the chance.

"Just post this letter, then," she said.

She went out and over the green and looked up, as usual, at the maypole, acknowledging its magic. There sat old Mazy on his usual bench, his head tipped back and eyes seeming to be closed. But as she drew near he suddenly opened his eyes wide and his head came up.

"Good day, Polly Flint," he said.

"Good afternoon," replied Polly politely, and was going to walk straight on past him, when she felt something catch at her ankle, and stumbled and fell.

"Oh!" she gasped. "Whatever?"

And she saw that he had used the crook of his long stick to trip her, and she stared up into his dark face with terror.

"The Catcher!" she thought. "Oh, my moon and stars – he must be The Catcher!"

Chapter Five

"Don't you do that!" gasped Polly, getting up and looking around for her dropped letter.

"Just a little game I play," he said. "No need to be afeared of Old Mazy. Harmless enough."

She stared at him. Could it be he she had seen striding like a giant through the woods?

"Reflections were there today?" he asked her. "Voices?"

"No!' said Polly loudly, rubbing at her knees. "No, there weren't!"

"My old eyes aren't so good, you see," he went on. "These days, I only seem to be able to see things that are really there. Do you take my meaning, Polly Flint?"

"No!" she stammered, and backed away a little, wary of the curved stick. "No, I don't!"

"Ah, but I think you do," he said softly. "Heard the bells, didn't you? Saw the children in the wood?"

"I must've been mistaken!" she cried. "I—I'm always imagining things. You ask my Mam!"

"Oh, I shan't do that," he said. "No need at all of that. I shall just do as I always have. Watch—and wait."

"I've to go now." Polly backed right off. "Got a letter to post!" and she ran all the way there and back again. She took care to take the other side of the green, but gave a sideway look as she went by, and saw the bench empty.

"Gone!" she thought. "Gone down to Rufford? Oh, and I can't even warn 'em! Oh – blow the jumble!"

Back at Forge Cottage she called "Aunt Em!" and receiving no reply went out to the back and found her struggling to pull something out of the shed.

"There!" she gasped, with a final yank.

"Whatever?" Polly gaped. It was a pram, a big pram with enormous wheels, and covered with dust and cobwebs which Aunt Em was already busily flicking away.

"Is that for the jumble?" she asked.

"For collecting," said Aunt Em. "Comes in very handy for collecting."

"But where's it from?" asked Polly. "It does look old!"

"It was mine," said Aunt Em, "when I was a baby. And your mam's. Used to push her in it, I did."

"But whatever did you keep it for?" cried Polly. "That was years and years ago!"

"Waste not, want not!" said Aunt Em, blushing red and looking awkward all the same.

"She could never've thought *she'd* get a baby to put in it!" thought Polly. "That'd be the day – her to have a baby!"

And she giggled at the thought, and Aunt Em heard the giggle, and said "Look sharp, now – out the way!"

They set off round the village and within an hour the pram was filled to overflowing. Polly watched her aunt pushing the enormous pram before her, and more than once thought, "She looks as pleased as punch with herself! You'd almost think there *was* a baby in there!" and allowed herself another giggle at the thought.

"Now, then," said Aunt Em, pushing the laden pram up the step. "That'll do for now. We'll sort it all out later. But what I'll do, Polly, as you've been such a good help, I'll come a little walk along with you, down Rufford."

"Oh!" Polly's hand flew to her mouth to stifle her gasp of dismay.

"What if they're there? What if she *sees* them?"

"Well, don't that please you, miss?" demanded Aunt Em, huffy at Polly's want of proper gratitude.

"Oh – yes, yes," lied Polly. "That'll be smashing, Aunt Em."

"We shan't take that dog," said Aunt Em, eyeing the hopeful Boz. "I can be doing without him dancing round my feet."

"Oh, he's ever so good," Polly assured her. "He don't do that. And I'm going to train him to do ever so many other things!"

Aunt Em contented herself with a snort. Boz – or Baggins – stayed behind.

It was strange to Polly to enter Rufford for the first time not alone.

"It's my kingdom," she thought, "and now she's setting foot in it."

But because it *was* her kingdom, Polly soon began to find herself enjoying pointing out this and that to her companion.

"That's the Silver Pool," she told her, as they approached it. "See? Because of them birches."

"Very nice," said Aunt Em.

"And look – see that? A tunnel, going right through from one side of the island to the other. Ain't decided what that's for, yet. So I call it the Secret Tunnel."

"Very nice," said Aunt Em.

"And here's the bluebells!" Polly cried at last. "That I told you about. I brought you some, remember. Look at 'em – miles of 'em."

"Oh, very nice," said Aunt Em. Even she could not remain unmoved by that glorious blueness. She sighed. "Fair *handsome*," she said. "You've got to admit."

They walked on.

"And now, I shall show *you* something," said Aunt Em.

"What?" cried Polly jealously. This was her kingdom, and she could not bear to think that Aunt Em might know it better than she herself.

"You know who lived there," said Aunt Em, waving towards the Abbey in the distance. "A lot of monks, in the olden times. Though I daresay I'm wrong to say as much to you, if you're to start seeing monks all over everywhere!"

'Oh, I shan't do that," promised Polly. "I've never seen a monk in my life."

"Well, then," said Aunt Em. "You just look at that!"

She pointed. Polly turned and gasped.

"A prison!"

"Prison?" said Aunt Em. "No such thing. You do get carried away, Polly, you really do. It's the Icehouse."

They approached along a dank and shady path.

Polly sniffed, and the air seemed already to have an icy tang.

"Still think it looks like a prison," she said.

Cautiously she went up to the massive iron grille and smelled age and cold and darkness. She could not make out the bottom of what seemed an enormous dungeon hollowed beneath the ground. She tested for echoes, and heard her voice flying about her.

"Where the monks used to keep their ice," she

heard Aunt Em say from behind her.

"Keep ice? What, all year round? In here?"

"What they say. All I know is, that in the winter they'd dig great blocks of ice, and keep it down there."

"Crikey!" Polly was impressed. "A sort of old-fashioned fridge!"

"Don't believe in fridges, myself," said Aunt Em. "Larder's cool enough for milk and meat, and such. And no one's ever died for the lack of an ice-cream, so far as I know."

"Hoo! Hoo!" Polly called the echoes out again from the stone.

She shivered and stepped back.

"Don't like it," she said. "Spooky!"

"No one's asking you to like it." Aunt Em was huffy again. "Just trying to teach you summat, that's all."

They walked back along the mossed path and over the Broad Rise with its view of the Abbey over the high yew hedge.

"Long way to carry ice," Polly thought. "Or might there be a tunnel? An underground tunnel . . . ?"

She heard the crying of a baby then, and stiffened. She looked rapidly about her.

"Can't see one," she thought. "Gosh – let them not be there now, let 'em not! If they are – and she sees 'em – they'll think I gave 'em away!"

On the other hand, she reflected, Aunt Em was so very firmly planted in this world, that it was very unlikely that she should even suspect the existence of another.

They were walking back along the edge of the lake

now, and still there was no sign of Babby Porter, though Polly could still hear the sound of a baby crying faintly from somewhere among the trees.

"I'll have to sit down now," she heard Aunt Em say. "Give my legs a rest a minute."

She made towards a wooden seat nearby. Polly looked up and let out a gasp of horror.

There, sitting on the far end of the bench, hunched in her bedraggled plumage with her arms wrapped around herself in an attitude of extreme sulk – was Granny Porter.

Polly's mind whirled. What if Aunt Em saw her – and worse, got into conversation with her? Or – worst – what if Aunt Em didn't see her – and *sat* on her!

Polly closed her eyes in anguish at the thought of Aunt Em descending on to that raggedy lap. Slowly she let out her breath and opened them again.

The two ladies were now sitting one on either end of the bench, both staring out at the lake and both apparently oblivious of the other's presence.

"She can't have seen her, surely!" thought Polly. "She'd never've sat next to her – her being so clean, and all!"

For whatever Granny Porter was or was not, she was undeniably grubby. She was, in fact, what even Alice herself, who was clean without being overly so, would describe as downright mucky.

Both ladies were facing towards the lake but in quite a different manner. Aunt Em was watching the broods of tiny ducklings. Granny Porter was wearing a stare that indicated that she was *seeing* nothing at all, but sunk in terrible and gloomy thought.

"Look, Aunt Em!" Polly almost shrieked. "Look at

them!" She pointed in the direction away from Granny Porter. "Look at them little ducks over there! Ain't they sweet? And see *there* – other side of that island! Look at – "

"I'm quite capable of looking for myself, thank you, Polly," said Aunt Em. "Do stop *dancing*, child! Sit down here alonger me, and shush up a minute."

Polly eyed with consternation the narrow space between her aunt and the hunched figure beside her. Just then, Granny Porter did at last turn her face, to give Polly a look of pure malevolence.

"You sit there," the look seemed to say, "and *then* see what happens!"

And then, right behind the frayed bonnet, two faces peered from the thicket. Sam and Gil. They were making furious gestures at her, and pointing to the motionless back of Granny Porter.

"Trying to tell me to get her to come?" Polly wondered. "Daren't speak, I don't suppose, with Aunt Em being there. But *I* can't speak to her, either."

So she too started to make grimaces at Granny Porter and stabbed her finger urgently in the direction of the thicket.

"Do stop *fidgeting!*" said Aunt Em, without moving her gaze from the lake.

Granny Porter watched Polly narrowly. Then, very slowly she turned her head. Gil and Sam made vigorous beckoning signs. She turned back towards the lake.

Then, with deliberate slowness, she rose and hobbled off to join them, turning to give Polly one last ill-tempered look before disappearing into the shrubbery.

"Oh!" gasped Polly. "I think I *will* sit down – my legs feel all wobbly!"

Aunt Em and she eventually wandered back home to tea and hot crumpets, and spent an evening that was almost companionable, sorting out the pram full of jumble.

Next day was Sunday. Polly itched to be down in Rufford, but knew that she would have to wait until after dinner.

"Can I just teach Boz some tricks before we go to church?" she begged.

"You can if you don't get yourself dirty," said Aunt Em, "and don't annoy the neighbours. Not that I've any belief that *that* animal'll ever do a trick."

"He will then!" Polly was indignant on Boz's behalf. "You watch this. Ought to have a biscuit, really, but I'll bet he'll do it without!"

She faced him.

"Boz, sit!" He sat. "Now, sit up!"

Boz sat up, wavering precariously on his hind quarters.

"There!" she cried triumphantly.

"It's to be hoped you'll not waste any more biscuits on that!" said Aunt Em, and marched back into the kitchen to attend to her roast.

"You're a clever boy," Polly whispered, "Boz – or Baggins – whichever!"

She picked up a ball and went out on to the quiet Sunday morning green.

"We're going to do Fetch," she told him.

She had thrown the ball for him only a few times when she saw Davey Cole approaching, a canvas bag slung over his shoulder, delivering newspapers.

"Here's the hag's." He passed the paper to her. "Why don't you get that lump of fur to take it?"

"I haven't trained him to, not yet," said Polly with dignity. "But I shall."

"Try it," he said. "He might have already been taught it, before you found him."

"All right."

To her delight, and also to her amazement, Boz-Baggins took the newspaper in his mouth and trotted to the open front door.

"There you are! I bet he could do any trick there is, if I taught him."

"Bet he couldn't!"

"What kind of trick, anyway?" Polly felt inclined to take up the challenge, if it was feasible.

"This!" He pushed his face close to hers and crossed his eyes horribly. Then he ran off over the green.

"Easy!" he yelled as he went. "Easy as winking!"

She pulled a face at his retreating back. She saw him again later, as she reached the church porch with Aunt Em. She knew there was no hope of escaping again, to listen for the Grimstone bells, but she glimpsed him, evidently lurking in wait at the far end of the church. She gave him a quelling and pious look as she entered, straight-backed, by her aunt's side. She had, in any case, the moment the Wellow bells started to ring, hastily and secretly put her ear to the ground in the garden, and *thought* she had heard the answering peals below. She did not, in fact, need to hear them now. She knew for certain that there was a village there below, and that it had, indeed, slipped the net of time.

After dinner Polly set off for Rufford with Boz. As she crossed the ford she looked upstream toward the mill race, and saw, ankle deep in the water, a small boy and girl, one with a jam jar, the other with a net.

"Could it be . . . . ?" she wondered.

They stood dappled by the sunlight that filtered through the overhanging trees. The girl certainly had an old-fashioned look in her grey dress with a white smock over, and the boy's knee length trousers, tied round the waist with twine, were baggy, as if several sizes too big for him. As she watched and wondered, they looked up and saw her. They paused for a moment, then turned and scampered off in a shower of spray.

"Must've been," she thought. "Why else would they run off?"

And as she turned into Rufford she wondered again where was the entry to that secret village? A tunnel seemed most likely, one that looked, perhaps, like any ordinary hole in the ground.

"I wonder if *you* know." She eyed Boz. "If you really were Baggins, you might've been down there. Boz – find a hole – find!"

He tore off. Polly had to run fast to catch up with him, and when she did so she saw that he had run to the foot of an old tree stump, and his plumed tail was waving furiously.

"It's a kind of burrow!" Polly exclaimed with delight.

"Dig, Boz, dig!"

Snorting, he disappeared half way into the opening, and threw back earth with his front paws. Back he came again – but not before Polly had glimpsed daylight through the other side of the stump.

"Here – let me look!"

Boz backed out and Polly stooped and peered. She was right. The tunnel went straight from one side to the other of the stump.

"Never mind," she said. "See if you can find another. Hole, Boz, hole!"

He *did* find another – and another, and another. It was clearly a favourite pursuit of his.

Polly decided to abandon the search for a secret tunnel.

"Though it's still a mystery!" she said out loud. "Must be *somewhere* they come and go."

By now she was on the lake path, and looking up saw what she had never seen there before – a boat.

"Didn't think boats were allowed," she told Boz, who was drinking greedily at the water's edge. "Just for ducks, and such, I thought this lake was."

It was a small wooden rowing boat, unpainted and shabby. And seated in it were two small figures, and suddenly Polly was alert and straining to see them better. They looked like the children she had seen earlier fishing in the ford stream. They were rowing, it seemed, towards the largest of the islands. Polly kept pace with them along the bank, and came to the point where she could see right through the curious arched tunnel that ran from one side to the other.

"That's that tunnel I've wondered about," said Polly to Boz. "*Now* what'll they do?"

The little boat turned.

"Going into it!"

She watched. Now the boat was in the gloom of the arch, the figures of the children barely more than outlines against the light beyond. And then – gone! One minute they were there – the next, gone!

Polly blinked hard and rubbed her eyes.

"Gone? Can't've gone! But where – ? Quick, Boz, round to the other side!"

She ran as fast as she could along the bank, over the little wooden bridge, past the smallest island and right to the spot where she could see light through the tunnel, see straight through.

She stood breathless and scanned incredulously the whole wide, bare expanse of lake.

"Vanished – into thin air!" she exclaimed. And then, very slowly, "Or – out of time!"

The answer seemed so simple. What was it that Old Mazy had said, more than once?

"Water always finds its own level."

The boat and the children had effortlessly slipped into another time and another place. She stood and she stared and she shivered with a long, cold thrill of excitement that was half fearful.

"You'd best just go round back where you were, Polly," she told herself. "Just to make absolutely *positive* sure."

But she was already sure in her bones, even as she retraced her steps, and not in the least surprised to find the water beyond the island innocent of anything more than a brood of ducks. They swam slowly and calmly, each leaving a clear and separate V in its wake.

"And now – where are *my* gypsies?" wondered Polly Flint. "Anywhere, they could be. Like finding a needle in a haystack, or a pin in a pint of peas."

It was, in fact, to prove nothing like so difficult, because it happened that the Time Gypsies were looking for *her,* and at that very moment were no more than a few yards away.

"Aooch!" she squealed, as something touched her arm – a little dirty hand in a raggedy sleeve.

"Hist!" Granny Porter tugged hard on Polly's arm. "Here! Come you here!" And then the ragged creature got behind and pushed her, with little rude shoves.

Polly allowed herself to be nudged and pulled into a little thicket. There she saw Sam and Gil sitting, with Babby Porter lying on the ground between them. They looked unsmilingly up at her.

"You bad bad gel, you bad bad gel!" Granma Porter gave Polly a series of little sharp prods and slaps – she was fairly dancing with fury.

Polly shrank back out of her reach.

"Why? Why? What've I done?"

"What've you done? What've you done – *you* know what you've done. You bad bad gel, you bad bad gel!"

It was as if she would have gone on for ever, pinching and slapping, had not Gil said:

"Leave her *be*, Granny!"

"Yes, *leave* her, Granny Porter, do!" cried Sam. "If she's more power than you – *then* where'll we all be?"

The old woman gave Polly a final shove and stood back, breathless. She shook her fist.

"All night!" she shrieked. "All night! Dew in my boots, dew in my shawl – aches pains and horrible screws in every joint – toes ankles knees elbows – "

"What do you *mean*?" interrupted Polly desperately.

"Now don't you go playing Pretty Polly with me," she retorted. "*You* know what you've done – if you didn't, you couldn't have done it!"

Polly was still trying to work out the meaning of this enigmatic utterance when Gil said,

"We don't *know* she did it. Now hold off her, do, will you? My head's fair splitting."

Polly looked at him. He did indeed look pale. He had a tired, unshaven look such as she had sometimes seen Tom wear when he came for breakfast after the night shift.

Grandma Porter gave a final flap of her shrubbery sleeve in the direction of Polly, and turned her back. Polly, left facing the bonnet, was at a loss how to address it.

"We've been here all night," said Sam. "All night – d'you know that?"

"But why? And what's that to do with me?"

"It's to do with summat," said Gil. "That is certain. But it was bound to come to this, I suppose, in the end. All that patched up half-baked guesswork witchcraft."

"You watch your tongue, Gil Porter," warned the bonnet.

"I don't necessarily say you," he said. "Though it's as likely you as another of 'em."

"'Tain't, 'tain't," came a muttering from the bonnet. "Proper, I am."

"I'm afraid," said Polly, "that I don't know what anybody's talking about."

"Ah, well," said Gil. "It's a long story. It's to do with a village called Grimstone – "

"I've heard of that!" put in Polly eagerly.

"And how an old woman happened on a book of spells – "

"Me!" croaked the bonnet. "Me! I found it!"

"Found a book of spells," repeated Gil wearily, "and instead of keeping her trap shut, went blabbing all round the village, until next we knew, there was every woman in the place writing down spells and charms and runes – just as if they was recipes, and every one of 'em fancying herself a witch, every one of 'em."

"And then – come May Day – whoosh!" Sam threw up his arms. "Dancing round the maypole, dancing the Gypsy's Tent and – whoosh!"

"What?" cried Polly eagerly. "Whoosh what?"

He shrugged.

"That's just it. There's no one knows – or least, if they do know, won't tell. Only thing certain is – we slipped the net of time."

"Though there is some rules," said Gil. "Like we can only slip back into time between May Day and Midsummer's Eve."

"And like we can only slip back into time betwixt dawn and sunset," added Sam.

"And that we must never touch bread or morsel from the folks in time," said Gil, "else we stop in time for ever."

"Like Baggins!" Polly cried. "Because I fed him!"

"That's it, exact," Gil nodded. "But *us* – we ain't touched no food, not one of us."

"Not a crumb, not a crumb!" The bonnet now wheeled about. "So why, tell us why, tell us why!" Three times her grimy forefinger stabbed toward Polly.

"Why what?" she faltered.

"Why," said Gil grimly, *"we couldn't get back last even."*

"Got in the ferry boat same as usual," Sam said.

"And into the Time Tunnel, and next thing we knew, we were out the other side – and still *here!*"

"'Twas lucky we'd brought a crust or two with us," said Gil. "Else not even Babby Porter here'd have had never a bite."

"And all night long," said Sam, his voice hushed and fearful, "we lay listening for the Catcher!"

"Every snap, every rustle!" shrieked Granny Porter. "Shiver and shake from dusk to dawn, aches and pains and screws in the joints!"

"I'm sorry, I really am!" cried Polly. "But I can't think it's anything to do with me!"

Gil heaved a deep sigh.

"Aye, well," he said, "they'll maybe manage to get us out. They'll be babbling and casting around down there, every woman jill of 'em, and maybe one of 'em'll hit on a way."

"Whist!" hissed the old woman. "There's one of the rules you ain't told." She lowered her voice and thrust her head nearer to Gil's. "You know the one!"

"Ah!" He shook his head. "Only *think* that's a rule, Granny. It's not certain."

"I'll tell her," Sam said. "But just a minute, first."

He got to his feet and moved a few yards away from them among the trees.

"Baggins – here!"

Immediately Boz-Baggins ran to him and stood wagging his tail.

"There!" he said triumphantly. "See that?"

"Boz!" called Polly, jealous. Back he ran.

"See?" she said to Sam.

"Came to me of his own free will," said Sam deliberately. He was not talking to Polly, but to the others.

"Aye, he did," Gil agreed.

"He goes to anyone, if they call him," said Polly defensively.

Gil looked her straight in the eye.

"We *think*," he said slowly, "think, mind you, that if one living being from above earth would come willing with us into the Time Tunnel, then we should be back in Grimstone again."

"Try the dog! We'll try the dog!" screeched Granny Porter.

Polly stepped back quickly.

"No!" she cried. "No, you shan't!"

She looked at the three faces, and was frightened by the intentness she read there. She spun on her heels and fled, calling "Boz! Boz!"

He raced ahead of her, and she heard shouts behind, "Baggins! Baggins!" and knew that the others were in pursuit.

And so Polly Flint fled blindly through her kingdom, as eager now to escape the Time Gypsies as she had ever been to pursue them.

Chapter Six

Once she was safely back, Polly's conscience began to nag. She kept seeing glimpses of the Time Gypsies' faces, tired and white, and even, in Sam's case, scared.

"And poor little Babby Porter," she thought. "Will he *die*, I wonder, if he don't get back?"

She asked herself this and a hundred other questions, and did not know the answers to any of them.

"There are times," she thought, "when I think I ought to stop meddling with time!" – and the relentlessly counting clock in the hall seemed to echo the thought.

Every now and then she wondered whether it *was* all her fault, but each time pushed the thought away.

"Not my fault. None of it – all the fault of them silly women, trying to be witches, when they're not!"

All the same she plucked up courage to say to Aunt Em when she came to say goodnight:

"Aunt Em .... I know it's a silly question. But has .... has there ever been any witches in the family?"

Aunt Em drew a very heavy sigh.

"I sometimes wonder," she said wearily, "I really do, whatever daft notion you'll come up with next. No. There has not. And nor will there ever be, there being no such things, as you know as well as I."

"No, Aunt Em," said Polly, and was for once pleased with her aunt's reply.

"Nowt to do with *me*, then," she thought, as she settled herself to sleep. "And they're not even my friends, not really. They wanted to take Boz – and they shan't!"

But she could not sleep. She kept picturing the Time Gypsies out there somewhere in the dark, spending a second night away from home, trying to sleep, but listening for every tiny sound that might mean the approach of The Catcher.

"It'll be pitch dark," she thought, "and owls hooting, and all the little creatures scurrying out from under the banks. And they can't escape. They're prisoners in time." And then she thought, "Dad – he's a prisoner, too. He's just as much a prisoner as them, lying there in that high white bed, never to walk and never to fish."

When at last she fell asleep she dreamed. She dreamed that as the Time Gypsies lay sleeping, that terrible shadowy figure of The Catcher came striding through the woods and discovered them. And how he netted them – first Babby Porter, and then the others, one by one. And as he netted them he threw them into that barred dungeon deep in the woods, and gloated as they cried, "Let us out! Let us out!"

In there, too, were all the other timeless children, the May Dancers, who had played hide and seek with her among the trees, and danced in her honour.

"Let us out, let us out!" they pleaded.

And then, incredibly, another face appeared behind the grille, and it was that of Tom, vainly trying to wrest the iron bars apart as the children flapped vainly about him like imprisoned butterflies.

"Poor little things! Poor little things!" Polly woke crying, and her cheeks were wet with tears.

For a time she lay there, remembering it all. Then, as she came slowly to, she became aware of a light, soft pattering, a rustling and whispering. She knelt up to draw back the curtain, and saw the window beaded with rain. It was falling steadily in the early grey light, and spattered in puddles that already lay black or silver as the light struck them.

"Oh no!" she gasped, dismayed. "They've been out all night, in this!"

She dressed rapidly and went down, sticking out her tongue at the maddening clock as she passed it. Aunt Em already sat at the table, sipping tea.

"Good morning, Aunt Em," she said.

"Not very," she returned. "There's a letter on your plate."

Polly opened it.

"Dear Poll," she read, "you'll know this writing as your mother's, but the words are mine. I'm still lying here the wrong way up, but now the doctors have done something, and they think I will be better. To stand, I mean, Poll, and to walk again . . ."

She read no further.

"Aunt Em!" she cried. "He's going to walk! Dad's going to walk!"

"Well, I should be pleased to think so," said Aunt Em, who was not easily moved to joy, nor indeed any strong emotion. "But don't go counting chickens. Only *might*, it says in my letter."

"But he will," said Polly stubbornly. "I know my Dad."

129

She read on.

"You'll have to take me then to that lake of yours, and I can maybe tell you the names of some of them birds of yours. I've still got my own birds in my own head, and always shall, I hope, but it'll be a right pleasure to see some real ones."

Aunt Em's voice interrupted.

"You'll not be thinking of going down Rufford in all this wet?"

"Oh, I shall!" said Polly swiftly. "I get a big enjoyment in rain!"

"Then you've a different idea of enjoyment from mine."

"But what I thought was," said Polly, launching her plan, "that I'd go round knocking some more with the pram, first. There's lots of houses not done yet."

"But the stuff'd get wet," objected Aunt Em.

"Not if I lay something over it," said Polly. "And I could take an umbrella. We collected some umbrellas first time round."

Aunt Em hesitated. Polly held her breath, and listened to the clock. The success of her scheme depended on the answer.

"It would be a help," Aunt Em admitted. "And I suppose a spot of rain won't do any harm, at your age."

"Oh, thank you, Aunt Em!" cried Polly joyously. Aunt Em looked startled at this reaction.

So Polly, wearing her oilskins, set off round the village, pushing the enormous pram, and Boz trotted by her side. Aunt Em had been dubious about allowing this, given the probable state of his paws when he returned, and had finally agreed, Polly guessed, because she was nervous of being left alone with him.

Polly enjoyed knocking on doors and making her request.

"What we *particularly* want," she said at each house, "are warm clothes, rugs or blankets, and umbrellas."

Then she would add, "It's for a very good cause."

And so it was, of course. It was, in her opinion, for a much better cause than the W.I. . . At many houses she was told what a good girl she was to work so hard, especially in the rain, and given biscuits, sweets and chocolates. These she pushed into her pockets.

The rain came faster. Polly pushed up a big old umbrella that was not without leaks, but served to keep the contents of the pram relatively dry. Nobody was about, it seemed a ghost village. Even the bench by the Red Lion was empty. But she did see Davey Cole. He had a catapult, and was aiming at the maypole.

"Wouldn't do that if he knew what *I* know," thought Polly.

He looked up, saw her, and stared.

"Look at that!" he shouted to the deserted green. "What you got in there? Rags and bones?"

Polly looked straight ahead and walked on.

"Rags and bones may break your bones, but words will hurt you never," she quoted inaccurately to herself.

"Polly Flint, always skint! Polly Flint, always skint!" he yelled after her.

"Lot *he* knows about rhyming!" she thought. Then she heard the shrill voice of a woman, and looked back

131

over her shoulder to see Davey being called back into the house by his mother.

This was very fortunate for Polly, because she wanted no witnesses for what was to happen next. She looked over her shoulders, left and right. A car splashed by. She began rapidly to push the pram beyond the last house in the village and towards the ford that she would have to cross to reach Rufford.

The wooden footbridge was too narrow for the pram, so Polly had to push it through the ford, the water perilously near the top of her wellingtons. She needed both hands to force the wheels against the weight of the water, so balanced the umbrella precariously on top of the pram.

Then she was over. She ran the few remaining yards with the umbrella swaying wildly, and then was within the shelter of the trees.

She stood for a moment debating with herself which direction to take. She decided that as the tunnel that ran through the largest island was their only lifeline, the Time Gypsies would not have strayed far out of sight of it.

She pushed the pram up the lakeside path, and began to walk towards the island. And as she did so, she slowly became aware that never before had her world been quite so particularly secret, and hers and hers alone. The rain dripped steadily from bough to earth, the surface of the lake was pewter and puckered, all its reflections gone. And as she gazed ahead, blinking through the rain, it seemed to Polly that she could herself at this very moment have gone hundreds of years back in time, and never would know it. There was not one thing, one single sign, to tell her that she was in the twentieth century. Trees, water, birds floating and flying, whitish sky and silvery fall of rain – all were timeless, unchanging, usual as the very air she breathed.

So strongly did this thought come upon her, that she actually stopped, and searched the distances for some sign that she had not herself somehow and by some haphazard magic slipped the net of time. With relief she saw the metallic tower of a pylon, and the reassuring lines of wires. She walked on.

She stopped level with the Time Tunnel and could see straight through to the other side, despite the curtain of rain. Then, out of nothing, appeared the shape of a boat, of figures rowing. It came out of the murky tunnel and into the wide daylight. Polly was witnessing in reverse the very magic she had seen the day before. On impulse, she pulled the pram off the path and in among the trees, and crouched there beside it, one hand on Boz's chain. She heard only the steady pattering of rain, and then, faintly, the creak of rowlocks, the splash of oars.

Craning, she watched as the little boat drew in to the bank. Two children clambered out – bare armed, bare legged in the rain, wearing only the little ragged tunics she had seen them in on the day they had danced for her, by the Silver Pool. They made fast the boat, took from it a small bundle, and disappeared from view.

Polly straightened up. She looked at the pram and hesitated. Then her eye fell on Boz.

"Stay!" she commanded in a whisper. "Stay – and guard!"

She walked away. There was no tell tale clink of

chain that would have meant Boz was following her.

"I *knew* he could do anything I told him," she thought. "Told that Davey Cole so!"

She moved from tree to tree, always alert for sound or movement. She caught a glimpse of bluish grey, and then the flash of limbs. From where she hid she watched the two children noiselessly flitting back the way they had come, toward the lake.

Polly was torn between following them, watching them row out and witnessing again that strange vanishing under that magical arch, and searching for the stranded trio who were surely hidden somewhere near.

"I'll go back and get Boz and the pram," she decided. "Then watch 'em go. 'Tain't every day you see folks disappear. Then go and find others. Best of both worlds."

She found Boz still sitting patiently by the laden pram.

"You needn't ever think," she told him, "I'll let them Time Gypsies have *you*."

The pair stood side by side watching the little boat swing to enter that mysterious no-man's-land that lay greenish and silent beyond the mouth of the tunnel.

"No man's water," murmured Polly. And then the boat vanished.

> *"Under the tunnel of time they go*
> *To the secret village way below."*

Slowly she shook her head, and turned her back on the lake to scan the woods. Pushing her way through soaked foliage she found the hollow where yesterday they had hidden.

"Gone from there," she thought. "But not much farther off, I should think. Not far from that tunnel."

She was right. The Time Gypsies had evidently been alerted to her approach by the unwieldy and noisy presence of the pram.

"Baggins! Here – Baggins!"

Polly, loosening her hold on the pram handle, saw Sam's face peering from a nearby thicket, disembodied, like that of the Cheshire cat. She raced after Boz-Baggins, terrified that he might be kidnapped – or dognapped – and used as a kind of time hostage by the desperate trio.

She burst into the clearing where the Time Gypsies had hidden themselves. It had at first sight a curiously homelike and sheltered look. A large, whitish outcrop of rock formed one solid wall, the others being of tightly interlaced boughs and undergrowth. The overhanging trees formed a roof of sorts. All this Polly took in only as an impression, there being no opportunity for a closer inspection.

Granny Porter was up in arms in the instant.

"That dog!" she shrieked. "Lay hold of that tricksy creature, can't you, Gil? Catch him! Catch him!"

Boz was jumping joyously and unafraid around Sam and Gil, and Polly felt a pang.

"He *has* been theirs," she thought, "wherever or whenever they found him."

She advanced into the clearing and stood awkwardly, hardly knowing how to manage the encounter.

"It's only me," she said unnecessarily. "Are you all right?"

"We're managing," said Gil.

"That we ain't!" shrilled Granny Porter. "The

135

things you say! I ain't been wuss in years – I ain't been wuss in *hundreds* of years!"

Here she fixed Polly with a challenging glare.

"Let's see what we have here," Gil said. "This'll maybe cheer you, Granny."

She snorted, to indicate the unlikelihood of any such thing, and shuffled and shrugged within her tattered plumage. Gil, meanwhile, was unwrapping a cloth-bound bundle that Polly recognized as the one the children had brought out of the boat. The folds fell away to reveal a round, crusty loaf, a lump of cheese, some flat brown scones or pancakes, eggs, and two earthenware flagons.

Sam, at any rate, cheered visibly. He reached out for the loaf, tore a piece away, and began to ram it into his mouth, at the same time breaking off morsels of cheese and stuffing them in after.

Almost simultaneously out grabbed a grimy, leather-mittened hand, and Granny Porter was feeding with the same greed and rapidity. The pair of them sat with bulging cheeks and smacking lips, and Polly watched and wondered what Aunt Em would make of their table manners. Gil, meanwhile, uncorked the stoneware flagons, and sniffed at each.

"Cider!" he said, and then, "Milk! Come you on here, then, Babby Porter!"

He reached and picked up the baby and put the narrow neck of the jar to his lips. A noisy sucking ensued. The Porters were, Polly decided, the noisiest eaters she had ever encountered.

As she stood watching this strange feast, a sudden thought struck her. She put a hand in either pocket and pulled out the haul of goodies she had saved from her rounds.

"Here!" She held them out. "Look – you can have 'em! Biscuits, look, and chocolate, and – "

She broke off. Granny Porter, her cheeks still bulging, and rendered incoherent by crumbs, was making muffled noises and stabbing her finger towards Polly's outspread palms. At last, as the rest watched, mystified, she swallowed hard and screamed.

"Ware crusts! Ware crumbs! Ware goodies!"

Then Polly remembered. "Take neither crust nor crumb from mortal hand."

"Oh!" She clenched her fists and snatched them back. Slowly she loosened them, and the contents fell to the ground, where Boz took a lively interest in them. "I'm sorry – I forgot! I never meant – "

"Want you ever to get back?" Granny Porter, ignoring Polly, was leaning toward Sam, who was still made speechless by quantities of bread and cheese, and merely nodded vigorously in reply.

"She's slippery!" hissed Granny Porter. "She's cunning!"

"I'm not! Look!" Polly looked about her and then stamped, vigorously and deliberately, on the scattered sweets and biscuits. "I forgot, didn't I? Anyone can forget. I never meant – "

"How she got the dog," said Gil slowly.

"And how she means to get *us*!" Sam supplied, through a mouth now miraculously emptied.

Polly looked at them, all three.

"I *never* meant that," she said at last. "I never meant anything, except to be friends. *I* don't belong here, any more than you do. And all I wanted – "

She broke off. She felt the rise of shaming tears.

"*Anyway*," she said. "Look at these, and see if you want 'em!"

She pushed her way out of the clearing to where stood the laden pram, umbrellas hanging rakish and askew. It looked so unlikely, so absolutely foreign among all the wild greenery that she giggled, despite herself.

"Jumble!" she said. "For the W.I.!" And then, "Women's Institute – or Witches' Institute!"

With difficulty she manoeuvred the pram under the spreading boughs. As she and it burst together into the secret clearing all three Time Gypsies, their hunger now evidently satisfied, looked towards her, with gratifying interest and astonishment.

"There!" exclaimed Polly triumphantly. "What do you think of *that*?"

The ensuing silence seemed to indicate that they thought little – or nothing – of that. Their looks expressed only extreme mystification.

"It's all for *you*!" cried Polly. "For while you're stuck up here, in the wood. Look!"

And she started to toss the items from the pram, one by one.

"Rug – blanket – got a few holes, but it don't matter – another rug – cushion – what's this? Oh, dressing gown – that'll be handy. Another rug, umbrella, umbrella, umbrella. Might have holes, but *all* the rain can't come in through them. *Another* cushion – ever so comfy you can be now!"

She paused. The pram was empty now, and the Time Gypsies were surveying her with unwinking –

but uncomprehending – gaze. She looked back at them.

"Oh, don't look at me so!" she half sobbed. "Can't you see I'm on your side?"

"*Them*," said Granny Porter, jerking her head towards the heap of jumble on the ground, "is home things, living things, *stopping* things."

"And we ain't stopping!" Sam cried. "We ain't!"

"But they'll do till you get back," said Polly. "You can be warm and comfy."

"What's warm, what's comfy?" snapped Granny Porter. "And what's *those*!"

She gestured towards the heap, then got up, slowly and complainingly. She shuffled over to the pile and picked up an umbrella. She twirled it, this way and that, held it aloft, where it was poised for an instant, and then brought it down – thwack – on a bed of nettles.

"Not a wand," she said to herself, "not a wand – but what?"

"Look – I'll show you!"

Polly picked up another umbrella. The others watched as she pushed it open.

"Magic!" exclaimed Sam, in awe.

"*No!*" cried Polly. "To keep the rain off – look!"

She held the umbrella above her head, and the heavy drops of rain that penetrated the roof of overhanging trees spattered heavily and noisily upon it.

"Keep Babby Porter dry!" she said, and placed the opened umbrella over him, where he lay, wide eyed and placid after his recent feed.

"There!" Polly turned toward her audience. "He'll be kept dry now, you see."

"I do believe he will," said Gil slowly.

"Sticks isn't *meant* to open out like mushrooms!" Granny Porter was not to be won over thus easily. "*I've* never see a stick open out, I never!"

"There's one here." Sam picked another from the heap. "Is this one?"

"I'll show you," offered Polly eagerly. And she pushed his finger up so that the umbrella unfurled, and he looked disbelievingly up at the multi-coloured spread of it, and was clearly enchanted by it, and began to caper about, crying, "It's a rain shield, it's a rain shield!"

"Umbrella," said Polly.

"Umbrella," he echoed, "a rain shield umbrella!"

"Hist you and hush you up!" Granny Porter was on her feet now, dodging back and forth to wrench the handle from his grasp. "Let it go, let it go – there!"

She tugged it from his hand, and as she did so, a spoke bent and broke.

"No – oh, now you've broke it!"

"Never mind," said Polly. "I've got another – and another."

She pulled them from the pile to prove it. But again a silence and a wariness had fallen upon the Time Gypsies.

"Safe from rain," said Gil. "But it's not rain that threatens."

They looked at him then, all three, while Babby Porter, forgotten, gazed at his bright new canopy.

"Time that threatens," said Gil. "What's to keep us safe from time?"

"And the Catcher," put in Sam.

"Oh, what'll become of us, what'll become of us."

Granny Porter rocked back and forth, dismal and fraught.

"I wish I'd never come!" burst out Sam. "I wish I'd stopped and never come out of Grimstone at all!"

"*That's* not true, Sam," said Gil. "All the children come into time, at the May Dancing. Like moths to the flame the children run, century in and century out."

"Is that true?" asked Polly, wondering. "Do you always come? Every May Day there has been?"

"Always," he replied. "Leastways, always the children. It's part of the spell – or seems to be."

"I think it's a marvellous magic," Polly said, "for a village to be there, way down below, and the children dancing and the bells ringing – and do you know, I've *heard* them bells, heard 'em, with my own ears!"

"And so you might," nodded Gil, "for ring they do."

"But my Aunt Em don't hear them," said Polly, "and nobody else, that I know of. My Aunt Em don't even believe you're there!"

"Then your Aunt Em's a silly old woman!" said Sam.

"*She'd* never believe you could skip in and out of time," Polly said. "And she's got a clock, a great big clock, and all day long and all night long it ticks the loudest tick you've ever heard – tick tock tick tock till it nearly drives me silly!"

They were listening now, intent and unsmiling.

"My Aunt Em," Polly went on, encouraged, "is the biggest believer in time I have ever met. And that clock – the one I told you about – has never lost *one single second*! Can you believe it?"

141

"A Catcher," Gil looked uncertainly at the others. "Another Catcher?"

"Oh, she's not *magic*!" Polly cried. "Not Aunt *Em*! She sat right next to you," turning to Granny Porter, "and never even knew!"

"I never said magic," Gil said. "I said Catcher."

"Who – who is The Catcher?" Polly was timid now, treading on dangerous ground. "I think I've seen him – I know I have, striding, with a great net. But why does he come? Why does he – ?"

"The Catcher," said Gil, "is the one who comes and who would have us all trapped in the net of time. As long as we run free – as long as the children of Grimstone run free as they do, in and out of days, in and out of years – "

"Then he'll *snatch*!" screamed Granny Porter. "He'll run and he'll chase and he'll *snatch*, till he has us all tangled again in the net of time!"

"I think I see," said Polly Flint slowly. "I think I've been seeing for a long time now – ever since I saw that angel. I saw a coal miner as well, for that matter, and I saw things in the fields there back home, and heard voices in the woods. And now I'm seeing you, and I know you're real, and a million Aunt Ems couldn't tell me you're not."

She looked round and saw that all three of them, except Babby Porter, of course, were listening, really listening for perhaps the first time since she had met them.

"In fact," she finished, "my Aunt Em is so locked up in time, so trapped, she can't see and she can't hear and she don't believe *owt*!"

"Could it," said Gil, "could it be that her *clock* has us caught?"

Granny Porter shook her head to and fro.

"If you think it is," said Polly, "I'll stop it, I will. Though I daresay she'd kill me, when she found out."

Sam suddenly stood up.

"I reckon I like her," he said, meaning Polly. He looked directly at her. "It's not your fault. I know it's not."

"Oh thank you!" cried Polly. "Thank you!"

"There's no need playing silly sweethearts!" snapped Granny Porter.

"Shall you come for a walk alonger me?" Sam asked Polly.

"Oh yes, yes!"

"You stop 'em, Gil," ordered Granny Porter.

"I shan't stop 'em," said Gil. "No harm to be done."

As Polly and Sam pushed their way out of the clearing they could hear Granny Porter's complaining croon.

"No harm done, but harm to come . . . no harm done, but harm to come . . ."

The voice faded. They stopped, looked at one another, and smiled.

"Don't she rattle!" said Sam. "Don't she just *rattle*!"

"Worse than my Aunt Em," said Polly. "And I never thought anybody could be that."

They walked on a little through the drenched woods, and there was a healing silence. Only the birds spoke, and the trees.

"Wish my Mam was here," said Sam, at length.

"Your Mam?" Polly was taken aback. "Oh – I didn't know! I thought – "

"Down there, still," he said mournfully. "Never came up with us. Said she'd milking to do."

Polly looked at the beautifully calm and reflecting lake and thought, "Think – *cows* under there! Not reflecting cows, but proper – with milk to give!"

Aloud, she said, "*Shall* you ever get back, do you think?"

"Oh, don't say that!" He was aghast. "Don't say it!"

"I'd help you," Polly said. "Any way I could. And my Mam and Dad, when they get back. They would."

They were climbing the stone steps that led to the wide lawns in front of the Abbey. Here and there were stone statues and urns, and Polly caught sight of two slight figures mounted and swaying on a plinth.

"Oh – look!"

Sam followed her pointing finger.

"It's Tommy and Jess!"

He began to race off towards them. Polly felt cut off. She was in one world, she felt, and he in another. She saw then, on a seat nearby, a woman with an easel, painting. As Polly watched, the woman looked up, directly at the statue where Tommy and Jess were entwined, and then back to her canvas.

"That statue . . ." Polly thought. "She's painting that statue . . . ."

She looked at the Time Gypsies, waving now toward the approaching Sam, and then again at the painter.

"Does she see 'em? Chance to find out . . . After all, ain't *sure* Aunt Em didn't see Granny Porter . . ."

144

Polly advanced slowly towards the artist, and just then she looked up, saw Polly, and smiled.

"Can I look?" Polly asked, and it was the hugest question she had ever asked in her life.

The woman nodded.

Polly approached and looked, half expectant, half fearful. What she saw was a painting of the lawn and trees beyond, and the very statue where now the Time Gypsies were swaying and climbing, but not a sign of any human being.

"It's very good," Polly said.

"Thank you."

"Er – didn't you want to put them in, then?"

"Put what in, dear?"

"I mean – well – don't you bother putting people in?" Polly was hard put to frame her question tactfully. "I'm not very good at drawing people, either."

The woman laughed.

"If there were any to *put* in!"

Polly heard voices and laughter and looked back toward the statue, to see that now dozens of Time Gypsy children – or so it seemed – were converging on the statue from all sides. Some of them danced and fiddled as they came, others ran ahead to form a ring about the statue.

"She don't see them," Polly thought. "Or hear them. She really don't. And what *that* means, is that they *ain't* here even if they *are* . . ."

She shook her head.

"You work *that* out, Polly Flint!" she told herself. At that moment Sam cupped his hands to his mouth and bawled,

"Baggins! Baggins! Here!"

Boz-Baggins tore off over the wide lawn, haloed in a spray of raindrops.

"What has your dog seen, I wonder?" said the artist, startled. "A rabbit, perhaps."

"I expect so," Polly agreed. "He's very keen on rabbits."

But to herself, she thought, "Rummest-looking lot of rabbits *I've* ever seen!"

She watched as Boz-Baggins ran from one Time Gypsy to the other, wagging his tail and even jumping up.

"He really is behaving very oddly," she heard the woman say.

"Oh! Oh – he's always like that. Daft as a brush! I'll go and fetch him. Thanks for letting me see your painting. Goodbye!"

She started off to join the others, but as she approached the Time Gypsies scattered as swiftly as they had assembled, and by the time she reached the statue, only Sam was left.

"Why've they all run off?" she asked.

Sam shrugged.

"Scared."

"Of *me*?"

"You can see 'em, see. They ain't used to that. Taken *me* some getting used to. And with us four getting stuck, they think it's to do with you."

"I keep telling you, it's not!"

"I dunno," Sam said. "Not o' purpose you didn't, anyhow."

Polly became aware of voices again, and laughter, and she turned to see that the Time Gypsy children were crowding around the artist and her easel, while she painted on, oblivious.

"Just you look at *that*!" Polly exclaimed. "And hark at the noise, blowing through leaves! It's as hard for me as it is for you. I can't *believe* that she don't see and hear them!"

"Would you help?" asked Sam suddenly. "Really help?"

"Of course, I want to."

"Not just bringing blankets, and such," he said. "Really help."

Polly glanced sideways at him, and saw how serious he was.

"What do you mean?" She was half fearful.

'What Granny Porter said yesterday ... about someone from above earth going willingly into the Time Tunnel ..."

"Oh!" Polly gasped. "I don't know if I'd dare! What if I couldn't get back – then I'd be stuck, same as you! I'd have to stop in Grimstone for ever and ever!"

"I could marry you," he said simply. "You'd be all right."

Polly laughed delightedly, and then saw his hurt expression and immediately straightened her face.

"I'm not laughing at you," she said, "really I'm not. It's just the idea! And what about my Mam and Dad? They've only got me."

But Sam had gone stamping on ahead.

"Leave it!" his voice came. "We'll *live* under a bush all our lives, that's all!" He paused. "Not even all our lives – till The Catcher gets us!"

Polly ran and caught up with him, seizing her chance.

"And what will happen if he does?"

"Nobody knows. There's tales flown here and there

147

for hundreds of years." He lowered his voice. "There's some says that the minute that net drops over your head – pouff – you're gone! Gone to a pile of dust!"

"Oh no!" Polly was aghast.

"And there's others say that if once he nets a Time Gypsy, we're all finished, every one of us. It'll put all Grimstone under his spell, and – "

"Look!" Polly pointed toward the lake.

Sam followed the direction of her finger. There were four little boats crossing steadily from bank to island.

"What of it?" he said. He added bitterly, "Going back, *they* are."

"But there's four boats! Boats aren't allowed. Why don't the keeper stop 'em?"

"Because he don't *see* 'em, of course!"

"Don't see the children, I know that. But the boats!"

"You still don't understand, do you?" said Sam wearily.

Polly shook her head. Evidently she did not.

"Look," he told her, "the lake's the same place for you *and* us. Only the *time* that's different."

Polly stared.

"Of course!"

And she seemed to hear again old Mazy's voice: "Water always finds its own level . . . ."

When they returned to the clearing, Granny Porter's mood had not improved.

"She let you back, then?" she snapped.

"I saw the others, some of 'em," Sam told her.

148

"They'd messages."

"Messages?" screeched Granny Porter. "Messages? *They'll* not get us out!"

"Mam says to make sure Babby's his crust to chew on," Sam told Gil. "And says not to lose heart."

"I've lost heart," moaned Granny Porter, rocking her raggedy person to and fro. "Gone to turnip, my heart has. Drat that babby, drat it!"

Babby Porter had woken up and was crying again.

"It's all wickedness and woe, wickedness and woe! You can stand there, oh yes, all very well for you. You ain't stuck from home, and like to be for ever, oh no!"

"Yes I am, then!" cried Polly. "I *am* stuck away from home, *and* on my own. I've got sad things in my life, as well as you! And my dad was in an accident, and can't walk, and that's worse than *anything* that's happened to you!"

"There's no use your rattling on," said Granny Porter. "My old head don't work when that babby's bawling."

Polly had an inspiration.

"Shall I take him a walk?" she asked. "In the pram?"

They looked mystified.

"In that!" She pointed. "That's what it's for, really. Pushing babies in. It rocks them, and they go to sleep."

"You could run off with him," said Granny Porter. "Or feed him, like you did that dog."

"Oh I wouldn't, you know I wouldn't! Look – I'll leave Boz here with you, if you like – Baggins. Then you'll know I'll come back."

"She would, Granny," said Sam. "She wouldn't lose her dog for *that* squally lump."

149

"Go on, then!" she snapped. "Get off, get off!"

She turned her back. Sam picked up his fiddle and started to play, a slow, sad tune. Gil was staring into space as if in a dream.

"All right, I will!"

No one replied. The bow pulled mournful notes from the strings.

So Polly lined the pram with a rug, pulled out a cushion from the pile, and picked up Babby Porter, still squalling.

"You *are* a lump!" she told him, as she pulled the rug over him. Then, to the others, "I shan't be very long. Just long enough to get him back to sleep. Boz – stay!"

"He's all right," said Sam, without pause from his fiddling. "Come on, then, Baggins old lad."

Polly enjoyed pushing the pram now that it had a baby in it.

"Wonder how many hundreds of years old you are," she mused. "And another thing I wonder. If I was to meet somebody – would they see you and hear you? If not, they'd think I was plain daft, walking along and talking to an empty pram!"

The rain had stopped now and the sun came out so that the soaked grass and every leaf of every tree flashed and glittered. Polly's spirits rose.

"It ain't such a bad old world," she told Babby Porter. "My Dad's going to walk again, for practically certain positive! You might even get to *see* him, if he comes here soon!"

Babby Porter looked neither pleased nor displeased at this prospect. He simply lay and gazed up into Polly's face, and she found herself flattered by this.

"Least *you* like me," she told him, after a time. "And as for old Granny Porter, bet she don't like anybody. Same with my Aunt Em. Proper battleaxe she is."

But Babby Porter was not listening. His eyes were closed and he was breathing peacefully. Polly gave herself the entire credit for this, and carefully turned the pram to retrace her steps.

A shadow fell across the pram. Polly gave a little shriek and clapped a hand to her mouth. She was looking up into the smiling face of Old Mazy.

"Oh! You made me jump!" Her mind was working rapidly. Could he – would he – see the slumbering Babby Porter in the depths of the big hood?

"Giving someone a push, are you?" he asked.

Polly took a deep breath.

"Oh no! Don't even *know* any babbies – babies, I mean. Just some old rugs and that, for the Jumble."

He stooped from his enormous height and peered in. Polly held her breath. He straightened up again.

"You'll not collect a deal in *these* parts," he observed, eyeing her closely. "Not many doors to knock on here."

Polly's legs felt silly with relief. She started to push the pram on.

"Just having a bit of a walk, that's all," she called over her shoulder. "Got sick of collecting."

He did not reply. Polly dared not turn her head at first, and when at last she did, he had disappeared.

"Not following me, then," she thought. "Don't even know he *is* The Catcher, anyhow. Not for sure."

She hummed a little under her breath as she approached the clearing where the Time Gypsies were encamped. At last, she felt, they trusted her. They would never otherwise have let her go off with Babby Porter.

She pushed aside the overhanging leaves and was stung by a cold spray.

"Hallo!" she called. "Hallo! It's me!"

There was no reply. She was right through the thicket now. Her heart gave a tremendous lurch. The clearing was empty.

"Boz!" she called. "Boz – here!"

She looked about her and saw that the pile of rugs was still there, and the cushions and umbrellas and oddments of clothing.

"Where are they?" She spoke out loud. Then, "Oh! Oh no! The Catcher!"

She had a swift picture of that shadowy figure, net upraised. Old Mazy was abroad in the wood, that she knew.

"But he didn't see Babby Porter – least, didn't seem to."

She stood bewildered.

"Oh, where are you?" she cried desperately. "Where *are* you?"

She heard only the spattering of moisture from the soaked foliage.

"Lake's most likely," she thought. "I'll look. Can't leave *him* here, though. And can't go very fast, either, pushing that great pram."

For a moment she hesitated. Then she reached and picked up the pinkly slumbering Babby Porter, and began to run, through the thicket, past the bluebell acres and down to the edge of the lake.

She stood aghast.

"No!" she screamed. "No!"

There, in a wooden rowing boat, was Granny Porter, making for the island and the arch. And there, sitting in the bow like a figurehead, was Boz-Baggins.

Chapter Seven

That ferry to another time and another place went heedlessly over that bright water and there was nothing Polly Flint could do to stop it.

She screamed, "Stop! Stop!"

Granny Porter made not a sign. The boat went, slow and implacable, towards that fateful tunnel.

"You're a bad old woman!" Polly screamed. "A bad, wicked old woman! You come back!"

There was no reply. The bundle of tatters topped by the large bonnet was mute. Even Boz did not bark, or make any sign of recognition.

"Lost!" She was almost in tears. "He'll go under that tunnel, and then I'll never see him again!"

It was only Babby Porter's renewed squalling that reminded Polly that she had him – was, indeed, holding him.

"Left holding the baby!" She half smiled through her tears.

An idea struck her.

"You come back this minute," she yelled, "or I'll drop Babby Porter in the lake!"

She held him aloft to demonstrate the seriousness of the threat, but the boat was turning now by the island, only yards away from that eerily green arch.

"I mean it!"

Slowly the boat swung.

"Oh! She can't hear me!" Polly was sobbing in earnest now. "Oh – goodbye, Boz! Goodbye!"

She could not bear to watch. She could not bear to see him dissolve into air, and know him gone beyond call, forever. She turned away, half blinded by tears. They splashed on to the grubby face of Babby Porter, who cried anew.

"I didn't mean it," she told him, ashamed. "Don't cry. I shan't really drop you in the lake."

She fished for a hanky and dried his face, and then her own. Slowly she turned to face the lake again.

It was deserted, as she had known it would be. Only the wild birds went sailing, making their v-shaped wakes, or dipping and pecking and doing all the other things they did every day of the year. There was no sight, no sound, of the boat that was bearing Granny Porter and Boz-Baggins to another world, another time.

Polly turned and walked slowly away.

"Only had him for a bit," she thought, "but I'll never forget him, never."

Then her mind, numbed with shock, began to work again.

"But I've got him!" looking down at Babby Porter. "And where's the other two – Sam and Gil?"

They must, she decided, be already back in Grimstone.

"Went ahead and took Boz, then sent him back for Granny Porter."

Stunned as she was, she did not stop to wonder how Boz could have brought the boat back alone through the tunnel, and to the waiting Granny Porter on the bank.

"But what about Babby Porter? They'll be back for him, surely! Can't go leaving a baby behind!"

She had reached the clearing, and pushed her way through to where the pram stood.

"You really are a lump," she told Babby Porter as she lowered him into it. "My arms fair *ache!*"

He gazed up at her, content again.

"It's near time for my dinner," she told him. "Must be, by now. My Aunt Em'll be caterwauling. But what'll I do with you? If she do see you, she'll want to know where I got you from, that is for certain positive. You don't go fetching babies home like a bunch of bluebells.

"But if she doesn't see you, she might go dropping a heap of jumble right on top of you!"

Polly began to push the pram out of the thicket with no very clear idea of where she was going, or what she was going to do.

"And you'll get hungry soon," she told him. "And *then* what'll I do? If I feed you, then you'll stop in time forever. . . ."

She turned the matter over.

"My Mam and Dad might be pleased – always wanted a lot of children. Only thing is, where will I say I got you from? They'd never believe me, not in a million years. Not even my Dad, and he's a big believer in things. Even believed in my angel . . ."

She looked again at Babby Porter, cocooned in his grubby bundle.

"But he'd never swallow you!"

He gazed solemnly up at her.

"Crikey – wonder if you need your nappy changing?"

Babby Porter was becoming more of a liability by the minute.

"Oh dear!" Polly was close to tears again. "Don't know what time it is, but it must easily be dinner time. What'll I *do*? Oh, they have landed me! And I thought they was my friends. Thought Sam was, anyhow. They tricked me. They tricked me on purpose! I wish The Catcher *had* got 'em, I do! Serve 'em right!"

She stopped pushing. She had arrived, without realizing it, at the dark corner under the yews where stood the row of little animal graves. She went over and walked along the line.

"'Boris'," she read. "'Faithful friends are hard to find.' Oh, true – that's true it is, and I've lost you now, forever!"

She lifted her head and saw, half blinded by tears, a blurry black shape beyond the railings. She brushed her sleeve across her eyes and stared, incredulous.

There, sitting as he had been that day when she first found him, eyes fixed on her under that tufted fringe – was Boz.

"Oh!" she gasped. "Can't be!" And then, joyously, "Boz, Boz!"

Then he was at her feet, tail wagging furiously, licking her hands, and warm, solid and undeniably *there*!

"Oh Boz – I thought I'd lost you! Thought I'd never see you again! But where've you come from? Just saw you go under that tunnel, I did, with that mucky old woman. Can't be in two times at the same time, surely?"

He gazed up at her.

"Oh, if only dogs could speak! Couldn't be a Boz *and* a Baggins, could there? Twins?"

As she pondered the matter, a voice called:

"Baggins! Baggins!"

It was Sam's voice, close by. Polly, astounded, scrambled to her feet.

"Here!" she called. "Here, Sam!"

The next minute he was there, torn shirt and breeches and mud-stained face as usual. Polly's mind reeled.

"But I thought – I thought you'd – "

"Gone," he supplied. "I know. We heard you screaming."

"But how? Hadn't you gone into the Time Tunnel?"

"Not us," he said. "Only Granny. Couldn't stop her. She'd got Baggins and shoved off before we knew."

"Oh – oh, I'm *glad*!" Polly threw her arms about the startled Sam and kissed him, mud and all.

"Hold on now," he said, bashful and pulling free. "'Tain't mistletoe time!"

"'Tis for me! I can't believe it! I've got Boz back, and now you can take Babby Porter. Where's Gil?"

"Coming. He stopped over the other side of the lake, to wait on the boat coming."

"She went right through that arch, and straight out at the other side!" Polly laughed with delight. "And I never saw, because I had my eyes shut! Couldn't bear to see Boz disappear."

"All right for you to laugh," Sam said. "'Tain't you that's stuck."

"I'm only laughing because I'm glad you didn't trick me. That we're still friends."

"Listen!" Sam told her. "Oh – it's them."

Floating through the trees came the unmistakable voice of Granny Porter.

"Catched in the net, catched and caught! Dear dear oh deary me! Catched in the net, catched and caught and cooked!"

"Now hush you, Granny," they heard Gil say.

"She's a bad old woman, that Granny Porter," said Polly. "She would've got off and taken Boz, if she could."

"She's bad on top," Sam conceded. "But not underneath."

The familiar bunch of walking shrubbery, topped by its tattered bonnet, was in sight now.

"Here!" Sam called.

The bonnet lifted. Granny Porter's eyes looked straight into Polly's, and the strangest thing happened.

The little grimy fingers in their leather mitts clutched at Gil's sleeve, and the bonnet came down again, and "Oh, she'll scold and scratch, scold and scratch out my eyes! I'm frightened and feared, frightened and feared!"

"Of *me?*" thought Polly Flint. "Can she mean me?"

"I'm a bad old woman, I am, I am," wailed the bobbing bonnet. "I ought to be pelted and pinched and ducked!"

"What does she mean, 'ducked'?" whispered Polly.

"In the lake. Ducking stool."

"But she's old!" Polly was shocked.

Sam shrugged.

"Been ducked times a-plenty, she has," he said. "Bound to be – a tongue like hers! 'Sides – the wash don't do her any harm!"

Then, in an instant and a flurry of rags, Granny Porter was right by Polly, clutching at her with her tiny hands.

"Oh deary, oh deary, I'm sorry, I am!" she wailed. "I'm a bad old woman, I am! But don't let 'em duck me!"

"Oh, *poor* Granny Porter!" Polly turned to Gil. "You won't let them, will you?"

He made a gesture that seemed to mean that he had no say in the matter, one way or the other.

"I know I'm bad," whimpered the derelict bonnet. "But I'm an old woman, and I hankered so to be back by my hearth in Grimstone. I'm frit here, frit!"

As Polly stood awkwardly searching for the words to comfort her, she was all at once aware of a stir in the woods.

"Listen!"

She turned left and right and caught glimpses of running children.

"The May Dancers!"

They ran from the trees and encircled the five of them.

"Not lost!" Gil said. "Not yet."

Then they were tugging at his sleeve, pulling him apart from the others, and he allowed himself to be led until he was a little way off. One of them Polly could see was whispering in his ear, while the rest huddled and hovered close about him, they flapping moths and he the flame.

Polly watched them.

"Always secrets, with you," she said. "And me left on the outside."

"Could be a spell!" Granny Porter was all a-twitch again, her tears forgotten. "Could be the way back they've found. Could be cooking little cakes on my own griddle, this very night!"

"And me rabbiting," said Sam hungrily, "with the rest. For the moon's full!"

Hearing them speak so, Polly felt a pang. She had a sudden strong awareness of their other life in Grimstone, their real life.

"For this, up here, is only like a dream to them," she thought.

She could almost see Grimstone as it would be when they came to it at evening, little lamps lit and reflecting in the lake, and owls hooting beyond and the lonely bark of a fox. She could almost smell the delicious warm scent of cakes baking on a griddle, and see the bare, moonlit acres where Sam and his friends would go snaring rabbits and creeping along the black-shadowed hedgerows.

"I hope you *do* get back!" she found herself saying, without really meaning to have said it at all.

"Oooh, it's The Catcher I fear," moaned Granny Porter. "'Tis that net of his that tangles in my dreams."

"I almost think," said Polly slowly, "that I know who he is."

They looked at her, all three, for Gil had now pulled away from the May Dancers. Polly heard again the weird music they made as they blew through leaves, or played their flutes or fiddles.

"I'm not positive certain," she said, "but I think it might be a man in the village they call Old Mazy."

There was an enormous silence.

"Old Mazy!" screamed Granny Porter, with a force that would have blown out candles, had there been any there.

"*Him!*" Sam was incredulous, but not more so than Polly herself.

"You know him?"

"Him that got left," said Granny Porter. "Him that come up after the May Dancing don't know how many centuries back. And was seen in Grimstone never again."

"Must've eaten summat," supplied Sam. "That's what we thought."

"That was afore we knew the rule," Gil said. "It was him getting caught back in time *gave* us the rule. He was spotted, see, eating a crust a farmer woman gave him."

"But why does he go after you with that net?" Polly was dizzy.

"I reckon," Gil said slowly, "he thinks it's the only road to get back. I reckon he thinks that if he catched a Time Gypsy, he'd get to Grimstone in his place."

"And he needn't!" Polly cried. "You said that if a single person from above earth was to come with you, willingly, then – "

"We'd be home!" shouted Sam. "Whee!" and he spun with such force that he fell to the ground, and the circling children gave a patter of applause.

"Find him!" screeched Granny Porter, dancing

madly on the spot and kicking her muddy little boots. "Find The Catcher!"

"Now steady," Gil said. "If we're mistook, we're done for." He addressed Polly. "What do you know of Old Mazy? Why've you got him notched as The Catcher?"

"Because he seems to have known," she said, "right from the start. He told me he could hear the church bells ringing below on *any* Sabbath – and he told me to listen, and I did, and I heard 'em, too. And it's only him who knows of the Time Gypsies. And my Aunt Em says he only comes to Wellow this time of year – then goes off."

"Betwixt May Day and Midsummer Eve," nodded Gil. "It fits."

"And he said to me that he'd do as he always does – watch and wait."

"It's him!" screeched Granny Porter. "It's The Catcher! Old Mazy, that got hisself catched in the net of time, and couldn't get free! And now he can, he can, he can – and so can we!"

She danced a triumphant jig and her rags flew.

"Oh, you're a duck!" she told Polly. "Oh, you're a proper little duck of a gel, and haven't I said so, all along!"

"You *never!*" thought Polly, but held her tongue.

"You *never!*" said Sam indignantly on her behalf. "You called her black and blue!"

"Oh, 'twas only a manner of speaking," said Granny Porter blithely.

"The others . . ." Sam looked towards where the May Dancers were still grouped a little way off. "What do they want?"

164

"Shouldn't be needed, not now," Gil said. He looked straight at Polly. "They say that the women have worked at that book of spells day and night. And they say that if you was willing to come alonger us, of your own free will, as you'll remember – they was all but certain they could spin you back into time, after."

"How?" Sam demanded.

"The May Dances," said Gil simply. "If she – " jerking his head towards Polly – "was to join in the May Dancing with the rest, we could spin her off into time again."

"But May Day's gone," Sam said.

"They know that," Gil told him, "in Grimstone, same as we know it here. *Despite* of that they reckon they could spin her back. Anyhow, hardly matters now. Old Mazy can work it for us."

"Oh, but what if I could!" said Polly softly. "Oh to see it – to see it with my own eyes!"

"Could still," Sam suggested.

"Could I? Could I?"

Gil nodded.

"But there'd be the risk. Of not spinning back."

"Them's daft, patched-up witches down there," said Granny Porter jealously. "Not proper, like I am, they ain't. Don't you go laying store by *their* spells."

> *"Who can tell, who can tell –*
> *Will it work, that secret spell?"*

The Time Gypsies looked at Polly in surprise.

"Sorry," she said. "Rhyming. I get it off my Dad. Listen, when I get back now, up the village, shall I tell Old Mazy, if he's there?"

The Time Gypsies looked at one another.

"Aye," said Gil, having read those looks. "And our thanks to you for your pains."

"And shall I say tonight?"

"Tonight," Gil nodded. "Before the sun sets."

"And when the moon rises in Grimstone, white and full!" crooned Granny Porter.

"I'll have to go," Polly said. "What's the time?"

They looked askance.

"I haven't got a watch," she explained, and in the instant realized that nor, of course, had they. "Ask a silly question...! Here!" She thrust Babby Porter into Gil's arms. "Take him. I'll have to run!"

She started to run, and the pram rocked wildly.

"Let him be there, let him be there!" she prayed as she ran.

She went so pell mell and so blind that she did not see the hooked stick go out to catch her ankle, and down she went as she had before.

She looked up, and there was the face of Old Mazy, but this time it was not smiling. And this time he put out a hand and wordlessly pulled her to her feet.

They stared into one another's eyes.

Then, "Help me," said Old Mazy. "Help me, won't you?"

Polly nodded.

"You've seen 'em, haven't you? Spoke with 'em. The Time Gypsies?"

Again she nodded.

"And I can't, I can't! The years go by, and every year they're fainter, till now I can glimpse only flickers, see only their shadows and hear only whispers. And I try to catch 'em – for I'm homesick! Centuries homesick I am to be again in Grimstone."

166

"I know," said Polly. "And I am going to help you."

He hardly seemed to take in what she said.

"The pain of it," he said, "to wander the world, and belong nowhere. A stranger in time, I am, and without a friend. And year after year I come back for the May Dancing, and year after year I come but a fingertip away... But they slip through my fingers, and through my net, and I'm left alone, and all I have left are dreams of timeless Grimstone, and even they grow cold...."

"Listen," said Polly, and her heart now ached for his loneliness. "They sent me to tell you. They're caught in the net of time themselves, the same as you are – least, four of 'em are. Granny Porter, and – "

"Granny Porter!" Old Mazy was jubilant to hear a well-known name. "Her – that old leathery thing, with – "

"Quick!" said Polly. "Yes, her. And they can only get back, they say, if one person from above earth goes willing with them. And they say that's you."

"Go with them? Willing? When all my heart's desire these hundreds of years – "

"I know," Polly told him. "You thought you had to catch one. But you don't."

He was shaking his head back and forth, back and forth, dazed.

"They want to go tonight," she told him.

"Tonight?"

"Before sunset," she said. "You know that."

"Betwixt dawn and sunset we slip the nets of time ..." he murmured.

"They say be there," Polly said, "on the bank of the lake, by the Time Tunnel."

"And I shall run free!" he cried. "Free again in time, and back in Grimstone and the lost land!"

"I've to go," Polly said, catching hold again of the pram. "But be there. And . . . and . . ." she hesitated, then called over her shoulder, "*I* may be, as well!"

On she went and past the maypole, and she looked up at it as she always did, and thought:

"Dare I? Dare I?" and sped on to Forge Cottage and the black looks that awaited her.

Aunt Em cast a cold look over Polly and the almost empty pram.

"And that, I suppose," she said, "has taken you all morning to collect. And half the afternoon, if it comes to that. Have you no idea of time?"

"Know more about time than *you* do," Polly thought. "That *is* for positive certain!"

Aloud she said, "It's with me not having a watch. And I did collect more than this, but it – "

She trailed off, as she realized that it would be impossible to explain to Aunt Em that she had emptied the pram in order to walk a Time Gypsy baby.

"Well, I left it somewhere," she ended lamely. "It – it was too heavy to push, so I left it. But I'll go and fetch it, I will, later on."

"That," said Aunt Em, "you will not. It'll come to no harm between now and tomorrow."

Polly visualized the damp and muddy clearing.

"That," she thought, "is what you think!"

"And you'll not go out again today," continued Aunt Em, ignoring Polly's gasp of dismay. "You'll go in and eat your dinner – which is stone cold. It's stone cold chips and stone cold sausage. Your favourite, Alice told me, and so I made it, though I don't hold with fried food. And now you'll eat it, stone cold. And you'll not set foot out of this house again today."

"But why not?" Polly cried. "I'll eat the stone cold sausages and chips – I like 'em cold, I do, nearly as well as hot. But why can't I go out?"

"Don't you stand there," said Aunt Em, "answering back your elders and betters."

So Polly went through and ate her stone cold meal.

"I'm a younger and worser, I suppose," she thought. "Why does getting older make you better?"

By mid-afternoon Aunt Em's mood seemed to have improved. She and Polly went into the garden and picked flowers, and arranged them in vases which they then stood about the house.

"They're lovely," Polly said. "Anyone'd think it was someone's birthday!"

Aunt Em seemed pleased with this remark.

"I'm going to make tarts now," she said. "Should you like to help?"

So Polly, still hoping for a reprieve, still hoping that she would be released before the day ended, helped with the tarts, and became remarkably floury in the process. She was also caught in the act of licking a spoonful of jam.

"Licking's dirty," said Aunt Em. "Polly – *don't!*"

"Shall I *ever* be Polly do?" she wondered.

"Hmmm!" Once the oven door was shut, Aunt Em turned her attention to Polly. "A fine sight you look. Get upstairs, and change into something decent. Haven't you got a nice frock?"

Polly trudged up to her room and dutifully changed

into her best frock. She opened the window and leaned out and smelt the delicious May scent of grass and approaching dewfall, and stared in awe at the towering maypole.

"A maypole in the month of May
Is magical, or so they say . . ."

She murmured the rhyme softly.

"Aunt Em can't kill me," she told the maypole. "If she did, the police would get her. And I've made my mind up. I dare go into the tunnel. I'd dare anything, almost, to be out of time and in Grimstone with the Time Gypsies. Never, never in my whole life again I'll get the chance to be out of time and running free. I'm coming, never fear. I'm coming!"

She shut the window, straightened her face and her frock, and went back downstairs.

"Very nice," said Aunt Em, casting an eye over her. "You can do very well, Polly, if you try."

"All I've to do," thought Polly, "'is wait my chance – and run!"

She looked out at the square framed view of the sky from the window, and tried to judge how far away sunset was. The clock in the hall was no help at all at telling this particular kind of time.

"You'll have to stop, Boz," she whispered to him. "Daren't take you. You might end up as Baggins again!"

Meanwhile she sat and listened to the clock in the hall making time seem so dense and actual that she almost felt she could touch it. Aunt Em seemed fidgety – excited, even.

Polly had an unexpected stroke of luck. The telephone rang. Aunt Em came in and said that she had to go out for a few minutes, to a neighbour.

"I shan't be long," she promised. "You look after the house while I'm gone."

The front door shut. Polly was instantly ready to go.

"There'll be no one run off with the house," she told the grandfather clock, as she waited to give Aunt Em time to disappear, "but with any luck, someone'll run off with *you*!"

She peered cautiously about the green. No one was in sight but the ubiquitous Davey Cole.

"Where're you going?" he called. "I could come with you!"

"Not now!" she called back. "Meeting somebody else!"

With that she was gone to the unclocked, uncharted, uncertain place that awaited her – to Grimstone. The sun was already beginning to set as she crossed the ford and entered Rufford, and there were strong green night smells of earth and water, and they went to her head, so that she ran along the edge of the lake, all silvery now, to where she knew the Time Gypsies would be waiting.

And so they were, huddled by the bank, voices hushed in the twilight lull, though there was no one but herself to hear. As she came near she saw that there were two boats waiting, and Granny Porter, Old Mazy and Gil were already seated in one of them.

"She's come!" she heard Sam whisper. "Told you!"

Old Mazy lifted an arm in salute.

"At last – slipping the net of time!"

Polly hesitated. She looked at the boats, the water, the arched tunnel.

"Dad and Mam – what'd they say?" she wondered. The moment was almost too much for her to bear alone. "But *Dad's* been down in the depths of the earth, plenty of times. Dare I?" And then, "What I've dreamed of – yes, I dare!"

And Polly Flint stepped from the bank to the boat and was already in another time.

"You're brave!" she heard Sam's whisper. "But I knew you would! Here – take *him*!"

A sleepy Babby Porter was passed into her arms. And then Sam pushed off, and they were clear of the bank on the calm evening water, and the only sounds were those of the oars splashing and birds whistling in the woods. And already to Polly it was all timeless, all inevitable and meant to be, and she thought:

"It's where it was all leading, right from the beginning!"

And when the boats turned, in mid lake, for the fateful move into that shadowy tunnel, she felt not a trace of fear. And then they were in the tunnel.

It was the strangest thing. They came through the icy cold and dark of the tunnel and were still on the lake, but now the shores of the lake were lit by little glowing lamps, reflecting in the water, as she had imagined. And people waited on the banks to greet them, as if they were kings and queens.

She saw Old Mazy step first on to that timeless shore and heard his cry,

"At last! At last!"

Then she herself was handed from the boat and was standing, at last, on that long imagined turf, and knew, quite certainly, that she was out of time.

Slowly she looked about her and took it all in – the

curve of the hill, the little lighted dwellings, the church whose bells she had heard ringing with her ear to the turf.

She saw Old Mazy, his face so altered that she hardly knew it, and his hand being wrung by one after another of the villagers of Grimstone, glad to welcome him back to the place where time would never touch him again.

"How's it feel?" Polly heard Sam whisper by her ear.

Polly Flint let out a long breath.

"It's as if I already knew it, in a way," she said wonderingly, herself surprised that this should be so.

"Come along with me." He led her a little way off, to a clump of trees by the water's edge.

"Can you really believe it?" he asked her, "that you're running free in time? Or does it all seem like a dream – as it seems to me when we go above earth after the May Dances."

"Real . . . unreal . . . I don't know. Real, I think. But how will it seem tomorrow? Tomorrow I shall be back with Aunt Em and that awful clock."

An owl hooted in the woods beyond.

"You heard that?"

Polly nodded.

"But still you don't know if you're here – or there . . . So look. This is what we'll do . . ."

He drew then a knife from his belt, and advanced to a young oak tree that stood nearby, silvery in the fading light.

"You *would've* been my sweetheart, if you'd stopped," he said. "So look!"

And with the knife he carved a heart in the bark, and then their initials . . .

"S.P.," read Polly. "P.F."

He stood back and regarded his handiwork, satisfied.

"That'll stand for us both now," he told her. Then, "We've not long. Moon rise, nearly."

And at that moment she might perhaps have chosen to stay there for ever, to run for ever with the Time Gypsies in and out of days and in and out of years, but the hands of the children reached out to pull her, willy nilly, to where the maypole stood in the twilit meadow. Beyond it she could see the church whose bells she had heard ringing from above. There was the pole, garlanded and hung with bright ribbons, and the sky was streaked with red beyond.

The pipes and fiddles struck up, Polly was handed her ribbon, and half in a dream she began to dance. And the dance was "The Gypsy's Tent" and the tune "Polly Put the Kettle On," and she was caught up into it and drawn by the music and was barely even able to think, "I'm out of time! Here I dance on timeless turf with timeless boys and girls!" before she was spun, and she felt herself spinning, through time, through space – who knows?

She was at the lakeside. She blinked. She shivered. Polly Flint stared over the now near dark water to the island where she had so lately travelled under the shadowy tunnel. She shivered again.

"Alone!" she thought, and was for the first time afraid. Where were they now, her companions of an hour – or a moment – since? Where Gil and Sam and Granny Porter, and the squalling Babby?

"Back home now. Home, where they belong. And even Mazy..."

An owl hooted. The water lapped softly, birds stirred and fluttered in the reeds. The moon made a path over the lake.

"I'm all alone!"

But in that moment she heard a voice calling, "Polly! Polly!" and the voice was, incredibly, that of Alice, and Polly began to run towards it, and cried, "Coming! Coming!"

She saw ahead not one figure, but two, and the second was that of Tom, and he was standing and walking. And Polly Flint ran straight into his arms and knew that she, too, was home.

From that day on Polly Flint – or Polly Don't – walked tall in the world, secure in her dreams, and from time to time rhyming as she went. She and Tom and Alice (with Boz, of course) went back to their old home, with its criss-crossing pigeons in the yard, and fields nearby where even angels could come. And Tom went back to work at the pit, though he never again went underground.

And every year, near May Day, they went to visit Aunt Em in her polished kingdom, and every year Polly Flint came into her own again – queen of *her* kingdom. She went to hear again the bells of Grimstone ringing sweetly through the warm turf, to run her finger yet again over the initials carved in an ancient oak, and most of all, to await the coming of the May Dancers from their timelessness, so that she, too, might spin for a while out of the everyday, and into the secret world of the Time Gypsies.